Frommer's®

Istanbul
day BY day®

2nd Edition

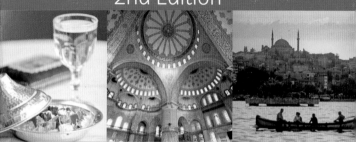

by Emma Levine

D1165204

John Wiley & Sons, Inc.

Contents

18 Favorite Moments   1

1 The Best Full-Day Tours   5
The Best in One Day   6
The Best in Two Days   12
The Best in Three Days   18

2 The Best Special-Interest Tours   23
Topkapı Palace   24
Arty Istanbul   28
Istanbul with Kids   34
Byzantine Constantinople   40

3 The Best Neighborhood Walks   45
Istiklal Caddesi   46
Eyüp's Sacred Sites   52
Tünel to Karaköy   56
Üsküdar   60
Eminönü to Sultanahmet   64
Fener & Balat   70
Beyazit's Bazaars & Mosques   74

4 The Best Shopping   79
Shopping Best Bets   80
Istanbul Shopping A to Z   84

5 The Best of the Outdoors   91
Gülhane Park   92

6 The Best Dining   97
Dining Best Bets   98
Istanbul Dining A to Z   101

7 The Best Nightlife 111
Nightlife Best Bets 112
Istanbul Nightlife A to Z 114

8 The Best Arts & Entertainment 121
Arts & Entertainment Best Bets 122
Arts & Entertainment A to Z 125

9 The Best Lodging 131
Lodging Best Bets 132
Istanbul Lodging A to Z 135

**10 The Best Day Trips &
Excursions 143**
Princes' Islands 144
Bursa 148
Edirne 154

The Savvy Traveler 159
Before You Go 160
Getting There 163
Getting Around 164
Fast Facts 166
Istanbul: A Brief History 170
Art & Architecture Highlights 173
Useful Phrases 176

Index 178

Editorial Director: Kelly Regan
Production Manager: Daniel Mersey
Commissioning Editor: Mark Henshall
Development Editor: Mary Anne Evans
Content Editor: Erica Peters
Photo Research: Cherie Cincilla, Richard H. Fox, Jill Emeny
Cartography: Simonetta Giori

British Library Cataloguing in Publication Data
A catalogue record for this book is available from the British Library

ISBN 978-1-119-97039-2 (pbk), ISBN 978-1-119-97234-1 (ebk),
ISBN 978-1-119-97235-8 (ebk), ISBN 978-1-119-97236-5 (ebk)

Typeset by Wiley Indianapolis Composition Services
Printed and bound in China by RR Donnelley

5 4 3 2 1

A Note from the Editorial Director

Organizing your time. That's what this guide is all about.

Other guides give you long lists of things to see and do and then expect you to fit the pieces together. The Day by Day guides are different. These guides tell you the best of everything, and then they show you how to see it in the smartest, most time-efficient way. Our authors have designed detailed itineraries organized by time, neighborhood, or special interest. And each tour comes with a bulleted map that takes you from stop to stop.

Hoping to gaze up at the domed ceiling at the Süleymaniye Mosque, check out Istanbul's contemporary art scene or watch fishermen where the Marmara Sea meets the Bosphorus? Planning to lose yourself in the music emanating from Galip Dede Caddesi, savor Turkish delicacies at the market in Gazlentep or take a dramatic cable car ride up Pierre Loti Kahvesi? Whatever your interest or schedule, the Day by Days give you the smartest routes to follow. Not only do we take you to the top attractions, hotels, and restaurants, but we also help you access those special moments that locals get to experience—those "finds" that turn tourists into travelers.

The Day by Days are also your top choice if you're looking for one complete guide for all your travel needs. The best hotels and restaurants for every budget, the greatest shopping values, the wildest nightlife—it's all here.

Why should you trust our judgment? Because our authors personally visit each place they write about. They're an independent lot who say what they think and would never include places they wouldn't recommend to their best friends. They're also open to suggestions from readers. If you'd like to contact them, please send your comments our way at feedback@frommers.com, and we'll pass them on.

Enjoy your Day by Day guide—the most helpful travel companion you can buy. And have the trip of a lifetime.

Warm regards,

Kelly Regan

Kelly Regan, Editorial Director
Frommer's Travel Guides

About the Author

Emma was born in Yorkshire, England, and fell in love with Istanbul on her first visit in 1989, and since then has been a regular visitor. After graduating in Graphic Design, she lived and worked as a writer and photographer in Mumbai, Hong Kong, and Istanbul, and has enjoyed many happy years having adventures around the world.

For much of her working life, Emma has specialized in documenting sporting culture of Asia, especially cricket culture in the Indian subcontinent, and traditional sports in countries including Iran, Pakistan and Kyrgyzstan in her book *A Game of Polo with a Headless Goat*. This book was later turned into a series of documentaries on National Geographic Channel, which she wrote and presented.

Emma is now based in North London, but still travels where and when possible.

Acknowledgments

For this update, huge thanks go to Joanna Marsh and Jill Guest from the press office of the Turkish Tourist Office in London. Also to Hulya, Ceyda and Evin at Redmint Communications in London. In Istanbul, thanks as ever to my lovely host Mick, always happy to give me a home from home.

Advisory & Disclaimer

Travel information can change quickly and unexpectedly, and we strongly advise you to confirm important details locally before traveling, including information on visas, health and safety, traffic and transport, accommodations, shopping, and eating out. We also encourage you to stay alert while traveling and to remain aware of your surroundings. Avoid civil disturbances, and keep a close eye on cameras, purses, wallets, and other valuables.

While we have endeavored to ensure that the information contained within this guide is accurate and up-to-date at the time of publication, we make no representations or warranties with respect to the accuracy or completeness of the contents of this work and specifically disclaim all warranties, including without limitation warranties of fitness for a particular purpose. We accept no responsibility or liability for any inaccuracy or errors or omissions, or for any inconvenience, loss, damage, costs, or expenses of any nature whatsoever incurred or suffered by anyone as a result of any advice or information contained in this guide.

The inclusion of a company, organization, or website in this guide as a service provider and/or potential source of further information does not mean that we endorse them or the information they provide. Be aware that information provided through some websites may be unreliable and can change without notice. Neither the publisher nor author shall be liable for any damages arising herefrom.

Star Ratings, Icons & Abbreviations

Every hotel, restaurant, and attraction listing in this guide has been ranked for quality, value, service, amenities, and special features using a **star-rating system.** Hotels, restaurants, attractions, shopping, and nightlife are rated on a scale of zero stars (recommended) to three stars (exceptional). In addition to the star-rating system, we also use a **kids icon** to point out the best bets for families. Within each tour, we recommend cafes, bars or restaurants where you can take a break. Each of these stops appears in a shaded box marked with a coffee cup–shaped bullet ☕.

The following **abbreviations** are used for credit cards:

AE	American Express	DISC	Discover	V	Visa
DC	Diners Club	MC	MasterCard		

Travel Resources at Frommers.com

Frommer's travel resources don't end with this guide. Frommer's website, **www.frommers.com**, has travel information on more than 4,000 destinations. We update features regularly, giving you access to the most current trip-planning information and the best airfare, lodging, and car-rental bargains. You can also listen to podcasts, connect with other Frommers.com members through our active-reader forums, share your travel photos, read blogs from guidebook editors and fellow travelers, and much more.

How to Contact Us

In researching this book, we discovered many wonderful places—hotels, restaurants, shops, and more. We're sure you'll find others. Please tell us about them, so we can share the information with your fellow travelers in upcoming editions. If you were disappointed with a recommendation, we'd love to know that, too. Please e-mail: frommers@wiley.com or write to:

Frommer's Istanbul Day by Day, 2nd Edition
John Wiley & Sons, Inc. • 111 River St. • Hoboken, NJ 07030-5774

18 Favorite **Moments**

18 Favorite **Moments**

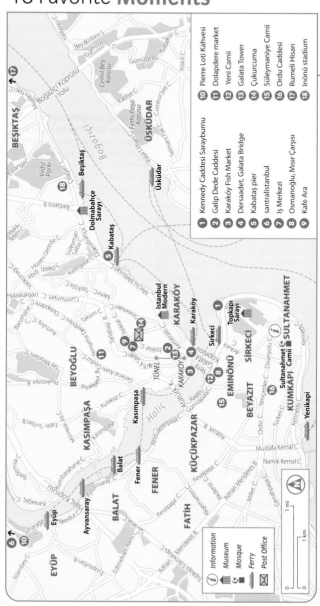

1. Kennedy Caddesi Sarayburnu
2. Galip Dede Caddesi
3. Karaköy Fish Market
4. Dersaadet, Galata Bridge
5. Kabataş pier
6. santralistanbul
7. İş Merkezi
8. Osmanoğlu, Mısır Çarşısı
9. Kafe Ara
10. Pierre Loti Kahvesi
11. Dolapdere market
12. Yeni Camii
13. Galata Tower
14. Çukurcuma
15. Süleymaniye Camii
16. Ordu Caddesi
17. Rumeli Hisarı
18. İnönü stadium

Previous page: Galata Tower.

I n 1989 I traveled to Istanbul for the first time. Gazing at Galata Bridge at sunrise, I breathed in deeply, turned to my traveling companion and declared of this magnificent city, "I think I'm in love." Over 2 decades later, Istanbul has emerged to be a true world city, with vibrant arts and nightlife to match its wealth of historic treasures.

① **Following the coastline from Kennedy Caddesi Sarayburnu (Seraglio Point),** where the Sea of Marmara meets the Bosphorus and the Golden Horn. From here you can see the old and new sides of Istanbul, and over to Asia. No wonder it was such a strategic point for a palace! *See p 75.*

② **Wandering down Galip Dede Caddesi** and listening to the sounds emerge from music stores—everything from electric guitars and drum kits to traditional instruments like *saz* and *ney*. I was even inspired here to buy a second-hand accordion! *See p 86.*

③ **Eating fresh grilled fish by Karaköy Fish Market.** It's a bit rough and ready, but on a warm summer's evening, with the Old City skyline ahead and a glass of fresh

Fishermen at Seraglio Point.

juice, it can't be beaten for price and pure enjoyment. *See p 59.*

④ **Playing backgammon at Dersaadet on Galata Bridge** with an Efes beer. As fishermen cram the upper level to dip their lines into the Bosphorus, I take a more relaxed approach to this iconic bridge, trying to beat the locals at their own game. It sounds a cliché, but this bar is also a fantastic spot to watch the sun set over the water. *See p 116.*

⑤ **Boarding a ferry from Kabataş pier for a cruise to the verdant Princes' Islands,** making the most of Istanbul's best form of public transport. The getting there is definitely part of the charm! *See p 147.*

⑥ **Perusing contemporary art at santralistanbul,** an old Ottoman power station with the height for mammoth sculptures and installations. It's an outstanding art space, and one of the most innovative galleries in the city. *See p 32.*

⑦ **Rummaging for bargain clothes at Iş Merkezi.** True, most of what's on offer is trashy, but a little perseverance can result in cut-price designer treasures, and it's a good bet for a good-value wardrobe revamp. And what's more satisfying than that? *See p 89.*

⑧ **Buying fresh pistachios from Osmanoğlu in Mısır Çarşısı.** It's turned me into a pistachio snob; nowhere else seems to have the same crisp, salty concentration of flavor as Turkish pistachios, especially those from the city of Gaziantep. *See p 9.*

Socks and runner beans at Dolapdere market.

⑨ **Sipping Turkish coffee at Kafe Ara,** surrounded by scenes of the city on the walls by Istanbul's photographer Ara Güler (b. 1928). A real "cafe society" feel. *See p 104.*

⑩ **Taking the teleferik to Pierre Loti Kahvesi on a warm summer evening.** After a fascinating morning people-watching around Eyüp Sultan Mosque and Meydanı, the short cable-car ride above the cemetery is a lovely, lazy way to reach the tea garden named after the romantic French author. *See p 54.*

⑪ **Buying flowery socks and fresh veggies at Dolapdere market,** where the Tarlıbaşı locals stock up on their weekly goodies. As an Istanbul shopping experience, this is a whole different ball game. *See p 90.*

⑫ **Climbing the stairs to Yeni Camii while dodging the pigeons.** This is one of the best spots to admire the Golden Horn and Galata Bridge, and the buzzing pier at Eminönü. *See p 65.*

⑬ **Ascending Galata Tower** and circling the gallery a dozen times for another memorable view. It still wows me after so many times—check out those rooftops! *See p 10.*

⑭ **Getting lost on the winding backstreets around Çukurcuma,** browsing antique shops, jewelry makers, and tiny art galleries. *See p 86.*

⑮ **Looking up at the vast domed ceiling at Süleymaniye Camii.** In this mammoth mosque it's possible to get a semblance of peace—and Sinan's ceilings are certainly something. *See p 8.*

⑯ **Stumbling across historic remains**—forgotten, yet, in a casual way, revered. At Beyazit, I love the stones from the Byzantine Triumphal Arch, piled up on the pavement of the busy Ordu Caddesi, so incongruous yet so typical of Istanbul.

⑰ **Scrambling along the walls at Rumeli Hisarı,** among wild flowers growing out of the towers—enough to bring out the kid in anyone. From the top, the Bosphorus views are astounding. *See p 39.*

⑱ **Cheering Beşiktaş soccer (football) club scoring the winning goal** at the spectacular İnönü stadium, with views of the Bosphorus and Dolmabahçe Palace clock tower. Like any major sporting arena, I feel a real buzz when walking down to the ground from Taksim Square with fellow Karakartal (Black Eagle) fans. *See p 129.* ●

1 The Best **Full-Day Tours**

The Best **in One Day**

1. Hagia Sophia
2. Sultanahmet Park
3. Süleymaniye Camii
4. Kurucu Ali Baba
5. Kapalı Çarşısı
6. Mısır Çarşısı
7. Bab-i Hayat
8. Rüstem Paşa Camii
9. Galata Köprüsü
10. Galata Kulesi
11. Istiklal Caddesi

(i) Information
🏛 Museum
☪ Mosque
✉ Post Office
P Police Station
⛴ Ferry
🚉 Train Station
— Funicular
T Tram

BEYOĞLU

Galatasaray
Lisesi

TÜNEL

Galata
Mevlevihanesi
Müzesi

TOPHANE

Nusretiye
Camii

Istanbul
Modern

GALATA

Arap
Camii

KARAKÖY

KARAKÖY

Karaköy

Haliç

Rüstem Paşa
Camii

Eminönü

EMİNÖNÜ

Yeni Camii

Sirkeci

Mısır Çarşısı

Bab-i Hayat

Sirkeci Tren
İstasyonu

SİRKECİ

PTT İstanbul
Müzesi

Süleymaniye
Camii

Kurucu Ali Baba

İstanbul
Üniversitesi

EMİNÖNÜ

SİRKECİ

Gülhane
Parkı

BEYAZIT

GÜLHANE

Topkapı
Sarayı

Beyazıt
Camii

Kapalı
Çarşısı

Arkeoloji
Müzesi

Aya İrini
Kilisesi

ÇEMBERLİTAŞ

BEYAZIT

Yerebatan
Sarnıcı

Hagia
Sophia

SULTANAHMET

Sultanahmet
Parkı

Türbeler
Müzesi

Sultanahmet
Camii

Cankurtaran

SULTANAHMET

0   1/4 mi

0   0.25 km

Previous page: Dazzling interior of the Blue Mosque.

Istanbul's history clusters around **Sultanahmet,** site of the ancient capital, and centerpiece to the Ottoman Empire. This area is referred to as the Old City, or Historic Peninsula of Istanbul's European side. Over the Golden Horn (an "arm" of the Bosphorus), and still in Europe, is the thoroughly modern Beyoğlu neighborhood. This busy tour gives you a taste of both. START: **Tram to Sultanahmet.**

① ★★★ kids Hagia Sophia (Ayasofya). One of Istanbul's most iconic landmarks, with a dusky red exterior and huge domes, there are usually snaking lines to enter this Byzantine church. An earlier church was built on this spot, its present form dating back to the mid-6th century when it was rebuilt by Emperor Justinian I. Your first impression, on entering its dimly lit first floor, is an ambience of awe under the magnificent 56m-high (184 ft.) dome. Restoration was completed in 2010, so now you can see the Muezzin's ornate loge, and the Omphalion, where Byzantine emperors were crowned. Peer through the wrought-iron grill into Sultan Mahmud I's library with its stylized Ottoman tilework. The upstairs gallery houses jaw-dropping 10th-century mosaics, including that of Christ flanked by Emperor Constantine IX and his wife, Empress Zoe. Close by you'll see Viking-era graffiti etched into the marble balcony. Pope Benedict XVI's 2006 visit reopened old wounds over whether Hagia Sophia should be a mosque (which was officially renamed as Ayasofya after the Ottoman conquest, and still called that in Turkish), a cathedral, or a museum. There were fears and protests that his praying there would provoke Islamic sensitivities. Thankfully, he didn't. ⏱ *90 min. Ayasofya Meydanı, Sultanahmet.* ☎ *0212 522 1750. Admission 20 TL, children under 13 years free; audio tours 10 TL Tues–Sun 9am–4:30pm (summer 9am–7pm). Tram: Sultanahmet.*

Take a break at Sultanahmet Park.

② ★ kids Sultanahmet Park. Take a breather in this tiny park, its fountain lying between the striking **Sultanahmet Camii** *(Blue Mosque, p 15)* and **Hagia Sophia.** Savor the precious location, and recharge the batteries with barbecued corn-on-the-cob (*mısır*) from the push-carts. It's a sublime location where everyone gathers to walk its well-laid paths. It's even better at night, when these monoliths are spot-lit; amazingly it's only in the past decade that **Hagia Sophia** has been lit up at night. It's popular for *iftar* (sunset "breaking the fast" meal during Ramazan), with picnicking locals. *Open 24 hr. Tram: Sultanahmet.*

❸ ★★★ kids Süleymaniye Camii (Süleymaniye Mosque).
One of the masterpieces of Mimar Sinan (1489–1588; *Sinan, Master Architect*, p 11), this Istanbul gem is relatively quiet. With a huge central dome and four slender minarets it was, like many great mosques, part of a *külliye*, a mosque complex once housing a *caravanserai* (resting place for travelers), hospital, *medrese* (religious school), and tombs. It was built in the mid-16th century under the order of Süleyman I, or Süleyman the Magnificent (*A Brief History*, p 170). The mosque's interior is breathtaking, its 53m-high (174 ft.) dome soaring above the subdued lighting from stained-glass windows made by Ibrahim "the Mad" (1615–48), so nicknamed because of his eccentricities. His tomb lies in the rose-clad graveyard; its marble pillars, hand-painted tiles from Iznik, and neat wooden alcoves are in sharp contrast to the modest tomb of his adored wife, Roxelana. You'll find fewer visitors here than at the **Blue Mosque** (p 15). ⏱ *1 hr. Prof Sıddık Sami Onar Cad.* ☎ *0212 513 3608. Admission free. Open daily 9am–dusk. Tram: Beyazit then 15-min walk.*

Intricate domes at Süleymaniye Camii.

❹ ★★ kids Kurucu Ali Baba.
The first tiny *lokanta* (simple restaurants) facing the mosque, this has served up simple, tasty *kuru fasulye* (white beans) since 1939. Perfect for a no-frills lunch with the locals. *1/3 Prof Sıddık Sami Onar Cad, Süleymaniye.* ☎ *0212 520 7655. Fasulye beans and rice 4 TL.*

❺ ★★ kids Kapalı Çarşısı (Covered, or Grand, Bazaar). You could happily spend half a day getting lost in the crowded market; even those who hate shopping will love the labyrinthine walk through a piece of history, with the boisterous shouts of traders, dazzling gold stalls, colorful ceramics, and mannequins draped with scarlet leather jackets. Its statistics are staggering: Over 4,000 shops, 60 lanes, and 550 years of hearty trading. Built by Mehmet II shortly after the Conquest of Constantinople in 1453 (*A Brief History*, p 170), its domed roofs and thick stone streets now house colorful machine-made ceramics, with souvenirs replacing traditional trades like quilt- and fez-making. Previously, natural daylight from the ceiling illuminated the entire market; now most rely on

electricity. **İç Bedesten** is the oldest part of the bazaar; once a warehouse, it's now the hub of stylish cafes, although some trades are still booming, like the carpet dealers and gold and leather stores. There's a more peaceful ambience in the leafy courtyard **Zincirli Han.** Admire the sturdy entrance gates (over 20 of them) and outside stalls, a little more earthy where locals grab a bargain, especially leather and denim clothes. If you have the energy, head north from the bazaar via **Valide Han** (*Neighborhood Walks*, p 78) to Eminönü, to Mısır Çarşısı, or take the tram. 🕐 *Anything from 1–3 hr. Open Mon–Sat 9:30am–7pm. Tram: Beyazit; or bus 61B from Taksim.*

Peaceful courtyard at Grand Bazaar's Zincirli Han.

6 ★★ kids **Mısır Çarşısı (Egyptian, or Spice Market).** This L-shaped market, built in 1660 to finance Yeni Camii (*New Mosque*, p 65) was once filled with piles of fresh peppercorns, cilantro (coriander), henna, and dried herbs brought from Egypt. Now this very touristy market is more likely to have boxes of apple tea, T-shirts, and gold shops, dotted with stalls selling syrupy *baklava* and *lokum* (Turkish delight). Inch your way past the crowds to see its delightful domed ceilings. If you want to hang out where the locals shop, concentrate on the stalls running around the outside wall of the market (including Osmanoğlu, my favorite for the freshest pistachios and dried figs) for a wondrous supply of Turkish cheese, olives, fresh fish, and *halva*. (*Neighborhood Walks*, p 65) 🕐 *1 hr. Open Mon–Sat 9:30am–7pm. Tram/bus to Eminönü.*

7 ★★★ kids **Bab-i Hayat.** Opened in 2007 and converted from a warehouse, this gorgeous domed restaurant looks out onto Mısır Çarşısı. Its

buffet lunch of Turkish traditional dishes is popular with local office workers. *39/47 Mısır Çarşısı, Eminönü.* ☎ *0212 520 7878. Buffet lunch 25 TL.*

8 ★★ **Rüstem Paşa Camii (Rüstem Paşa Mosque).** Stashed away above a row of workshops, hardly visible from street level, this mosque really is a hidden gem. It is delightfully located at the edge of busy Tahtakale, and you'll first walk through its tiny courtyard with potted plants lining the balcony. One of Mimar Sinan's smallest creations, it was built in 1560 and originally funded out of proceeds from nearby tradesmen. It's one of the best places to see the famous blue Iznik tiles, here covering the interior. The surrounding streets, filled with busy workshops making wooden backgammon sets (*tavla*), simple hammocks, and kitchenware, are lovely to explore. 🕐 *20 min. Hasircilar Cad.* ☎ *0212 526 7350. Open dawn–dusk. Tram/bus to Eminönü.*

Watching the fishing off Galata Bridge.

9 ★★ **Galata Köprüsü (Galata Bridge).** Many attempted, and failed, to build a bridge linking the Ottoman Palace of old Istanbul to the "new" neighborhoods of Pera, Beyoğlu and Galata, where merchants and diplomats lived. Leonardo da Vinci, no less, had his mid-16th-century designs rejected, and Michelangelo even turned down an offer to design a new bridge. At last, the early 20th century saw the first bridge completed, linking Eminönü to Karaköy over the Haliç (Golden Horn). The wooden bridge was destroyed by fire in 1992, replaced by today's bridge in 1994. It's almost 500m (1,640 ft.) long,

with fishermen on the upper level, and cafes and restaurants on the lower, looking down to the ships sailing the mighty Bosphorus. Today you may find yourself here at sunset, in a cafe playing backgammon (hugely popular here) while enjoying a beer; in the 19th century, Galata Bridge was the subject of myriad Turkish poems and songs. ⏱ *Varies. Tram; Eminönü or Karaköy.*

10 ★★ **Galata Kulesi (Galata Tower).** I always recommend this to first-time visitors (I've ascended it countless times) for the best 360-degree views of the city and a perspective of Istanbul's mammoth size. The 62m-high (203 ft.) conical

Sightseeing—the Basics

Most major attractions are open Tuesday to Sunday, 9am–5pm, some opening later in summer. Getting around the Old City is best done by tram or on foot. Most mosques are open to visitors from dawn to nightfall, excluding prayer times; dress modestly, covering arms and legs, and women should cover their hair. You'll soon get used to the street names in Turkish; the basic ones are Sokak (abbreviated to Sok)—road; Caddesi (Cad)—avenue; Meydanı—square. You'll be walking along plenty of those to visit mosques (*camii*), museums (*müzesi*), and covered markets (*çarşısı*)! For other Turkish words, see p 176.

Sinan, Master Architect

You're likely to be awed by the work of one man: master architect of the Ottoman Empire, Mimar Sinan (1489–1588). He was "adopted" as the Ottoman Palace architect by Süleyman I, under whose reign arts and architecture flourished. Under him, Sinan built hundreds of mosques, *hamams*, bazaars, and hospitals throughout Turkey but most famously in Istanbul. Ironically he chose the famous Byzantine Hagia Sophia basilica as inspiration for his mosques, to which he added the slender minarets (and rather ugly buttresses) afterward.

tower was built by the Genoese in 1348, when they took control of the trade colony of Pera. Take the elevator to the top to walk around the viewing gallery, overlooking disheveled rooftops, minarets, the Bosphorus, and even the Princes' Islands (*Day Trips & Excursions*, p 144). Time your visit for sunset if possible, although it's a popular time. If you don't fancy walking uphill to the tower, take the Tunnel (the old subway) from Karaköy to Tünel and walk down (*Neighborhood Walks*, p 56). ⏲ *1 hr. Büyük Hendek Sok, Galata.* ☎ *0212 293 8180. www.galatatower.net. Open daily 9am–8pm. Admission 11 TL, children under 6 years free. Tunnel to Tünel or tram to Karaköy and walk.*

☕ ★★★ kids **Istiklal Caddesi.** You're close to the dining and entertainment hub of Beyoğlu, so try one of its many restaurants around this busy main street. *See Best Dining for details, p 97).*

Climb Galata Tower for the best views.

The Best **in Two Days**

1. Topkapı Sarayı
2. Arkeoloji Müzesi
3. Derviş
4. Sultanahmet Camii
5. Yerebatan Sarnıçı
6. Istanbul Modern
7. Bosphorus Cruise
8. Anadolu Kavağı ferry pier

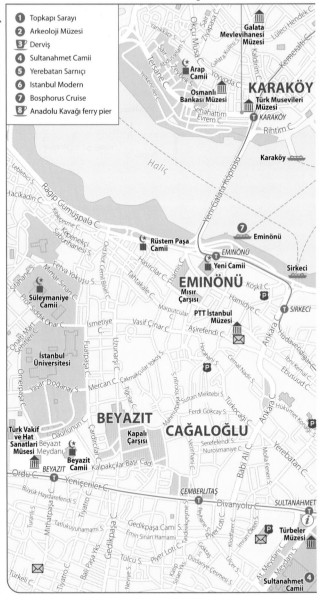

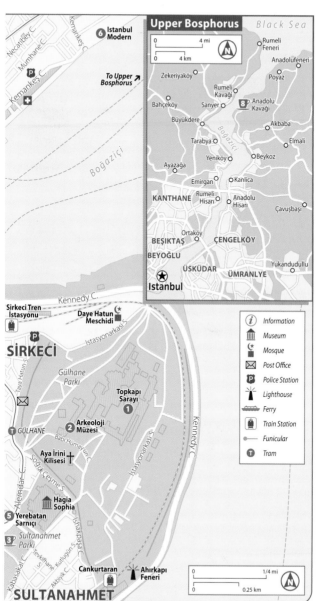

Upper Bosphorus

0　　　　　　4 mi
0　　　　　　4 km

Black Sea

Rumeli Feneri
Anadoluféneri
Zekeriyaköy
Poyaz
Rumeli Kavağı
Anadolu Kavağı ⑧
Bahçeköy
Sarıyer
Akbaba
Büyükdere
Tarabya
Elmali
Yeniköy
Beykoz
Ayazağa
Emirgan
Kanlica
KANTHANE
Rumeli Hisarı
Anadolu Hisarı
Çavuşbaşı
Ortaköy
BEŞIKTAŞ
ÇENGELKÖY
BEYOĞLU
ÜSKÜDAR
ÜMRANLYE
Yukandudullu
★ Istanbul

⑥ Istanbul Modern

To Upper Bosphorus ↗

Boğaziçi

Kennedy C.

Sirkeci Tren İstasyonu
Daye Hatun Meschidi
İstasyonarkası S.

SİRKECİ

Gülhane Parkı

Topkapı Sarayı ①

Babı Humayun C.

② Arkeoloji Müzesi

Aya İrini Kilisesi †

Kennedy C.

İstasyonarkası S.

Hagia Sophia

⑤ Yerebatan Sarnıçı

Sultanahmet Parkı ③

Cankurtaran
Ahırkapı Feneri

SULTANAHMET

ⓘ	Information
🏛	Museum
☪	Mosque
✉	Post Office
Ⓟ	Police Station
🔦	Lighthouse
⛴	Ferry
🚉	Train Station
●	Funicular
Ⓣ	Tram

0　　　　　　1/4 mi
0　　　　　　0.25 km

On your second day, dip back into Sultanahmet for more history, including Topkapı Palace, centerpiece of the Ottoman Empire, and Istanbul Modern's collection of contemporary Turkish art. If you have more time, try to visit the palace and Archaeology Museum on separate days. A Bosphorus Cruise is a perfect way to end the day. START: **Tram to Gülhane or Sultanahmet.**

Historic courtyard of the Archaeology Museum.

① ★★ **Topkapı Sarayı (Topkapı Palace).** Built by Mehmet II in 1478 and center of the Ottoman Empire until 1853, it's no wonder that it's usually a struggle to catch sight of the famous 86-carat tear-shaped Spoonmaker's Diamond and Topkapı Dagger inside the crowded **Treasury.** Other highlights include the **Harem** (well worth the extra ticket) with its series of tiled chambers—and probably the largest mirror I have ever seen. Don't miss the religious artifacts, including those belonging to the Prophet Mohammed. (*Special-Interest Tours*, p 24). ⏱ *2–4 hr. Bab-ı Hümayun Cad, Gülhane.* ☎ *0212 512 0480. www.top kapisarayi.gov.tr. Admission 20 TL, children under 12 years free; Harem extra 15 TL. Open Wed–Mon 9am–5pm; summer 9am–7pm. Tram: Gülhane or Sultanahmet.*

② ★★★ **kids Arkeoloji Müzesi (Archaeology Museum).** Part of the Topkapı Palace's complex, the museum is world class. It was established to prevent classical antiquities disappearing to Europe by curator and artist Orhan Hamdi Bey (1842–1910), best known for his painting *The Tortoise Trainer*, now in Pera Museum (*Arty Istanbul*, p 28). With around one million relics spread over three buildings, be selective, especially if you've just emerged from the palace. I suggest prioritizing the main building, which contains astounding exhibits; don't miss the huge Alexander Sarcophagus (4th-century B.C.) with carved marble scenes of battle, the mummy of Sidonion King Tabrit (500 B.C.), and the weighty significance of the Treaty of Kadesh (1269 B.C.), the world's earliest-surviving peace treaty. Across the courtyard, the **Museum of Ancient Orient** has fabulous Babylonian tiled friezes, and **Çinili Köşk (Tiled Pavilion)**, a small pavilion with an outstanding collection of Seljuk and Ottoman tiles. Take a breather in the charming courtyard cafe alongside cats and broken tombstones. ⏱ *90 min–2 hr. Osman Hamdi Bey Yokoşu Sok, Gülhane.* ☎ *0212 527 2740. www.istanbularkeoloji.gov.tr. Admission 10 TL, children under 12 years free. Open Tues–Sun 9am–5pm. Tram: Gülhane.*

3 ★ kids **Derviş.** This leafy courtyard is perfect to rest weary feet. Nothing extravagant, just tea, nargile (tobacco water-pipe), toast, and snacks, and bang opposite the Blue Mosque. On summer evenings, try to catch the Sound and Light show on the mosque walls. *1 Kabasakal Sok.* ☎ *0212 516 1515. Tea and nargile 8 TL.*

4 ★ **Sultanahmet Camii (Blue Mosque).** Being opposite **Hagia Sophia** might be handy for sightseeing, but the mosque's location was intentional. It was larger to emphasize the superiority of Islam over Christian Byzantium. The

The opulent Harem in Topkapı Palace.

approach to the mosque's courtyard from the Hippodrome (see *Neighborhood Walks,* p 68) is delightful as the full impact of cascading domes and six soaring minarets unfolds in front of you. The number of slender minarets created consternation when it was built, as the only other mosque with six minarets is at Mecca. Built in 1617 by Mehmet Ağa, a student of Sinan, this was the last of the Imperial mosques, commissioned by the 19-year-old Sultan Ahmet I (its Turkish name is **Sultanahmet Camii**). The courtyard, made from Marmara marble, is

Blue Mosque's distinctive minarets.

The mysterious Medusa's head at Yerebatan Sarnıçı.

actually the same size as the interior of the prayer hall and, ironically, more peaceful. Its most famous feature, the blue Iznik tiles that give the mosque its name, cover the upper levels and the domes' interiors—over 20,000 tiles in total—and are beautifully illuminated by 260 windows. Astoundingly each tile took 72 days to paint. Non-Muslim visitors will be ushered around the side of the courtyard and unfortunately only allowed at the back, which tends to get very crowded. It's

The Istanbul Modern.

difficult to see the tiles' detail, or the carved white *minbar* (pulpit) and *mihrab* (niche pointing to Mecca) at the front. During the summer, wonderful **Sound and Light** shows on the mosque's walls play from 9pm in various languages; great for kids.
🕐 *30 min. Sultanahmet Meydanı. Open 9am–dusk daily, except during prayers. Tram: Sultanahmet.*

⑤ ★★ kids Yerebatan Sarnıçı (Basilica Cistern). A great feat of Byzantine engineering, this is one of the city's most unusual and memorable sights, dating back to the 6th century. Back then, water came from the Belgrade Forest, some 19km (12 miles) away, through the 4th-century **Valens** viaduct constructed by Emperor Valens (p 42). The red spotlights' eerie glow is best experienced when the place is as empty as possible—try early morning or late afternoon. Make your way to the northwest corner for the two Medusa-head columns, thought to be late Roman, one upside down and one tilted 45 degrees. And the reason? No one really knows, except possibly to create even more intrigue surrounding the legendary woman who transformed people who looked at her into stone. No such grizzly results

here, as people throw coins into the carp-filled pool and make a wish. Scenes in James Bond's 1963 film *From Russia with Love* were filmed here. ⏲ *45 min. 13 Yerebatan Cad, Sultanahmet.* ☎ *0212 522 1259. www.yerebatan.com. Admission 10 TL, children under 8 years free. Open daily 9:30am–6:30pm (Oct–Apr 9:30am–5:30pm). Tram: Sultanahmet.*

⑥ ★★★ kids Istanbul Modern. When you whizz over the Golden Horn by tram to Tophane, near Karaköy, you leave behind centuries of history. Enter this converted customs house, opened in 2004, to see one of the country's finest art collections, from 20th-century Ottoman art to today, spread over its two floors. The huge gallery (it still looks like a warehouse from the outside) has a sublime waterfront location, so as you peruse the galleries of 20th- and 21st-century Turkish art, with paintings, sculpture, videos, and installations, you can take a seat and gaze out to the Bosphorus. (*Arty Istanbul, p 28.*) ⏲ *90 min. Meclis-i Mebusan Cad, Liman Işletmeleri, 4 Sahası Antrepo, Karaköy.* ☎ *0212 334 7300. www.istanbul modern.org. Adult 12 TL, children 13–17 years 6 TL. Thurs free. Tues–Sun 10am–6pm; Thurs 10am–8pm. Tram: Tophane.*

⑦ ★★★ kids Bosphorus Cruise. One of Istanbul's most popular trips; locals and visitors adore cruising the city's famous waterway, strategically important for centuries (*A Brief History*, p 170). Trips begin at Eminönü pier, with stops including Beşiktaş and Ortaköy (*Best In Three Days*, p 18) on the European side, Çengelköy on the Asian side, before terminating at **Anadolu Kavağı**. During summer, weekday trips leave at 7:15pm from Eminönü and make a wonderful evening, with enough

Savor the views from Anadolu Kavağı.

time for the steep climb to the 14th-century Genoese **Yoros Castle** for incredible views of where the Bosphorus meets the Black Sea. Enjoy dinner on the pier then return by ferry. If you're traveling during winter, I highly recommend taking this trip one sunny afternoon, and perhaps visiting one of the museums the following day. To spend more time at the castle (it's less than a 2-hour turnaround), take the ferry from Anadolu Kavağı to Sarıyer on the opposite side, and a fast bus back to Beşiktaş. From Eminönü there are also regular 1.5-hour round-trip cruises, with no stops, operated by fast, modern **TurYol**. ⏲ *varies. Check www.ido.com.tr. for times and prices. Ferries from Eminönü pier. Tram: Eminönü.*

⑧ ★ kids Anadolu Kavağı ferry pier. Passengers leaving the ferry may be bombarded with restaurants vying for business. Don't feel pressurized and look around. There are also simple stalls cooking fresh *balik ekmek* (fried fish in bread). *Snacks from TL 4; entrees (in restaurants) from TL 10.*

The Best **in Three Days**

Fener

Eğrikapı Rum Mezarlığı

Mısır Tarlası Mezarlığı

Savaklar C.

Hoca Çakır S.

Kuyulubahçe S.

Kariyemaret S.

Merdivenlikahve S.

Pasamaramı C.

Vaiz S.

Kariyebostani S.

Kariye Pembe Köşk
❷

Kariye Müzesi
❶

Türbe S.

Neşter S.

Şeyh Eyüp S.

Kariyecami S.

Kaleboyu C.

Fevzipaşa S.

Üçbeyi S.

Neşter S.

Tarlici S.

Vaiz S.

Abacılar C.

Yeşilcedirek S.

Selma S.

Tomruk C.

Draman C.

❻

0 ───── 200 yd
0 ───── 100 m

Abdi İpekçi C.

Hüsrev Gerede C.

Nüzhetiye C.

Abbasağa Parkı

Yahya Kemal Beyatlı Parkı

Barbaros B.

Muvezzi C.

Yıldız Parkı
❺

BEŞİKTAŞ

P

Süleyman Seba C.

Çırağan C.

Deniz Müzesi

Beşiktaş

Taşlık Parkı

Dolmabahçe C.

❹
Saray Müzesi Koleksiyonları

❸
Dolmabahçe Sarayı

Kadırgalar C.

İnönü Stadyumu

❾

Dolmabahçe Camii

Meclisi Mebusan C.

Kabataş

↙ To Fener

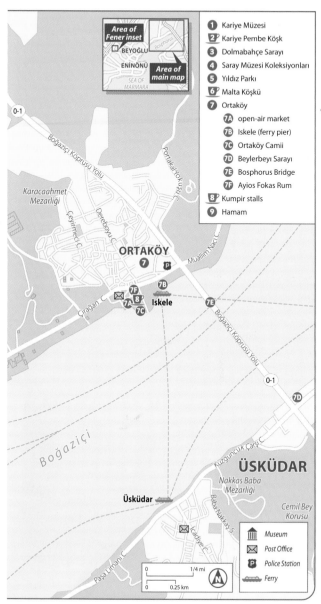

1 Kariye Müzesi
2 Kariye Pembe Köşk
3 Dolmabahçe Sarayı
4 Saray Müzesi Koleksiyonları
5 Yıldız Parkı
6 Malta Köşkü
7 Ortaköy
　7A open-air market
　7B Iskele (ferry pier)
　7C Ortaköy Camii
　7D Beylerbeyi Sarayı
　7E Bosphorus Bridge
　7F Ayios Fokas Rum
8 Kumpir stalls
9 Hamam

Area of Fener inset
BEYOĞLU
ENİNÖNÜ
SEA OF MARMARA
Area of main map
Bosphorus

0-1

Boğaziçi Köprüsü Yolu

Karacaahmet Mezarlığı

Çevirmeci C.

Dereboyu C.

Portakal Yokuşu C.

ORTAKÖY
7
P

Muallim Naci C.

Çırağan C.

7F
7A 8
7C
7B
Iskele

7E

Boğaziçi Köprüsü Yolu

0-1

7D

Boğaziçi

ÜSKÜDAR

Kuzguncuk Çarşı C.

Nakkas Baba Mezarlığı

Baba Nakkaş S.

Cemil Bey Korusu

Üsküdar

İcadiye C.

Paşa Limanı C.

0   1/4 mi
0   0.25 km
N

🏛 Museum
✉ Post Office
P Police Station
⛴ Ferry

Experience Istanbul's finest Byzantine art, then indulge in Ottoman affluence at Dolmabahçe Palace. Need some exercise? You can walk from here to Yıldız Park and onwards to Ortaköy, a charming waterfront neighborhood with plenty of dining options; and by walking you'll avoid crowded buses and traffic jams, busiest at weekends. START: **Bus 86 from Eminönü or 87 from Taksim to Edirnekapı, then 5-min walk.**

① ★★★ Kariye Müzesi (Kariye Museum). Built in the 11th century as Chora Church, the frescoes and mosaics added in the mid-1300s are some of the world's finest Byzantine art (*Special-Interest Tours*, p 41). When the church was converted to a mosque in 1511, they were plastered over, as representation of the human form is forbidden in Islam. Ironically this helped to preserve them. In the restored church, now a museum, gaze at the golden mosaics in the vaults of inner and outer narthexes, illustrating scenes from the life of Christ and the Virgin Mary. Above the entrance to the nave the figure of Theodore Metochites (1270–1332), the theologian who facilitated the church's redecoration, "presents" the church to Christ. No flash photography or tripods. ⏲ *90 min. Kariye Camii Sok, Edirnekapı.* ☎ *0212 522 1750. Admission 15 TL, children under 12 years free. Thurs–Tues winter 9am–5pm, summer 9am–7pm. Bus 86 from Eminönü or 87 from Taksim, then 5-min walk.*

② kids **Kariye Pembe Köşk.** Rest in a peaceful courtyard opposite the museum with tea, toasted sandwiches, or hot lentil soup. *27 Kariye Camii Sok, Edirnekapı.* ☎ *0212 635 8586. Tea and toasted sandwiches 10 TL.*

③ ★★ kids **Dolmabahçe Sarayı (Dolmabahçe Palace).** After lavish Topkapı Palace was built (*Special-Interest Tours*, p 24), the declining

Ottoman Empire ended its days here (*A Brief History*, p 170). Its highly ornate appearance is an eclectic mix of mid-19th-century baroque and rococo styles. The highlight is the **Selamlik,** home to the head of the house, with an ostentatious marble exterior and entrance hall with a superb gilded ceiling. The sultan received foreign visitors only from the 19th century, when the declining Empire depended on European trade. The Ambassadorial Reception hall was created to host guests; you can't miss one of the world's largest chandeliers, a 4-ton gift from Queen Victoria. Tours of the **Harem**—the private, far less ornate women's quarters—and Selamlik are only by

Ottoman Mehter music at Dolmabahçe Palace.

guided tour. You don't need a ticket to see the **Mehter band** (*Istanbul with Kids*, p 38) at 11am every Tuesday by the **Imperial Gate.** The pompous "changing of the guard" is performed by soldiers outside the gate every hour. ⏲ *2 hr. Dolmabahçe Cad, Beşiktaş.* ☎ *0212 236 9000. www.dolmabahce.gov.tr. Tour of Selamlik 15 TL, Harem 10 TL, tour of both 20 TL, children under 12 years free. Winter open 9am–4pm, summer 9am–5pm, closed Mon and Thurs. Tram/funicular: Kabataş.*

④ ★★ **Saray Müzesi Koleksiyonları (Palace Museum Collection).** The former palace kitchen opened as a museum in 2005 (originally known as Depo Müze), with over 40,000 pieces salvaged from Dolmabahçe Palace. Few visitors make it here, so it's easy to discover the Sultan's monograms on intricate glass flasks, 4m-high (13 ft.) cabinets with gold leaf, and gilded birdcages. I love the household items, like an 1870 Remington typewriter and central heating from 1912. There's a charming display of Ottoman family portrait photographs, and oil paints owned by Abdülmecid II (1866–1944). ⏲ *1 hr. Dolmabahçe Cad, Beşiktaş.* ☎ *0212 227 6671. www.millisaraylar.gov.tr. Admission 2 TL, children under 12 years free. Tues–Sun 9am–5pm. Tram/funicular: Kabataş.*

⑤ ★ **kids** **Yıldız Parkı.** The sultans once strolled and hunted here while living at Çirağan Palace—which later burnt down, and is now a deluxe hotel (*Hotels*, p 136)—and Yıldız Palace. These days it's local families on weekend visits. Enjoy dappled walks on peaceful weekdays, with courting couples seeking precious solitude. The steep road up from the main entrance leads to **Yıldız Porcelain Factory & Museum,** built by Abdülhamid II in 1896 to produce porcelain to rival

Once real deer were hunted at Yıldız Parkı.

Iznik's and still used today by artists. **Yıldız Sarayı Palace** has fascinating household items which belonged to later sultans who lived here, including Abdülhamid (1876–1909). Check out the 19th-century **Malta Köşkü** (⑥), with neo-classical, Islamic, and Ottoman styles, rococo arches, and baroque oval windows. Murat V (1840–1904) probably didn't notice, as he was imprisoned here by his brother Abdülhamid II for 27 years. **Çadır Köşkü** has a charming duck pond and cafe. ⏲ *1–2 hr. Yıldız Parkı. Çirağan Cad, Beşiktaş.* ☎ *0212 261 8460. Open daily dawn–dusk.*

⑥ **Malta Köşkü.** This chalet with a terrace commands great Bosphorus views—probably as close as you can get to a sultan's lifestyle. A lovely cafe with Turkish dishes, hot and cold. *Yıldız Korusu, Beşiktaş.* ☎ *0212 444 6644. Tea and pastries from TL 10.*

⑦ ★★★ **kids** **Ortaköy.** Once a fishing village, Ortaköy today is a busy neighborhood, especially at weekends. On summer weekends

Ortaköy Camii, picturesque neo-baroque mosque.

the **7A** **open-air market** (*Shopping, p 90*) has hats, hand-made jewelry, and old books. From the **7B** **Iskele (ferry pier),** ferries ply the Bosphorus and this is a popular stopping-off point. Perching over the Bosphorus is compact **7C** **Ortaköy Camii** (mosque; open dawn till nightfall) built in 1853 for Sultan Abdülmescit in neo-baroque style. Head upstairs to see restored frescoes, plus views of **7D** **Beylerbeyi Sarayı (Beylerbeyi Palace)** (*Neighborhood Walks Üsküdar, p 60*). At night, the lights on the mighty **7E** **Bosphorus Bridge** change color, graceful without being kitsch. Look out for **7F** **Ayios Fokas Rum's** beautiful bell tower (16 Muallim Haci Cad), a Greek Orthodox church previously central to the local Greek community. ⏱ *varies. Bus to Ortaköy.*

8 ★★ **kids** **Kumpir stalls.** An alternative to Ortaköy's trendy restaurants, these simple stalls sell filled baked potatoes (kumpir). Take a fruit-filled waffle to finish and dine on the wall while watching the boats. Bliss! *Mecidiye Köprüsü Sok, Ortaköy. Kumpir and waffle 6 TL.*

9 ★★ **Hamam.** You could substitute Ortaköy for a soak and scrub in a *hamam* (Turkish bath). With neighborhood baths throughout the city, **Çemberlitaş Hamam** is the most historic (and foreigner-friendly). Built in 1584 by Sinan, the huge marble slab and domes of the sıcaklık (hot room) are unchanged, as are the attendants' energetic scrubs and massages. Men and women bathe separately. Visitors are given wooden shoes, soap, and a *peş tamel* (wrap). You can choose extra treatments, from basic scrub to luxurious oil massage. ⏱ *1–2 hr. 8 Vezirhan Cad.* ☎ *0212 522 7974. www.cemberlitashamami.com.tr. Prices from 39 TL. Open daily 6am–12am. Tram: Çemberlitaş.* ●

Topkapı Palace

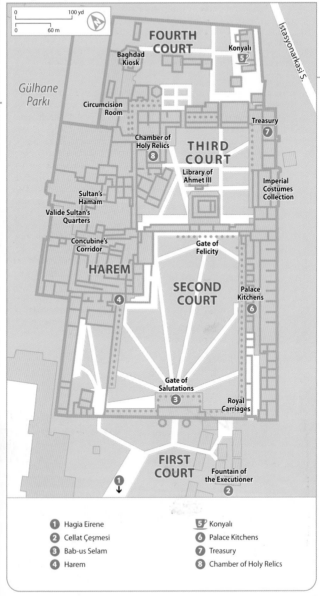

0   100 yd
0   60 m

FOURTH COURT

Konyalı **5**

Baghdad Kiosk

Gülhane Parkı

Circumcision Room

Treasury **7**

Chamber of Holy Relics **8**

THIRD COURT

Library of Ahmet III

Imperial Costumes Collection

Sultan's Hamam

Valide Sultan's Quarters

Concubine's Corridor

Gate of Felicity

HAREM

4

SECOND COURT

Palace Kitchens **6**

Gate of Salutations **3**

Royal Carriages

İstasyonarkasi S.

FIRST COURT

Fountain of the Executioner **2**

1 Hagia Eirene
2 Cellat Çeşmesi
3 Bab-us Selam
4 Harem

5 Konyalı
6 Palace Kitchens
7 Treasury
8 Chamber of Holy Relics

Previous page: Kanyon's superb contemporary architecture.

Probably Istanbul's most famous attraction, this sprawling 80,000 sq. m (861, 000 sq. ft,) palace complex was built by Mehmet II in 1478 at Sarayburnu, overlooking the meeting point of the Marmara, Bosphorus, and Golden Horn. Central to Ottoman sultans for almost 400 years, it housed thousands of people, with residences, offices, the seat of government, and soldiers' training ground. Spend several hours enjoying its treasures. START: **Tram to Sultanahmet.**

1 ★ **Hagia Eirene.** In the first courtyard, before entering the main gate, this 6th-century Byzantine church, presumably part of Hagia Sophia's complex, was never converted into a mosque—although used as a weapons arsenal in Ottoman times. Unfortunately, you're only likely to see the inside during rare concerts at the summer Istanbul Music Festival. Performers use the original five rows of built-in seats hugging the apse, above which is an 8th-century black mosaic cross on the wall. ⏱ *10 min.*

2 ★ **kids** **Cellat Çeşmesi (Fountain of the Executioner).** Although it resembles a disused water-fountain, its use was far more macabre. In the 16th century, this is where the executioner washed the blood off his sword and hands after a public execution, before re-entering the palace. ⏱ *10 min.*

3 ★ **kids** **Bab-us Selam (Gate of Salutations).** With distinctive twin conical towers, this leads into the second courtyard, where all visitors had to dismount, as only the sultan could ride through on horseback. It was also known as *kapı aralığı*, where high officials who had displeased the sultan were arrested and choked to death. The only thing to worry about these days is passing your bag through an X-ray machine—a far less horrible experience! Look up at the superbly extravagant gold-painted ceiling. On entering, look for the ornate **Royal Carriages,** created in Vienna for Abdulaziz (1830–76). Close by, the scaled-down model of the palace and its surrounds might help your navigation. ⏱ *15 min.*

4 ★★★ **kids** **Harem.** On the left of the third courtyard, this is well worth the extra ticket needed to

Bab-us Selam, where traitors were strangled.

It's a Concubine's Life

Although "harem" perhaps conjures up images of Oriental debauchery, it literally means "forbidden," and refers to the palace's private women's quarters. Life in this 300-room, enclosed complex was no picnic; girls and young women were brought from all corners of the Ottoman Empire to live a mundane existence, working as servants, sleeping in dormitories, and learning the palace ways. The only other people allowed in the harem were the sultan and his sons, plus hundreds of eunuch slaves (castrated boys), many from Ethiopia and Sudan, who guarded the women. Favored girls were "trained" as wives or concubines for the sultans by the Valide Sultan (sultan's mother, who really ruled the roost) and, ideally, would bear him sons.

explore the Harem's rooms—even though only a fraction is open to the public. Your journey into the "forbidden" quarter begins at the colonnaded, black-and-white cobbled **Corridor of Concubines,** where plates of food were laid out on marble counters. You'll gasp at the opulence of the **Imperial Hall,** complete with crystal chandelier and Sultan's sofa, where he entertained his best buddies. The Sultan's **apartments** and marble *hamam,* enclosed behind a golden door— allegedly for his own

The cobbled Corridor of Concubines.

safety—contrast sharply with the more modest living quarters of the concubines and eunuchs. But the prize woman, the **Valide Sultan** (Sultan's mom), enjoyed five-star living quarters, where her devoted son visited her every morning. *Tip:* Try to get to the Harem as soon as you arrive at the palace, as crowds build up during the day. (*It's a Concubine's Life,* above.) 🕐 *45 min.*

5 kids **Konyalı.** The palace's only restaurant is pricey, although the traditional Turkish dishes are good. The adjacent courtyard's cafe is slightly cheaper, with the same superb Bosphorus view. ☎ *0212 513 9696. Mains from 20 TL.*

6 ★ kids **Palace Kitchens.** In contrast to the lavish Treasury or the Throne Room, this is where the work was actually done. Heard the phrase "An army marches on its stomach"? Every soldier, and in this case sultan, needed food prepared here by several hundred staff for around 5,000 people each day— with 12 to prepare the sultan's sustenance alone. Under the domed stone ceilings, display cabinets glitter with silverware and crystal, and plates from Chinese celadon favored by the sultans because, allegedly, this type of ceramic changed color when in contact with poison. Now that's paranoia! 🕐 *20 min. See p 21,* ④.

⑦ ★★ **Treasury.** Most visitors line up for a glimpse of the famous curved **Topkapı Dagger,** from 1741 (made even more famous thanks to the 1964 film *Topkapi*), encrusted with diamonds and huge emeralds. Made for the Shah of Persia, in thanks for his gift of the **Nadir Shah throne** (in the fourth hall), he was assassinated before receiving it, so, you guessed it, Mahmud I (1696–1754) kept it for himself. If the eye-popping emeralds aren't enough, take a look at the 84-carat **Spoon-maker's Diamond.** The background to its name is a little hazy, but it may have been called after the scrap merchant who found it and received three spoons in return. You'll also see jeweled **golden candlesticks,** sent as a gift to the tomb of Mohammed, but returned to Constantinople after the evacuation of Medina in World War I. 🕐 *30 min.*

⑧ ★★ **Chamber of Holy Relics.** This is home to the palace's

The Palace Kitchens.

most sacred items, located inside the Privy Room where new sultans would seek blessing before the coronation ceremony. Religious items, plus holy objects found in Medina, were sent to sultans between the 16th and 19th centuries. The prized possession is believed to be the Holy Mantle of the Prophet Mohammed, given to Sultan Selim. Look out for the hair from the Prophet's beard, the sword of David, and seemingly ordinary kitchenware—from Abraham. Inside you'll hear the constant recital of verses from the Qur'an; on your way out look for the reader sitting at a tiny booth. 🕐 *20 min.*

Topkapı Palace: Practical Matters

Bab-ı Hümayun Cad. ☎ 0212 512 0480. www.topkapisarayi.gov.tr. Tickets 20 TL, children under 12 years free; Wednesday to Monday 9am to 5pm (winter), 9am to 7pm (summer). Tram: Gülhane/Sultanahmet. Perennially busy, especially in summer and at weekends, so beat the crowds by getting there at opening time or, in summer, late afternoons. Buy separate tickets for the **Harem** for 15 TL at its entrance (9am–4pm year-round), and separate **audio guides** for the palace and harem, available in many languages. Tip: If you're getting a taxi to the palace, ask the driver for "Topkapı Sarayı." If you just say "Topkapı," unscrupulous drivers might take you to the unrelated area of the same name!

Arty Istanbul

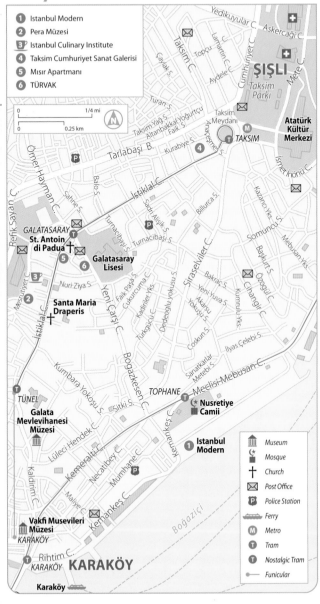

1. Istanbul Modern
2. Pera Müzesi
3. Istanbul Culinary Institute
4. Taksim Cumhuriyet Sanat Galerisi
5. Mısır Apartmanı
6. TÜRVAK

0	1/4 mi
0	0.25 km

ŞİŞLİ

Taksim Parkı

Atatürk Kültür Merkezi

TAKSİM

Taksim Meydanı

Tarlabaşı B.

İstiklal C.

GALATASARAY
St. Antoin di Padua

Galatasaray Lisesi

Nuri Ziya S.

Santa Maria Draperis

TÜNEL

Galata Mevlevihanesi Müzesi

TOPHANE

Nusretiye Camii

Istanbul Modern

Vakfı Musevileri Müzesi

KARAKÖY

KARAKÖY

Karaköy

Bogaziçi

🏛	Museum
☪	Mosque
✝	Church
✉	Post Office
🅿	Police Station
⛴	Ferry
Ⓜ	Metro
Ⓣ	Tram
Ⓣ	Nostalgic Tram
●	Funicular

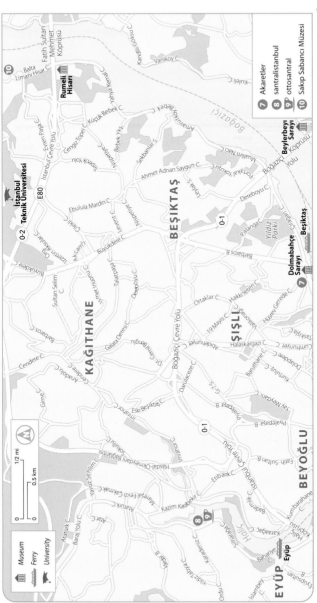

Legend:

7 Akaretler
8 santralistanbul
9 ottosantral
10 Sakıp Sabancı Müzesi

Museum
Ferry
University

1/2 mi
0.5 km

Place labels:

Balta Limanı Hisar C
Fatih Sultan Mehmet Köprüsü
Kandilli Göksu C
Vaniköy C
Rumeli Hisarı
Küçük Bebek C
Yahya Kemal C
Arnavutköy Bebek C
Evren Paşa
Cengiz Topel C
Nispetiye C
Bebek YKS
Sektbanlar S
Ahmet Adnan Saygun C
Muallim Naci C
Kuleli C
Boğaziçi
Beylerbeyi Sarayı
Boğaziçi Köprüsü Yolu
İstanbul Teknik Üniversitesi
E80
İstanbul Çevre Yolu
Tepecik Yolu
S. Kiraz Yokuşu
Dereboyu C
Ebulula Mardin C
Nispetiye C
Akçarı S
Büyükdere C
Levent C
BEŞİKTAŞ
0-1
Çırağan
Yıldız Parkı
Beşiktaş
0-2
Orta Uzettin Aksak C
Sultan Selim C
Büyükdere C
Talatpaşa C
Palangar C
Barbaros B
Dolmabahçe Sarayı
Ortaklar C
Hakkı Yeten C
Barbaros B
Cendere C
Galata Deresi
Dr. Cemil Bengü C
Boğaziçi Çevre Yolu
Abdulhamam C
19 Mayıs C
Valikonağı
Hüsrev Gerede C
ŞİŞLİ
Cumhuriyet C
Taşkışla C
KAĞITHANE
Dandarasa C
Halaskargazi C
Dolapdere C
Baruthane C
Kurtuluş C
Anavutça C
Cendere C
Girne C
İmrahor C
Eski Beşiktaş C
G-25
Yay Meydanı
Piyalepaşa B
BEYOĞLU
Hasdal-Okmeydanı Bağlantısı
Okluğu
İmrahor C
0-1
Fatih Sultan B
İstanbul Çevre Yolu
Etibank C
Bademlik C
Kumbarahane C
Atatürk C
Baraj Yolu C
Atar C
Mareşal Fevzi Çakmak C
Kazım Karabekir C
Karaağaç
Halıç
Haliç Köprüsü
8 9
EYÜP
Bahariye C
Eyüp
Yıldız Tabia C
İdlebeler B
İdlahmey C
Oruç C
Eyüpsultan B

Historic treasures cram the city, but to understand Istanbul's full breadth experience its artistic side. Over the last decade, new bijoux galleries have sprung up, mainly showcasing local artists. It's certainly been one of Istanbul's most exciting developments and has given the city a new cachet. START: **Tram: Fınıklı.**

❶ ★★★ Istanbul Modern.

When this contemporary art gallery opened in 2004 in a converted customs warehouse (p 17), it sparked a huge boost to the local art scene. The first floor's permanent exhibition, *New Works, New Horizons,* is a good start, highlighting prominent 19th-century Turkish painters and the development of modern and contemporary art. Look out for Ihsan Cemal Karaburçak (1897–1970), influenced by Cézanne, Gaugin, and Matisse from trips to Paris, and the huge works of Nejad Melih Devrim (1923–95), one of Turkey's earliest abstract painters. It's interesting to read how the first professional artists, including Osman Hamdi Bey, famed for his Orientalist style, operated under the new Turkish Republic from 1923, having been trained and financed under the Ottomans. Go downstairs, where the false ceiling made up solely of suspended books leads to the research area and temporary photographic exhibitions. The shop has an eclectic collection of prints, mugs, and even kits to paint reproductions of paintings on T-shirts. Tickets include entry to the cinema, often showing international art-house movies. ⏱ *90 min (see p 17 for details).*

❷ ★★ Pera Müzesi (Pera Museum).

Opened in 2005 in a Victorian mansion, this jewel of a museum contains the private collection of Suna and Inan Kıraç. After the permanent displays of delicate Ottoman ceramics, head to the upper three floors for changing

Turkey's first modern art gallery, Istanbul Modern.

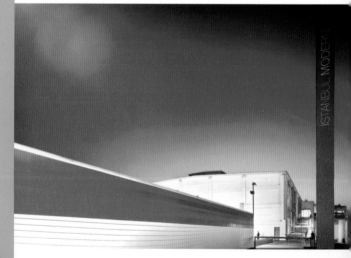

ISTANBUL MODERN

exhibitions, often by prestigious international artists such as Frida Kahlo and Diego Rivera. In the Ottoman painting exhibition, don't miss Osman Hamdi Bey's serene *Tortoise Trainer* (1906), Turkey's most valuable painting at $3.5m, depicting himself as a dervish "training" the tortoises with music. ⏱ *1 hr. 65 Meşrutiyet Cad, Tepebaşı.* ☎ *0212 334 9900. www.pm.org.tr. Admission 10 TL adults, 5 TL children 7–17 years. Tues–Sat 10am–7pm, Sun noon–6pm. Tram: Tünel, or Taksim and 15-min walk.*

3 ★★ kids **Istanbul Culinary Institute.** This stylish apprentice-run restaurant creates Ottoman cuisine with a contemporary twist, with a daily changing lunch menu, perhaps including pan-fried zucchini pancakes. Good value. 7:30am to 6pm Monday to Saturday. *59 Meşrutiyet Cad.* ☎ *0212 251 2214. Menus from 12 TL.*

4 ★ **Taksim Cumhuriyet Sanat Galerisi (Taksim Art Gallery).** Behind the omnipresent police vans is this multi-arched vaulted gallery, opened in late 2008, renovated from Istanbul's famous water tank (*Neighborhood Walks*, p 47). It houses a busy program of regularly changing exhibitions by contemporary Turkish and international artists. Its well-lit 22 rooms cover a mammoth 797 sq. m (85,578 sq. ft.), although each section is bijoux so it never feels overbearing. ⏱ *30 min. Taksim Meydanı, 2 Istiklal Cad.* ☎ *0212 245 7832. Admission free. Mon–Sat 10am–6pm. Bus/tram/funicular: Taksim.*

5 ★★ **Mısır Apartmanı.** On the top floor of this early-20th-century building, the über-stylish rooftop bar and restaurant **360Istanbul** (*Best Nightlife*, p 119*) opened in 2004,

The Pera Museum.

tempting more commercial art galleries here. Take the elevator to the top, then work your way down and look out for new galleries opening up. Highlights include: **Galeri Nev** (5/F; ☎ 0212 252 1525; www.galerinevistanbul.com), which represents over a dozen Turkish artists, plus photographer Robert Mapplethorpe and U.S.-born sculptor Mike Berg. With two changing exhibits by contemporary European artists or photographers, **Galerist** (4/F; ☎ 0212 244 8230; www.galerist.com.tr) has become even more iconic since exhibiting creations by Istanbul's top designer, Hussein Chalayan. Sneak onto its balcony for wonderful views over busy Istiklal Caddesi. Opened in May 2007, **Casa Dell'Art** (3/F; ☎ 0212 251 1214; www.casadell artegallery.com) represents around 15 young established Turkish artists and aims to promote them overseas. Each month sees an exhibition of two, perhaps figurative painting, installation, or photography. One of the building's oldest galleries, **Fototrek**

Some of the original machinery on show at santralistanbul.

Fotograf Merkezi (1/F; ☎ 0212 251 9014; www.fototrek.com), houses top-quality photographic exhibitions, usually of contemporary Turkish and European photographers, but occasionally of members of the photojournalist agency Magnum. ⏱ *1 hr. (See p 50 for details.)*

⑥ ★ TÜRVAK (Türker Inanoğlu Foundation Cinema Theatre Museum). This compact museum covers a century of Turkish cinema history, centered around the personal collection of film director Türker Inanoğlu, and is great fun even if you have no knowledge of its stars. Every square inch of wall space is crammed with photographs and prints of movie posters and stars, categorized not in chronological order but by venue. There's no information in English, sadly, but don't miss the posters on the first floor next to the elevator. Upstairs sees the Adnan Öztrak Television Hall with 1970s' cameras used by TRT (the state broadcaster), vacuum tubes, and digital-effect devices. There's a bright cafe upstairs. ⏱ *45 min. Yeniçarşı Cad 24, Beyoğlu.* ☎ *0212 245 8092. www.turvak. com. Admission 10 TL adults, 5 TL children under 12 years. Tues–Sun*

10am–6pm. Bus/funicular: Taksim, then 10-min walk.

⑦ ★ Akaretler. Officially named Şair Nedim Caddesi, this sloping street was once the neoclassical accommodation built in 1875 for Dolmabahçe Palace staff; after renovation, it's an über-stylish row of commercial galleries and high-end designer brands, centering on the **W Hotel** (p 142). At the time of writing, **Art On The Gallery** (no. 4; ☎ 0212 259 1543) had just opened with a flourish, and included works by Damien Hirst. **Rampa** (no. 21a; ☎ 0212 327 0800; www.rampa istanbul.com) is one of the biggest, with a huge space for large-scale works of its small stable of local contemporary artists, plus foreign artists including David LaChapelle. There's also a second space for prestigious **Galerist** (no. 4–8; see Misir Apartman). ⏱ *1 hour. Şair Nedim Cad, Beşiktaş. Tram: Kabataş, then 15-min walk.*

⑧ ★★★ kids santralistanbul. My favorite arts venue in Istanbul, this astounding space opened in 2007. The building transformed the old Silahtarağa Power Plant, the Ottoman Empire's first urban power station that provided electricity to the city from 1911 to 1983. Many of the original buildings had to be knocked down but were rebuilt to the same dimensions, giving mammoth scope and scale for large-scale art, sculptures, and installations. Its award-winning main gallery building covers 3,500 sq. m (37, 673 sq. ft.), housing several exhibits a year, mainly by Turkish contemporary artists. Don't miss the interactive Museum of Energy! (See p 36.) ⏱ *90 min. Eski Silahtarağa Elektrik Santralı, Kazım Karabekir Cad, Eyüp.* ☎ *0212 311 7809. www.santralistanbul.org. Admission 10 TL adults, 5 TL children 6–17 years. Tues–Fri 10am–6pm, Sat*

and Sun 10am–8pm. Free shuttle from Atatürk Kültür Merkez (Taksim) every 20 min (Tues–Sat), every hour Sun; boat from Eminönü to Eyüp; bus 44B or 47 from Eminönü, 36T from Taksim.

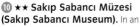 ★★ **ottosantral.** In the grounds of santralistanbul, it's all exposed pipes in this funky, industrial-looking restaurant, with a pricey menu of fresh salads, risotto, and unusual pizzas. Creative decor by day, achingly trendy DJ-bar by night. ☎ 0212 427 1889. Pizzas from 18 TL.

Dine at ottosantral, a restored power station.

⑩ ★★ **Sakıp Sabancı Müzesi (Sakıp Sabancı Museum).** In an Italianate 1920s' villa overlooking the Bosphorus, this world-class museum houses the private collection of the Sabancı family, a prestigious dynasty of Turkish industrialists. The permanent collection of Ottoman calligraphy in the elegant Atlı Köşk mansion (their former home) covers 500 years of works including rare manuscripts of the Qur'an, exquisitely displayed.

The annex holds temporary exhibits, often of modern European artists. Recent years have seen major retrospectives of Dalí and Picasso. From the museum, take a stroll in nearby pleasant Emirgan Park. ⏱ 90 min. 42 Sakıp Sabancı Cad, Emirgan. ☎ 0212 277 2200. http://muze. sabanciuniv.edu. Admission 10 TL adults, children under 15 years free. Open Tues–Sun 10am–6pm; Wed 10am–8pm. Bus: 22 or 42T.

Ottoman calligraphy at Sakıp Sabancı Museum.

Istanbul with Kids

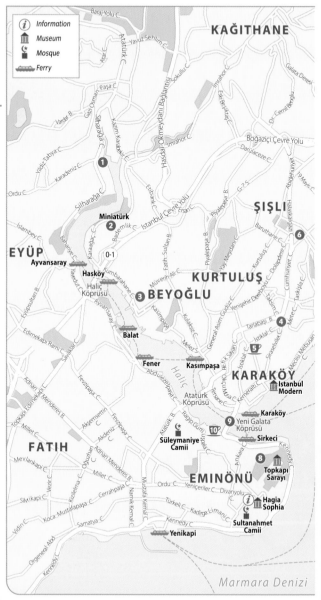

ⓘ	Information
🏛	Museum
☪	Mosque
⛴	Ferry

KAĞITHANE

Baraj Yolu C.

ŞİŞLİ

Miniatürk ②

EYÜP

Ayvansaray

Hasköy

Haliç Köprüsü

Balat

Fener

Kasımpaşa

KURTULUŞ

BEYOĞLU

KARAKÖY

Istanbul Modern

Karaköy

Yeni Galata Köprüsü

Sirkeci

FATIH

Süleymaniye Camii

EMİNÖNÜ

Topkapı Sarayı

Hagia Sophia

Sultanahmet Camii

Yenikapı

Marmara Denizi

Rumeli Hisarı Müzesi ⑦

Akçam S.
Çilekli C.
İsmet İnönü C.
Keçeleri C.
Tepeci Yolu
Cengiz Topel C.
Küçük Bebek
Büyükdere C.
Ebulula Mardin C.
Meydan S.
Levent C.
Nispetiye C.
Bebek Yks.
Yahya Kemal C.
Cevdet Paşa C.
Dereboyu C.
Nispetiye C.
Ahmet Adnan Saygun C.
Şekbanlar S.
Kandilli-Göksu
Boğaziçi Çevre Yolu
Barbaros B.
Leylak S.
Amavutköy Res.
Ortaklar C.
Ambarlıdere S.
Dereboyu C.
Portakal Oluğu C.
0-1
BEŞİKTAŞ
Cemil Topuzlu Parkı
Boğaziçi
Yankoy C.
Kuleli C.
Hakkı Veren C.
Çalıkonağı C.
Hüsrev Gerede C.
Palangaç C.
Maliim Naci C.
Kalantor S.
Barbaros B.
Çırağan C.
Yıldız Parkı
Boğaziçi Köprüsü Yolu
Valiboyu C.
Beylerbeyi Çamlıca C.
Maçka Parkı
Dolmabahçe C.
🏛 🚋 **Beşiktaş**
Gümüşsuyu C.
Dolmabahçe Sarayı
Cemil Bey Korusu
Reyospatu S.
Guzeldere C.
🚢 **Kabataş**
Fethi Paşa Korusu
Kadıye C.
Gümüşyolu
OFS.
Şamlı Ca C.
Üsküdar 🚢
Paşa Limanı C.
Cumhuriyet C.
Selmani Pak. C.
ÜSKÜDAR
Kuşbakışı C.
Şile Otoyolu
Paşa Limanı C.
Hakimiyet Milliye Gündoğumu C.
Selami Alefendi C.
Gazi C.
Kıskılı C.
Mahir İzi C.
Ord. Prf. Fahrenn. Kerim Gökay C.
Doğancılar C.
Halk C.
Çavuşdere C.
Allame C.
0-1
Uncular C.
Eski Toptaşı C.
Nuhkuyusu C.
Mütevellişeşme S.
Kuşyolu C.
Kısıklı C.
Aliuçler C.
Harem 🚢
Karacaahmet Mezarlığı
Tibbiye C.
Dr. Eyüp C.
Harem İskele C.
D100 E5
Ankara İstanbul Devletyolu
Harem İskele C.
Tibbiye C.
Aksoy C.
Aliuçler C.

Haydarpaşa 🚢

①	santralistanbul
②	Miniatürk
③	Rhami Koç Müzesi
④	Istiklal Nostaljic Tram
⑤	Dondurma stalls
⑥	Askeri Müzesi
⑦	Rumeli Hisarı Müzesi
⑧	Gülhane Park
⑨	Galata Köprüsü
⑩	Eminönü fishing boats

0 — 3/4 mi
0 — 0.75 km
N

Much of everyday Istanbul life is a kids' paradise, from watching the fishermen on Galata Bridge to world-class museums. Locals adore children, so don't be surprised when grown men coo over your baby. The list below is too much in one day, so pick and choose to suit ages and interests. All museums have family-friendly cafes, and many can be reached by boat, especially the Haliç (Golden Horn) Ferry Line. START: **Bus from Taksim or Eminönü.**

1 ★★★ **santralistanbul.** In addition to fabulous art exhibitions at this refurbished Ottoman power station (*Arty Istanbul*, p 28), the **Museum of Energy** has a Play Zone with 22 interactive machines, buttons, and games galore designed for ages 4 to 14 (although adults like me will love it too). Create magnetic sculptures and even your own electricity, then take a closer look at huge turbine generators dating back to 1911. One highlight is the Reactable, a new electronic "instrument." Kids can mess around in the Switch Gear Room, where the original connecting cables distributed electricity to the whole city; it's not interactive—so no danger of them fusing Istanbul. Decent kids' menu and pizza at **ottosantral** (p 33). ⏱ *1 hr. (See p 32 for details)*

2 ★★ **Miniatürk.** If you want to see Istanbul's best landmarks close up, this outdoor museum is the place where a few strides (even for little people) take you from Galata Tower to the Blue Mosque via Dolmabahçe Palace. There are 45 models of Istanbul's best-loved monuments, plus 15 from the Ottoman Empire, including the Egyptian pyramids, and a toy train ideal for small passengers to weave their way around the park. An indoor exhibition recreates the World War I battlefields of the Dardanelles Campaign, complete with machine-gun fire and bombs, while the playground, giant chess set, and lovely cafe make it a great family trip. ⏱ *1–2 hr. Imrahor Cad, Sütlüce.* ☎ *0212 222 2882. www.miniaturk.com.tr. Admission: 10 TL adults, children under 8 years free. Open daily 9am–6pm. Boat from Eminönü or Eyüp to Sütlüce; bus 47 from Eminönü or 54HT from Taksim.*

Tiny world wonders at Miniatürk.

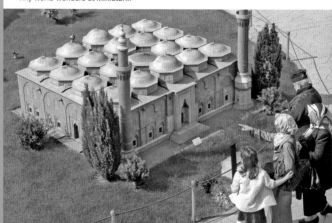

Boarding the Boeing at Rahmi Koç Museum.

❸ ★★ Rahmi Koç Museum.

Kids can jump aboard a Douglas DC-3 (1942) plane, gaze at huge anchors, and explore a plethora of cars ranging from Formula 1 and a 1908 Model T Ford to a 1958 German Amphicar. You can even enter their U.S.A.-produced submarine. Built in 1944 for service in World War II against the Japanese, it then saw 30 years service with the Turkish Naval Forces. This private collection of Turkey's great industrialist Rahmi Koç (b 1930) also houses sawmills and lathes grinding into action when you enter the workshop. You'll love pressing the buttons on the "How Does It Work?" exhibits to watch the mechanism in a cutaway car or domestic washing machine. At weekends, ride the 1960s' diesel train along the Golden Horn, between Hasköy and Sütlüce. ⏱ *90 min. 5 Hasköy Cad, Hasköy.* ☎ *0212 369 6600. www.rmk-museum.org.tr. Admission: 12.50 TL adults, 6 TL children 7–17 years. Submarine 6 TL adults, 4 TL children 7–17 years. Tues–Fri 10am–5pm, Sat and Sun 10am–8pm (winter 10am–6pm). Bus: 54HT from Taksim, 47 from Eminönü.*

❹ ★ Istiklal Nostaljic Tram.

This one-carriage red tram trundles along Istiklal Caddesi between Taksim and Tünel, a favorite with visitors, and locals avoiding the mass of pedestrians. Originally running along the 19th-century Grande Rue de Pera (the street's previous name), it was taken out of service in 1961 then restored, and re-introduced in 1990. Grab a window seat for a street-level view on the 1.6-km (1-mile) journey, taking about 10 minutes, with a stop halfway at Galatasaray Lisesi (*Neighborhood Walks Istiklal Caddesi*, p 46). The driver constantly clangs the bell—the original one—to shoo pedestrians out of the way. Use your *akbil* (transport

Nostaljic Tram running down Istiklal Caddesi.

Scramble the battlements at Rumeli Hisarı Müzesi.

token; *Savvy Traveler*, p 164) or pay the driver. ⏱ *10 min. Ticket 1.25 TL. Trams run from Atatürk Monument (Taksim Meydanı) to Tünel Meydanı, every 5–8 min, 9am–11pm.*

5 ★ **Dondurma stalls.** You can't miss the traditional dondurma (ice cream) stalls dotted along Istiklal—originally from the city of Kahramanmaraş. Dondurma (4 TL) is thicker, stickier, and stretchier than normal ice cream thanks to extra ingredients like mastic and sahlep (starch from orchids), and is served up by sellers clad in traditional Ottoman costume garb. Never has the serving of ice cream into a cone been so entertaining! *Istiklal Cad.*

6 ★ **Askeri Müzesi (Military Museum).** The army played a huge role in Istanbul's history (modern Turkey's founder Mustafa Kemal Atatürk, see *A Brief History*, p 170) was previously an army general), and this well-laid-out museum celebrates military history from the Ottoman Empire to the present day. Highlights include the Hall of the Conquest of Istanbul, recreating the battle scene and, from the same era, the mammoth chains placed at the entrance of the Golden Horn. Kids will love the dazzling Ottoman gold-plated armor and Yemeni daggers. People gather for the afternoon Mehter performances, the uniformed, pompous Janissary band (outdoor in summer, indoor in winter) that led the army into battle (below). ⏱ *90 min (inc Mehter). Harbiye.* ☎ *0212 233 2720. Admission: 3 TL adults, 1.30 TL children 6–12 years, extra for camera, video. Wed–Sun 9am–4:30pm, Mehter band 3–4pm. Metro/bus: Harbiye.*

Mehter—Band of the Ottoman Army

The world's oldest military band, the Mehter, accompanied Ottoman armies into battle to instill confidence and, ideally, strike terror into the enemy. These days, various bands perform marches and recitals at the **Military Museum** (daily) and **Dolmabahçe Palace** (p 20), plus at various special events. In full Ottoman costume, the band uses traditional Turkish instruments including *zurna* (reed instrument) and *davul* (large drum). Its stirring style and beat are thought to have influenced European classical composers like Mozart, Beethoven, and Haydn—though their music did not have to evoke such terror as their Ottoman counterparts' did.

7 ★★★ Rumeli Hisarı Müzesi (Fortress of Europe). This 30,000 sq. m (323,000 sq. ft.) landmark fortress overlooking the Bosphorus with its sturdy walls and watchtowers is fabulous for scrambling around, especially as it's surprisingly quiet (it also closes oddly early, even in summer). Built by Mehmet the Conqueror in 1452 in just 4 months (don't we all wish for builders like that?) it lies opposite his Anadolu Hisarı (Fortress of Asia) on the narrowest part of the water, and was part of the Sultan's plans for his Siege of Constantinople in 1453. Its three sturdy towers, 12-sided flag tower, and rows of canons dating back to Süleyman the Magnificent (p 171) make great exploring, though hold on to little ones if you're climbing up to the walls. Look out for the amphitheater, venue of occasional summer concerts, and enjoy views of the huge cemetery from Zaghanos Paşa Kulesi, the southwestern tower. **Kale Cay Bahcesi** cafe is a good lunch spot, at the bottom of the fortress. 🕐 *90 min. Yahya Kemal Cad, Sariyer.* ☎ *0212 263 5305. Admission 3 TL. Thurs–Tues 9am–4:30pm. Bus: 25 or 40E from Beşiktaş, 559C from Taksim then 10-min walk.*

8 ★ Gülhane Park. Although Istanbul sadly lacks green space, at least this clean, well-laid-out park, with broad avenues lined with ancient plane trees, provides some breathing space. Great for the kids to run around, it also houses a museum, historic artifacts, and a good hill-top cafe. (*The Best of the Outdoors, p 92.*)

9 ★★ Galata Köprüsü (Galata Bridge). One of Istanbul's great landmarks (*Best in One Day, p 6*), this makes a lovely end to the day. From the bridge, watch the row of fishermen cast lines, peering optimistically into the murky waters below. Kids can check out their pots of bait (usually maggots) and buckets of tiny fish. Breathtaking views take in ferries cruising up the Haliç (Golden Horn), the mêlée of people crowding into Eminönü's markets, and spot-lit mosques at night. This is one of my favorite places to hear the cacophony of sounds of *azan* (call to prayer) from myriad mosques. *Bridge joining Eminönü to Karaköy. Bus/tram: Eminönü or Karaköy.*

10 ★★ Eminönü fishing boats. Bobbing on Eminönü's waterfront are huge ornamental fishing boats, offering fresh fish cooked by elaborately dressed attendants in matching Ottoman costume. Feast on cheap *balık ekmek* (fresh fish in bread) with salad, or a corn-on-the-cob with a cool drink. It's an unbeatable people-watching spot for all ages. *Eminönü pier, west of Galata Bridge. Balık ekmek 4 TL.*

Hub of fishing on Galata Bridge.

Byzantine Constantinople

Legend:
- Information
- Museum
- Mosque
- Train Station
- Metro
- Tram

Map labels:
Karaköy · Eminönü · Sirkeci · EMINÖNÜ · Mısır Hamidiye Çarşısı · EMINÖNÜ · Daye Hatun Meschidi · Sirkeci Tren İstasyonu · SIRKECI · Topkapı Sarayı · Arkeoloji Müzesi · Gülhane · GÜLHANE · Yerebatan Sarnıçı · SULTANAHMET · Hagia Sophia · Sultanahmet Camii · SULTANAHMET · Kabasakal · Kennedy C · Yeni Galata Köprüsü · Haliç · Atatürk K. · Rüstem Paşa Camii · Süleymaniye Camii · İstanbul Üniversitesi · Kapalı Çarşısı · Beyazıt Camii · BEYAZIT · CEMBERLITAŞ · Kumkapı · KUMKAPI · Şehzadebaşı Camii · ŞEHZADEBAŞI · İstanbul Üniversitesi · LALELI · Laleli Camii · LALELI · Atatürk B. · AKSARAY · YENIPAŞA · Fatih Camii · FATIH · FENER · Sultan Selimiye Camii · Yavuz Selim C. · Namık Kemal · Mustafa Kemal C. · Egrikapı Rum Mezarlığı

Scale: 1/4 mi · 0.25 km · N

Numbered list:
1. Edirnekapı
2. Çakırağa Çay Evi
3. Tekfur Sarayı
4. Kariye Müzesi
5. Fethiye Camii
6. Zeyrek Camii
7. Zeyrekhane
8. Bozdoğan Kemeri
9. Vefa Bozacısı
10. Kalenderhane Camii
11. Yerebatan Sarnıcı
12. At Meydanı
13. Hagia Sophia
14. Büyüksaray Mozaik Müzesi
15. Bukoleon Sarayı

After Istanbul's mosques, it's time for pre-Ottoman monuments. Once named Byzantium, Emperor Constantine I made this the capital of the Roman Empire in A.D. 324, renamed it Constantinople, and adopted Christianity. Today's Istanbul boasts astounding Byzantine-era churches and cisterns. From Edirnekapı, you can walk between most venues. START: **Bus to Edirnekapı.**

① ★ **Edirnekapı (Charsius Gate).** The name of this gate on the 6.5km-long (4 miles) 5th-century city walls built by Emperor Theodosius II (408–450) now refers to the transport hub, best seen from the top of its poker-straight restored walls. Edge closer to the real thing, farther west, to see part of its original structure with Ottoman carvings over the arch. ⏲ *30 min. Bus: 87 to Edirnekapı.*

②2 ★ **Cakirağa Cay Evi.** This traditional teahouse is in keeping with the historic, earthy neighborhood. Sip tea inside or take a table under the canopy opposite. *Hoca Çakır Cad. Bus: 87 to Edirnekapı.*

③ ★ kids **Tekfur Sarayı (Palace of Constantine Porphyrogenitus).** Closed for restoration since 2006 (completion date unknown), this former Byzantine palace, built into the city walls, is now a mere

shell. Completed in the early 14th century, it later served as a brothel, pottery workshop, and poorhouse before being abandoned in the late 18th century. Pop into the cooing weekend **Pigeon Market** in the adjacent sports court for hearty trading—these birds cost up to $500. The ancient Middle Eastern hobby of pigeon racing lives on! ⏲ *15–30 min. Corner of Şişhane Cad and Hoca Çakır Cad. Bus: 87 to Edirnekapı.*

④ ★★★ **Kariye Müzesi (Kariye Museum, or Church of St. Savior in Chora).** Inside this modest-looking 11th-century church are world-class frescoes and mosaics, procured later by Theodore Metochites (1270–1332), writer and senior member of the Byzantine administration who died here in 1332. Among these stunning works, look out for his portrait in the inner narthex. Metochites took the genealogy of Christ as his starting point when commissioning mosaics for the domes and walls.

Ruins of Tekfur Sarayı, previously a palace, brothel, and workshop.

Christ adorns the dome at Fethiye Camii.

The two domes of the inner narthex hold the centerpiece—Christ, plus the Life of the Virgin series. It was converted to a mosque soon after the Conquest, but nothing remains here from the Ottoman period. ⏱ *60–90 min. See p 20.*

⑤ ★★ Fethiye Camii (Church of the Pammakaristos). From ④, walk down to Draman Caddesi, then Fethiye Caddesi (10 min; see detailed map, p 40). This rarely visited mosque, nestled in the conservative Çarşamba neighborhood, was built in 1292. It was a nunnery, seat of the Patriarchate (1456–1568), and converted to a mosque in 1573 by Murat III who renamed it Fethiye (victory) to celebrate his conquests over Georgia and Azerbaijan. In the late 20th century, its amazingly well-preserved Byzantine frescoes and mosaics were discovered beneath the stone-and-brick facade. The startling mosaic centerpiece of Jesus with the prophets of the Pentateuch covers the dome of the grave chapel. ⏱ *40 min. Fethiye Kapısı, off Fethiye Cad. Admission: 10 TL adults, 5 TL children under 13 years. Summer Tues–Sun 9:30am–7pm, winter 9:30am–4:30pm. Bus: 90 Eminönü to Draman.*

⑥ ★★ kids Zeyrek Camii (Monastery of the Pantocrator). It's a lovely cobbled uphill walk from the main road to Küçükpazar, a neighborhood of ramshackle wooden houses and kids playing soccer—a far cry from its prestigious past. This mosque (closed for restoration until 2013) was the original church of the monastery built between 1118 and 1124 by Empress Eirene Komnena. Mehmet II turned the monastery into a *medrese* (religious school) and the church into a mosque. If closed, try to find the caretaker (tip appreciated) to show you its high-ceilinged interior and ornate mosaic floors. ⏱ *20 min. Ibadethane Sok. Bus: Taksim or Eminönü to Atatürk Bulvarı.*

⑦ ★ Zeyrekhane. Opposite the monastery, sip coffee or taste Turkish dishes on the restaurant's terrace, a restored building within the old monastery complex. A perfect stop on a Byzantine tour. *10 Ibadethane Arkası Sok, Zeyrek.* ☎ *0212 532 2778. Bus: Taksim or Eminönü to Atatürk Bulvarı. Main courses from 15 TL.*

⑧ ★ kids Bozdoğan Kemeri (Aqueduct of Valens). You probably passed through these arches from the airport. The 4th-century two-tiered aqueduct was completed under Emperor Valens to carry water from Belgrade Forest to the palace, and was still in use centuries later. Follow it a few meters west to the arches' north side to the local teahouse, with tables outside during summer. ⏱ *20 min. Aqueduct parallel to Mustafa Kemalpaşa Cad, crossing Atatürk Bulvarı.*

⑨ ★★ kids Vefa Bozacısı. The well-trodden stone threshold indicates its age, a favorite since 1876 with original intricate tiled interior.

Locals' favorite venue for boza, the famous fermented millet drink.

Try a *boza*, made from fermented millet, fruity *şira* drink, or a simple ice cream. *104 Katıp Çelebi Cad. Bus: 87 to Edirnekapı. Boza 3 TL.*

⑩ ★★ Kalenderhane Camii.
Site of a church since the 6th century, once surrounded by monastery buildings, this is a rare domed Greek cross church. Its gloomy interior improved when the Ottomans installed windows after converting it to a mosque following the 1453 conquest. It was renamed when Mehmet II assigned it to the Kalenderi sect of the Dervish. Still functioning today, its distinctive gray-and-pink marble walls gleam from shafts of light creeping through high windows. Look for the fresco fragments above the main doorway, although most of the frescoes discovered during its 1966 restoration are now in the Archaeology Museum (p 14). From here you can walk to the tram for Sultanahmet. ⏱ *20 min. 16 Mart Şehitleri Cad. Open dawn–dusk. Tram: Üniversite.*

⑪ ★★ kids Yerebatan Sarnıçı (Basilica Cistern). The Byzantines used engineering know-how to bring water to the city (p 16), despite droughts and sieges. Founded in A.D. 532 by Emperor Justinian (487–565), this vast underground cistern held around 100,000 tons of water, with 336 9m-high (30 ft.) columns holding up the roof, thought to be built by 7,000 slaves. Once traversed by rowing boat, now by walkway, this is one of many cisterns lying under the city. Opposite the entrance, the blackened **Million Stone** is what remains of a monumental landmark, which once marked distances from Byzantine's capital to other prominent cities. You're now on **Divan Yolu,** one of the Empire's most strategic

Windows galore at Kalenderhane Camii, thanks to the Ottomans.

What remains of the great Bukoleon Sarayı.

streets, which led to Rome. ⏱ *45 min. See p 16 for details.*

⑫ ★★ kids At Meydanı (Hippodrome). Imagine thousands of fans cheering on chariot racing, or perhaps macabre jeering at public executions, in one of the Empire's largest hippodromes (*Neighborhood Walks*, p 68). Built in the 3rd century and enlarged by Constantine I, this was the site of 30,000 deaths during the A.D. 532 Nika Riots between rival supporters of the Blue and Green chariot teams, which had deep political roots. No horses or executions here today, just three ancient monuments, of which the **Egyptian Obelisk** was later adorned with scenes of Theodosius I (A.D. 346–95) at the Hippodrome's royal box. ⏱ *30 min. At Meydanı. Tram: Sultanahmet.*

⑬ ★★★ kids Hagia Sophia. Rebuilt by Emperor Justinian in A.D. 537, its hulking exterior contrasts with its ornate interior and breathtaking dome (p 7). It followed a basic rule of Byzantine architecture: A modest exterior to save your attention for inside. When you've savored the religious mosaics, return outside to see the Byzantine frieze of lambs, remains of the earlier 5th-century Hagia Sophia. ⏱ *90 min. See p 7.*

⑭ ★ Büyüksaray Mozaik Müzesi (Mosaic Museum). Nestled behind **Arasta Bazaar,** the stone walls are the only remains of Emperor Justinian's 6th-century Byzantine Great Palace, in ruins since 1206. The incredible mosaics you see today—huntsmen spearing gazelles and tussling elephants and lions—are some of the few remaining Byzantine non-religious mosaics, unearthed during excavations in 1912. The photographic display shows how these mosaics were discovered and restored. ⏱ *40 min. Arasta Çarşısı, Torun Sok. ☎ 0212 518 1205. Admission 8 TL adults, children under 12 years free. Tues–Sun 9am–4pm. Tram: Sultanahmet.*

⑮ ★ Bukoleon Sarayı (Bucoleon Palace). Originally part of the Byzantine emperors' Great Palace, this is its last remaining wall. Built by Emperor Theophilos in A.D. 842, the western facade was demolished in 1873 when the railway line to Sirkeci was built. From here it's a short walk to **Küçük Ayasofya** (p 68), or a pleasant stroll to the waterfront. ⏱ *10 min. Kennedy Cad. Tram: Sultanahmet.* ●

Istiklal Caddesi

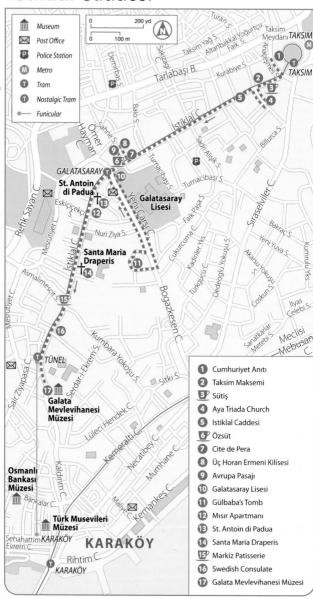

Museum
Post Office
Police Station
Metro
Tram
Nostalgic Tram
Funicular

1 Cumhuriyet Anıtı
2 Taksim Maksemi
3 Sütiş
4 Aya Triada Church
5 Istiklal Caddesi
6 Özsüt
7 Cite de Pera
8 Üç Horan Ermeni Kilisesi
9 Avrupa Pasajı
10 Galatasaray Lisesi
11 Gülbaba's Tomb
12 Mısır Apartmanı
13 St. Antoin di Padua
14 Santa Maria Draperis
15 Markiz Patisserie
16 Swedish Consulate
17 Galata Mevlevihanesi Müzesi

Previous page: Pretty tomb of Gulnus Emetullah Valide Sultan.

This 3km-long pedestrianized street (Independence Avenue) was once known as Rue de Pera, and is still modern Istanbul's main artery. It's the hub for shopping, soccer celebrations, and demonstrations for thousands of people, day and night, home to restaurants, churches, cinemas, mosques, and noble art nouveau architecture. START: **Bus, metro, or tram/funicular to Taksim.**

1 ★ Cumhuriyet Anıtı (Republic Memorial). This striking arch-shaped monument was commissioned by Mustafa Kemal Atatürk to commemorate the founding of the Turkish Republic and made by Italian sculptor Pietro Canonica in 1928. At last, the post-Ottoman era meant figurative expressions could now be used (previously forbidden in Islam). So one shows Atatürk the leader, with Ismet Inönü (the Republic's first president) and Fevzi Çakmak (soldier and ex-prime minister) marking the foundation of the young Turkish Republic. Around the other side, Atatürk stands with soldiers, representing the War of Independence. It's an unusual format—not surprising considering it was originally designed as a square-shaped fountain. ⏱ *10 min. Taksim Meydanı.*

Cumhuriyet Anıtı in Taksim Square.

2 ★ Taksim Maksemi (Water Distribution Center). This white, low, octagonal building, the first structure in Taksim Square, was the water distribution center ordered by Sultan Mahmud I in 1732. Recently it was restored and converted into the **Taksim Art Gallery** (p), although practically hidden by the phalanx of ever-present police and vans. The square is the hub of most political demonstrations, which are best avoided, especially on May Day. *Taksim Meydanı.*

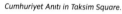

3 ★ Sütiş. With fabulous high ceilings and speedy service, this is a good stop for a dish of menemen (egg dish), Turkish breakfast, or coffee and traditional milk-based pudding. *7 Istiklal Cad.* ☎ *0212 251 3270. Turkish breakfast 10 TL.*

4 ★ Aya Triada Church. After a 5-minute walk, you'll see Istanbul's largest Greek Orthodox Church on the left, just off Istiklal Caddesi. This majestic white church was built in 1880 by Greek architect Kampanaki. It's officially only open for Sunday services, although you may be able to peep inside if the caretaker is around. If so, you'll love the sunlight streaming through the four large circular stained-glass windows, casting deep red and green light. With less dark wood and gold than many Greek churches, it

Aya Triada, Istanbul's largest Greek Orthodox church.

nonetheless has impressive frescoes above the gallery, and a painted dome. Mosaics of the Virgin Mary and Christ dominate the entrance hall. ⏱ *15 min. Entrance off Meşelik Sok, off Istiklal Cad. Services Sun 9–11am. Bus/tram/funicular to Taksim.*

⑤ ★ **Istiklal Caddesi.** Until very recently, this northern end of the iconic street had darkened covered alleyways (*pasaj*), running off the main drag. But with a huge facelift underway, most shops and alleys have been gutted. Shame, because it used to house the historic Emek Sinema, in existence since 1920 when it was known as Melek Sinemasi. At the time of writing, the carved stonework exterior remains—hopefully it just needs a quick clean-up without extensive changes. Look out for **Rumeli Han** on the right, one of the most adorned doorways with inscriptions in Arabic. A little further down, opposite **Alkazar Sinemasi**— screening Hollywood and Turkish movies—has a wonderful stonework facade, in keeping with Beyoğlu's ornate style. This was an important building in the 19th century, originally a theater set up by Turkish actor **Ayfer Feray** (1928–94), heartthrob for decades. ⏱ *10 min. 62 Istiklal Cad.*

⑥ ★ kids **Özsüt.** Cakes, puddings, and ice-creams… it's a sweettooth's dream! Take a coffee with traditional Turkish pudding aşure on a balcony seat—a great people-watching spot. *206 Istiklal Cad.* ☎ *0212 292 9678. Coffee and cake 12 TL.*

⑦ ★★ **Cite de Pera.** A fine reminder of the Grande Rue de Pera's glory years. And here's a little-known fact: Previously it was the Naum Theater hosting Italian operas, which burned down during the great Pera fire of 1870. Greek-Turkish banker Hristaki Zografos Efendi bought the land, and the restored building was named Cite de Pera. In the 1940s, florists traded from the first-floor stores, and it was known as Çiçek Pasajı (Flower Passage), a name still used today. When the building collapsed in 1978 and was then renovated, it was filled with noisy *meyhanes* (traditional restaurants). These days it's a shadow of its former self with a few

Historic Cite de Pera, now Çiçek Pasajı.

Everyone's favorite meeting point, the Galatasaray Lisesi gates.

bars and restaurants (with better restaurants nearby) but still worth a look inside. I'm not as keen on the colored glass in its renovated window, but love the ornate stone carvings above the entrance. ⏱ *10 min. 172 Istiklal Cad.*

❽ ★ Üç Horan Ermeni Kilisesi (Armenian Church of Three Altars). A real hidden gem on **Balık Pasajı**, this church behind heavy wooden doors (usually open to the public) celebrated its 200th anniversary in 2008. With a plain exterior and graceful interior, the story goes that an unknown sick man prayed to be cured, promising to build a church with three altars if his prayers were answered. Peek inside to see the famed altars. ⏱ *15 min. 24 Sahane Sok, Balık Pasajı. Services Sun 9am–noon. Open daily 8am–5pm.*

❾ ★ Avrupa Pasajı. Don't be distracted by the passageway's grubby glass ceiling; instead look up above the shop entrances to small black statues of angels lining what was the original exterior. This tiny arcade is the place to browse for antiques—or more precisely interesting ephemera. ⏱ *15 min. Off Sahane Sok. Most stores open daily 10am–7pm.*

❿ ★★ Galatasaray Lisesi. A massive landmark, its gate and pillars being my favorite Beyoğlu meeting-point, this school was established in the 15th century, when Sultan Beyazit II (1447–1513) responded to an old man's wish to build a school for educating "promising young men." Fast forward to the late 19th century when Sultan Abdülaziz acquired the help of Napoleon III in transforming the school to the contemporary French lycée system, a huge influence on modernizing Ottoman Turkey. Since 1992, it's been part of Galatasaray University, and is co-educational with entrance exams required, even at primary level. Visitors are allowed to enter the grounds (9am–5pm), or just peer through the ornate gilded gates. ⏱ *15 min. Istiklal Cad.*

⓫ ★ Gülbaba's Tomb. Take a 10-minute detour down Yeniçarşı Caddesi to see the little-known tomb of the man who inspired the Lisesi (above), a humble reminder of a promise kept by Sultan Beyazit. The working-class neighborhood is lively, and the grave—the only one there—is well kept, often tended by the local children. You'll be one of the few visitors to make it here! ⏱ *10 min. Gül Baba Sokağı.*

12 ★★ **Mısır Apartmanı.** The white six-story apartment block was built in 1920 by Hovzep Aznavur, a prominent Armenian architect who also built St. Stephen of the Bulgars (p 73). It's one of my favorite Istiklal buildings, representing the old Pera with a funky facelift. Take the lift to the top floor and walk down, popping into the small private art galleries inside (*Arty Istanbul*, p 31) or lunch in the stylish **360Istanbul** on the top floor (*Best Nightlife*, p 119). This building was the winter residence for 19th-century Abbas Halim Pasha, son of an Egyptian prince (*Mısır* is Turkish for Egypt). Later converted into housing and office space, it was recently converted once again into modern apartments and given a new lease of life. ⏱ *30–60 min. 163 Istiklal Cad.*

13 ★ **St. Antoin di Padua.** This one is easy to miss: It's through a triple-arched gateway and down a set of steps. The huge neo-Gothic Catholic church, built in 1913 by Giulio Mongeri, replaces the original one here from 1725. The interior is dominated by a statue of Christ on the cross suspended from the ceiling. The leafy courtyard is delightful, with circular stained-glass windows

and flowerpots up on the ledges of the entrance archway, originally part of apartments built as a source of income for the church. The statue of Pope John XXIII, who served Istanbul's Catholic community (1935–44), was unveiled by Pope Benedict XVI on his 2006 visit. ⏱ *15 min. Istiklal Cad. Open daily 8am–7:30pm.*

14 ★ **Santa Maria Draperis.** Like St. Antoin di Padua (above) the entrance is hidden from view, from the days when it was forbidden for churches to have visible spires. This Franciscan church, dating back to 1789, has a gorgeous bell tower, visible from the courtyard. ⏱ *15 min. 215 Istiklal Cad. Open daily 10am–noon and 2–6pm. Sun and Tues 2–6pm.*

15 ★ **kids** **Markiz Patisserie.** Now called Yemek Külübü, this was loved by Pera's bohemian elite, including young author Orhan Pamuk. The huge art nouveau tile panels by French artist J.A. Arnoux once depicted all four seasons, although only spring and fall remain. *172A Istiklal Cad.* ☎ *0212 252 2701. Sandwiches from 6 TL.*

Pope John XXIII welcomes worshippers to St. Antoin di Padua.

Santa Maria Draperis, hidden from view.

⑯ ★ Swedish Consulate.
Among the street's many consulates, mainly European, this is one of the most attractive. Resembling a summer palace, it was built on land bought in 1757, and was Sweden's first state-owned property overseas. Its chapel, built in 1858, is still used by the Protestant congregation. ⏱ *15 min. 247 Istiklal Cad, Tünel.*

⑰ ★★ kids Galata Mevlevihanesi Müzesi. Reopened in 2011 after major restoration, the museum housed in the 1491 *tekke* (lodge) built for the Mevlevi (Whirling Dervishes) contains traditional musical instruments, illuminated Qur'ans and costumes. Many of the lodge's Sufis are buried in the serene graveyard, including the tomb of Galip Dede, the revered 17th-century Sufi poet, and the ornate fountain of Hasan Ağa (1649). This is the venue of the famous *sema* ceremony, where white-clad Dervishes perform their trancelike "whirling" meditation that brings them closer to God. Scheduled every Sunday at 5pm; phone

to check. ⏱ *30 min. 15 Galip Dede Cad.* ☎ *0212 245 4141. Admission 5 TL adult, children under 8 years free. Open Wed–Mon 9:30am–4:30pm. Bus/funicular Taksim, then walk or Tunnel: Tünel.*

Ornate entrance to newly-restored Galata Mevlevihanesi Müzesi.

Eyüp's Sacred Sites

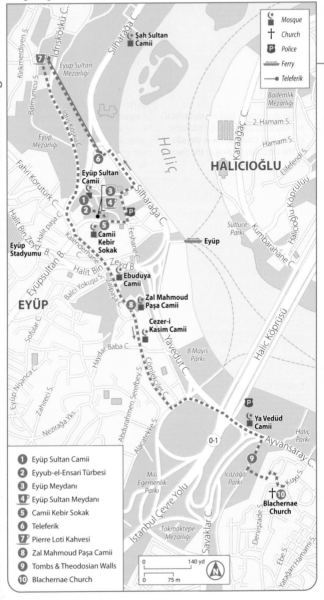

Legend:
- ★ / 🕌 Mosque
- † Church
- 🅿 Police
- ⛴ Ferry
- ●— Teleferik

Map labels:
Kırıkmerdiven S. · İdrisköskü C. · Silharağa C. · ★ Şah Sultan Camii · Eyüp Sultan Mezarlığı · Balmumcu S. · İdris Köskü C. · Eyüp Mezarlığı · Haliç · Bademlik Mezarlığı · 2. Hamam S. · Hamam S. · Karaağaç C. · HALICIOĞLU · Ellifendi S. · Haliçoğlu Köprülü · ⑥ · Eyüp Sultan Camii · ①② ③ ④ · Fahri Korutürk C. · Halit Bin Zeyd · Halit-paşa C. · Kalenderhane · ⑤ Camii Kebir Sokak · Feshane C. · 🅿 · Sütlüce Parkı · Kumbarahane C. · ⛴ Eyüp · Eyüp Stadyumu · Halit Bin Zeya B. · Eyüpsultan B. · Balcı Yokuşu S. · Zalbaşa C. · ⑥ Ebuduya Camii · EYÜP · Sofular C. · ⑧ Zal Mahmoud Paşa Camii · Haliç Köprüsü · Eyüp Nişanca C. · Zahireci S. · Haydar Baba C. · ★ Cezer-i Kasim Camii · Neziraağa Yks. · Abdurrahmen Serefbey S. · Çömlekçiler S. · Yavedurt C. · 8 Mayıs Parkı · Alacatekke S. · 🅿 · ★ Ya Vedüd Camii · Haliç Parkı · Ayvansaray C. · İstanbul Çevre Yolu · Mili Egemenlik Parkı · 0-1 · İcazağa Parkı · ⑨ · Dervişzade C. · † ⑩ Blachernae Church · Savaklar C. · Tokmaktepe Mezarlığı · Ebe S. · Yatağan Hamam S.

Scale: 0 — 140 yd / 0 — 75 m

① Eyüp Sultan Camii
② Eyyub-el-Ensari Türbesi
③ Eyüp Meydanı
④ Eyüp Sultan Meydanı
⑤ Camii Kebir Sokak
⑥ Teleferik
⑦ Pierre Loti Kahvesi
⑧ Zal Mahmoud Paşa Camii
⑨ Tombs & Theodosian Walls
⑩ Blachernae Church

Join religious pilgrims in Eyüp, located beyond the city walls. It's best known for the sacred Eyyub-el-Ensari tomb, and at weekends, small boys in white satin costumes fill the square, ready (or not?) for their circumcision ceremony (*sünnet*). You could reverse this tour to end at Pierre Loti cafe at sundown. START: **Bus 55T from Taksim or 99A from Eminönü to Eyüp.**

1 ★★ kids **Eyüp Sultan Camii.**
The mosque you see today, completed in 1880, replaces the first imperial mosque, built by Mehmet II in 1458 after the fall of Constantinople. Its vast courtyard was the site of the Ottoman Girding of the Sword of Osman, the enthronement rite where the sword of 13th-century leader Osman Gazi was passed on. Local people watched the ceremony and in so doing accepted that the ruler had possession of the city. ⏱ *20 min. Eyüp Meydanı. Open daily dawn–dusk.*

2 ★★ **Eyyub-el-Ensari Türbesi (Tomb).** Adjacent to the mosque, this shrine is one of Islam's holiest sites. Standard-bearer and companion of the Prophet Mohammed, Eyüp Sultan (as he was later known) was killed in the 7th century during battle and buried on the city's outskirts. Before conquering the city in 1453, Mehmet II rediscovered Eyüp's grave and built a shrine and mosque. The tomb attracts many worshippers, especially on Fridays; non-Muslims are welcome wearing modest clothing (*Savvy Traveler Clothing*, p 166). Inside, vivid blue Iznik tiles in Ottoman baroque style contrast with the silver sarcophagus. Look out for the footprint of Mohammed in marble stone, framed in silver and embedded in the tomb's left-hand wall. ⏱ *15 min. Eyüp Meydanı. Open daily 9am–5pm. Free.*

3 ★★ kids **Eyüp Meydanı (Eyüp Square).** Take a breather to people-watch in this enthralling public square, adjacent to the tomb. During weekends, family groups gather for photographs along with their small sons decked out in white satin *sünnet* (circumcision) suits. These lads—usually aged between 4 and 8—seemingly have no fear of their impending op, but love the attention. ⏱ *15–30 min.*

4 ★ kids **Eyüp Sultan Meydanı.** Plenty of busy food options in the main square, including Karadeniz Pide and Et Lokantasi—or choose ice cream and waffles if you need a sugary snack. **Pide 5 TL.**

Dazzling tiles outside the tomb.

5 ★★ kids **Camii Kebir Sokak (Camii Kebier Bazaar).** This lively bazaar lines both sides of the pedestrianized street in front of the mosque, catering for religious visitors. Multi-colored headscarves swirl in the breeze, copies of the Qur'an are piled up on the stalls, jewelry and trinkets add a touch of glamor, and a crackly cassette player usually blasts out Qur'anic or musical recitals. ⏲ *30 min. Camii Kebir Sok. Open daily 9am–6pm.*

6 ★★ kids **Teleferik (cablecar).** From Camii Kebir Sokak, turn left past Sultan Mehmed Resad Han Tomb, turn right at the end, and left onto the main road. You're now at the cable-car station, completed in 2006, for the 3-minute journey up Pierre Loti Hill through the huge Eyüp Sultan Cemetery. It's a good choice if you don't fancy the half-hour hike (even though the walk is wonderful). If you walk down through the cemetery, take a closer look at the Ottoman-era gravestones. Expect long lines for the *teleferik* at weekends, and late afternoons in summer. ⏲ *30–60 min. 1.75 TL. Running daily 8am–10:30pm.*

Religious books and headscarves fill the bazaar.

Shade, view, and a glass of tea at Pierre Loti Kahvesi.

7 ★★★ kids **Pierre Loti Kahvesi.** Named after the pining Turkophile French novelist who penned *Aziyade* in 1879 about his lover, this cafe has Golden Horn views and a shady terrace, one of Istanbul's best. *Balmumcu Sok, Gümüşsuyu Cad.* ☎ *0212 581 2696. Tea 1 TL.*

8 ★★ kids **Zal Mahmoud Paşa Camii (Zal Mahmoud Paşa Mosque).** Walk through the cemetery and across the main square, down Kalenderhane Caddesi, then down Hz Halid Bulvarı, a street dotted with quaint wooden houses. On the left is this dark-stone mosque complex, built by Sinan (p 11) in 1571, which also contains the tomb of Zal Mahmoud Paşa, Süleyman I's teacher. Mahmoud, a servant, was in love with Süleyman's sister but stood no chance—until he strangled Süleyman's son to thwart an uprising. Mahmoud was rewarded with the title *Zal* (hero), and marriage to the woman of his dreams. ⏲ *15–30 min. 36 Feshane Cad.*

9 ★ Tombs & Theodosian Walls. From the mosque, walk south down Çomlekçiler Caddesi, under the Haliç Bridge spanning the Golden Horn. This heads into the Ayvansaray neighborhood, marked by the Old City walls built by Theodosius II in A.D. 412 to seal Constantinople against invasion. From the main road, turn left into the grounds of the tiny mosque, Hacı Husrev Mescidi, and take the main gates on the left. Walk through the gorgeous rose gardens, under the stone arch and past the tomb of Ebu Şeybetul el Hudri Hz. To your left, steps take you along Ayvansaray's old walls; scramble to the top for views over the stone houses in this traditional area. 🕐 30 min.

Walk through the old Ayvansaray streets.

10 ★ Blachernae Church. After descending the city walls, turn left down Toklu Ibrahim Sokak and follow Kafesci Yumni Sokağı. At the end, to the right you'll see the secluded Blachernae Church. Originally built in A.D. 451 and once a venerated Byzantine church, it was rebuilt several times. Today it houses the Blachernae *ayazma* (sacred spring), thought to have healing powers. The waters dripped into a reservoir behind the building, accumulated in a large pool, and then through holes in the hands of a marble relief (replaced after breakage in 1960) of the Virgin Mary. Byzantine times saw emperors plunge three times into the pool. Now, the holy water is poured for Greek Orthodox worshippers to drink. Services are held every Friday at 9:30am. 🕐 *15 min. Ayvansaray Kuyusu Sokağı, off Mustafa Paşa Bostani Sok. Open 8am–5pm.*

What's in a Name?

In 2007, a row over a name opened a can of worms: The hillside topped by Pierre Loti Kahvesi was known as Pierre Loti Heights, but the mayor of Eyüp wanted it changed to Eyüp Sultan Heights, after the sacred man (**2**), so put up a new sign at the teleferik. Local opinion in this conservative enclave divided along secular and religious lines, with some saying Pierre Loti was part of the city's cultural history, and others feeling that to name it Eyüp Sultan was in keeping with Turkish history. The sign has since been changed back, and all seems to be calm—for now.

Tünel to **Karaköy**

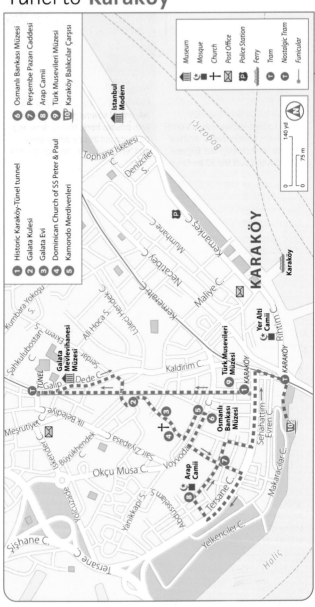

1 Historic Karaköy-Tünel tunnel
2 Galata Kulesi
3 Galata Evi
4 Dominican Church of SS Peter & Paul
5 Kamondo Merdivenleri
6 Osmanlı Bankası Müzesi
7 Perşembe Pazarı Caddesi
8 Arap Camii
9 Türk Musevileri Müzesi
10 Karaköy Balıkçılar Çarşısı

Museum
Mosque
Church
Post Office
Police Station
Ferry
Tram
Nostalgic Tram
Funicular

Istanbul Modern

Tophane İskelesi

Denizciler S.

Boğazısı

KARAKÖY

Karaköy

Kemankeş C.

Mumhane C.

Necatibey C.

Maliye C.

Kemeraltı C.

Lüleci Hendek S.

Ali Hoca S.

Serdar C.

Kaldırım C.

Dede C.

TÜNEL

Galata Mevlevihanesi Müzesi

Şahkulubostan C.

Kumbara Yokuşu S.

Ekrem C.

Galip

İlk Belediye C.

Meşrutiyet C.

İskender C.

Büyükhendek C.

Şair Ziya Paşa C.

Voyvoda C.

Okçu Musa C.

Yanıkkapı S.

Abdüsselam C.

Tersane C.

Yelkenciler C.

Yolcuzade S.

Şişhane C.

Tersane C.

Haliç

Yer Altı Camii

KARAKÖY

Rıhtım C.

Sebahattin Evren C.

Makaracılar C.

Arap Camii

Türk Musevileri Müzesi

Osmanlı Bankası Müzesi

140 yd
75 m

N

This neighborhood walk centers on Galata, part of Beyoğlu in today's bohemian Istanbul, and the epitome of 19th-century European culture. A run-down neighborhood 20 years ago, today it is gentrified with affluent restored housing, its steep cobbled streets housing a mix of stylish coffee shops and traditional workshops.

START: **Tunnel from Karaköy to Tünel.**

❶ ★★ kids **Historic Karaköy–Tünel tunnel.** Beginning at Karaköy, take a ride on the world's second-oldest subway system (after the London underground), and the shortest. French engineer Eugene Henri Gavand built the 573m-long (1,880 ft.) funicular in 1874 with a steam engine and gas lamps, after seeing locals struggle between Galata and Pera. If you're staying in Beyoğlu, start your walk from Tünel. ⏱ *15 min. Sebahattin Evren Cad. www.iett.gov.tr/en. Jeton or akbil (ticket) 1.25 TL. Mon–Fri 7am–9pm, Sat and Sun 7:30am–9pm.*

❷ ★★★ kids **Galata Kulesi (Galata Tower).** Ascend the tower for Istanbul's best panoramic views (*Best in One Day*, p 10). But first from the outside you can visualize an unusual flight. In the late 17th century, Hazerfan Ahmet Çelebi (1609–40) became one of the world's first aviators, using artificial wings to power his flight as he leapt off the tower over the Bosphorus. Apparently, he was inspired by Leonardo da Vinci's studies of birds in flight. *(p 10).*

❸ ★ **Galata Evi (Galata House).** From the tower, head left down Galata Kulesi Sokak to this historic residence. Converted by architects Mete and Nadire Göktuğ in the

1990s into a restaurant, it was originally an early-20th-century British jail, one of several political powers with prisons here. Have a drink and poke around its tiny dining areas and terrace, and try to spot the prisoners' graffiti. ⏱ *15–30 min. 61 Galata Kulesi Sok. ☎ 0212 245 1861 (restaurant reservation). www.thegalatahouse.com.*

❹ ★ **Dominican Church of SS Peter & Paul.** Like the churches on Istiklal Caddesi (p 46) this one, built by 19th-century Italian architect Gaspare Fossati, is also hidden behind high walls, out of sight. After arriving in Istanbul, the friars of the order of Preachers established themselves in

Inside the courtyard of Dominican Church of SS Peter and Paul.

Galata, and their original church was converted into what is now Arap Camii (p 58). Look out for the icon of the Virgin Mary, Odighitria, framed in a case of embossed silver. ⏱ *15 min. Sen Piyer Kilisesi, 44 Galata Kulesi Sok. ☎ 0212 249 2385. Open Mon–Fri 7–8pm, Sat 3:30–5:30pm, Sun 10am–noon.*

❺ ★★ **Kamondo Merdivenleri (Camondo Staircase).** From Galata Kulesi Sokak, turn left onto Kart Çınar Sokak and on the right you'll see a curvaceous double staircase. Built in 1860 by Avram Camondo, head of

Once the Turkish bank HQ, now a museum.

the Jewish banking family (see box, below), this led from Voyvoda Caddesi to the family home on Felek Sokak (now the Galata Residence hotel, see p 138). Built soon after his son Moise was born, its hexagonal design meant there wasn't far to fall if a child slipped. Camondo, a leading merchant in the city, was the first foreigner given the right to own real estate during the Ottoman Empire, and this staircase was his gift to the city. ⏱ *10 min. Off Voyvoda Cad.*

⑥ ★★ kids Osmanlı Bankası Müzesi (Ottoman Banking Museum). From the bottom of the steps, turn right and cross the road to this great little museum. Housed in the former Ottoman bank

headquarters (next to the Central Bank of Turkey), this was Constantinople's first "modern" bank. Venture into the vaults storing banknotes from 1875. Thought the 2009 global downturn was bad? Nothing like the crisis during the 1877–78 Russo-Ottoman war, judging by original loan contracts between the bank and the Ottoman government. Sultans had to follow the same banking rules as mere mortals; even the harem eunuchs had savings and loans here. ⏱ *1 hr. 32 Mete Cad.* ☎ *0212 292 7605. www.obmuseum.com. Adults 3 TL, children under 7 years free. Open daily 10am–6pm. Tram: Karaköy.*

⑦ ★ Perşembe Pazarı Caddesi. From the museum, turn left and left again onto this historic trading street. One of the area's busiest and most charming streets (except on Sun), this is chock-full of *hans*, sturdy 18th-century merchants' houses. On the corner of Bakir Sokak, peep at the arched ceilings in the workshops of Genoese **Saksi Han** and look out for **Ceneviz** (Turkish for Genoan) **Han** at #17, and **Serpus Han.** ⏱ *10 min.*

⑧ ★ Arap Camii (Arab Mosque). Approach from Tersane Caddesi for a dramatic first glimpse. The mosque's deep-red minaret was once the bell-tower of the church, built by the Genoese; later it was the original church for Black Friars.

The Camondo Dynasty

Istanbul's Jewish community was largely established by those fleeing the 1497 Spanish Inquisition, when Jews were forced to convert to Christianity or face death. The Camondo family, well-known bankers, fled to Vienna, and then came to Istanbul following the Austrian takeover in 1798. Once again they soon flourished as merchants and philanthropists, respected by their adopted country despite being "minorities." Such was the esteem shown to Avram (⑤) that, after he moved to Paris in his 80s and died there in 1873, his body was flown back to Istanbul for a state funeral.

Mehmet II turned it into Galata Camii in the 1470s, known as Arap Camii when Beyazid II assigned it to Moors (Muslims from the Spanish region), fleeing the 15th-century Spanish Inquisition. (Closed for restoration at the time of research.) ⏱ *15 min. 15 Futuhat Sok. Open dawn–dusk.*

❾ ★★ Türk Musevileri Müzesi (Jewish Museum of Turkey). End your walk here, if it's open. Hidden up an alleyway, the museum is housed in the former 17th-century Zulfaris Synagogue and gives a fascinating insight into local Jewish history. Its displays reveal how Sephardic Jews—those from Spain and Portugal—considered the Ottomans as saviors in 1326 when they were freed from Byzantine oppression in Bursa; more so when welcomed by Beyazid II (1448–1512) when forced to flee Spain and the Spanish Inquisition. More recently, Atatürk invited Jewish scientists from Nazi Germany, and several Turkish diplomats saved Turkish Jews during the Holocaust. Look out for displays of silver used inside for synagogue services, and displays highlighting the historic cultural similarities between Muslims and Jews. ⏱ *1 hour. Selanik Pasajı, Percemli Sok, Karaköy Meydanı.* ☎ *0212 292 6333. www.muze500.com.*

Silver Torah adornments at the Jewish Museum.

Admission 10 TL adults, 3 TL children 12–17 years. Mon–Thurs 10am–4pm, Fri and Sun 10am–2pm. Closed Sat and Jewish hols. Tram/tunnel: Karaköy.

❿ ★★ kids Karaköy Balıkcılar Çarşısı (Karaköy Fish Market). Enjoy simple fresh grilled fish with salad and bread on wooden rickety tables next to the market. Stunning views of the Old City skyline. Open late in summer; cash only. *Fish with salad from 7 TL.*

Football flag flutteres in Galatas' traditional banking area.

Üsküdar

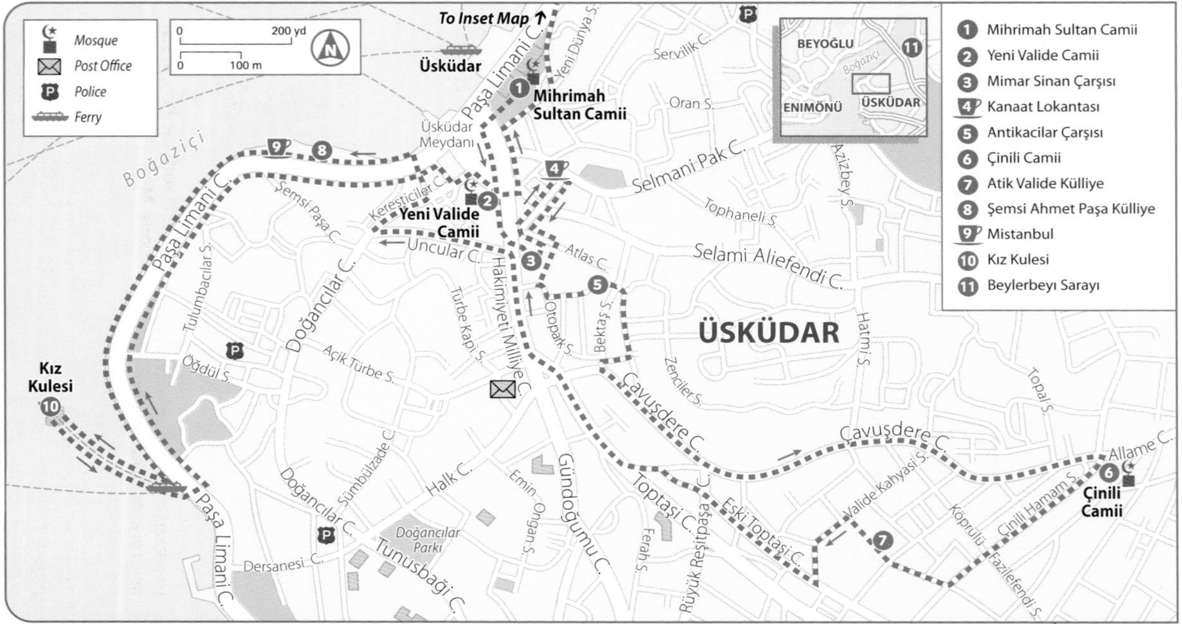

1. Mihrimah Sultan Camii
2. Yeni Valide Camii
3. Mimar Sinan Çarşısı
4. Kanaat Lokantası
5. Antikacılar Çarşısı
6. Çinili Camii
7. Atik Valide Külliye
8. Şemsi Ahmet Paşa Külliye
9. Mistanbul
10. Kız Kulesi
11. Beylerbeyi Sarayı

Çinili Camii

Topal S.

Allame C.

Eski Hamam S.

Köprülü

Fazilefendi S.

Çavuşdere C.

Valide kahyası S.

Hatmi S.

Azizbey S.

Selami Alifefendi C.

Tophaneli S.

ÜSKÜDAR

Zenciler S.

Çavuşdere C.

Toptaşı C.

Eski Toptaşı C.

Büyük Reşitpaşa C.

Ferah S.

Oran S.

Servilik C.

Yeni Dünya S.

Mihrimah Sultan Camii

Atlas C.

Bektaş S.

Otopark S.

Gündoğumu C.

Emin Ongan S.

To Inset Map ↑

Üsküdar iskelesi

Üsküdar Meydanı

Yeni Valide Camii

Hakimiyeti Milliye C.

Uncular C.

Türbe Kapı S.

Halk C.

Tunusbağı C.

Doğancılar Parkı

Sümbüzade C.

Kefçedede C.

Açık Türbe S.

Doğancılar C.

Doğancılar C.

Dersanesi C.

Şemsi Paşa C.

Tulumbacılar S.

Paşa Limanı C.

Öğdül S.

Paşa Limanı C.

BOĞAZİÇİ

Kız Kulesi

BEYOĞLU

ÜSKÜDAR

BOĞAZ

EMİNÖNÜ

200 yd

100 m

N

- Mosque
- Post Office
- Police
- Ferry

Hop over to Istanbul's Asian side, which might surprise first-time visitors: It's a relatively modern area with fewer historic landmarks and less contemporary style than the European side. Nonetheless, Üsküdar is a charming neighborhood, easily accessible by ferry, and filled with lovely mosques. START: **Ferry from Eminönü, Beşiktaş or Karaköy to Üsküdar.**

① ★★ **Mihrimah Sultan Camii (Mihrimah Sultan Mosque).** Dominating your first sight of Üsküdar from the ferry is this mosque built by Mimar Sinan (p 11) in 1548. Also known as Iskele ("docks") Camii, it was built for Süleyman I in memory of his favorite daughter, Mihrimah, on a raised platform to protect it from the water. With no space for a central courtyard, Sinan used a protruding roof to cover the *şadırvan* (ablutions fountain). Outside, the stunning rococo Ahmed III fountain is an architectural masterpiece with calligraphy, masonry, and art. 🕐 *20 min.*

② ★ **Yeni Valide Camii (Yeni Valide Mosque).** Walk to the south side of the plaza to the mosque, built for Gülnuş Emetullah Valide Sultan, mother of Sultans Mustafa II and Ahmet III. She was buried in 1716 in the simple adjacent tomb, which I love, far removed from the glamorous tomb of Süleyman's wife Roxelana (p 75). An iron domed roof, rather like a birdcage, lies over the open stone tomb, usually overgrown with roses. 🕐 *20 min. Uncular Cad.*

③ ★ **Mimar Sinan Çarşısı.** From the tomb, cross the main road Hakımıyeti Milliye Caddesi to this pleasant fountain courtyard, a popular relaxation spot. The market isn't much of a shopping experience, but the building and location are charming. Sinan built this in 1583 as the hamam of the Mihrimah Sultan complex. With separate men's and women's bathing areas, it became derelict and impossible to reconstruct, but in

Mihrimah Sultan Camii, named after Süleyman's daughter.

the 1960s it was restored as a covered bazaar by Mehmet Bozkurt. Look out for the early-18th-century *çeşme* (fountain) outside. 🕐 *15 min. Hakımıyeti Milliye Cad. Open daily 9am–6pm.*

④ ★★ **kids Kanaat Lokantası.** This has been a locals' favorite since 1933, with hearty traditional dishes like *tandir* (tandoori) lamb and döner kebab with tomatoes and butter. *25 Salmanipak Cad.* ☎ *0216 553 3791. Main courses from 10 TL.*

⑤ ★★ **kids Antikacilar Çarşısı (Antique Market).** Return to Mimar Sinan Çarşısı and continue up to the quaint three-domed **Karadavud Paşa Camii.** Turn left up the side street opposite, following it to the left then right, toward a garish yellow building. Opposite is the

antique market, housed in an unassuming two-story building. Browse its two levels of around 40 stores with dusty antiques, including Ottoman carved wooden doors, tables, brassware, and lighting. Most goodies on show are between 70 and 140 years old, with craftsmen restoring older pieces on the lower-ground floor. 🕐 *30 min. 32 Buyük Hamam Sok, corner of Bulgurlu Mescit Sok. Open daily 10am–7pm.*

6 ★★ **Çinili Camii (Tiled Mosque).** From the market, turn right onto Evliye Hoca Sokak and left onto Cavusdere Caddesi. It's a pleasant 20-minute uphill walk along a residential street to this tiny neighborhood mosque. Hardly visited and closed between prayer times, the caretaker may open up (tip appreciated) to show you its interior adorned with Iznik tiles. Dated 1640, it was built under Mahpeyker Kösem, a wily woman with political ambitions, especially after the death of her husband, Sultan Ahmed I. 🕐 *20 min. Çinili Mescit Sok. Open prayer times.*

7 ★ **Atik Valide Külliye.** From the main gate of Çinili Camii, turn left down Çinili Hamam Sokak (the

hamam is on your right), then right down Kartalbaba Caddesi. You'll see the impressive *külliye* (mosque complex) ahead, Mimar Sinan's final major building, completed in 1583. Built for and funded by Valide Nur Banu, wife of Selim II and a former slave in Topkapı Palace, it's one of Istanbul's most impressive complexes. It contained the Ottoman Empire's first mental hospital, and became a tobacco warehouse in 1935. The huge courtyard has an ancient hollow cedar tree, next to the *şadırvan*. 🕐 *20 min. Kartalbaba Cad. Mosque closed outside prayer time.*

8 ★★ **Şemsi Ahmet Paşa Külliye.** Turn left out of Atik Valide Külliye, under the arch and down the steps ahead onto Eski Toptaşı Caddesi. Veer left, continue to Hakımıyeti Milliye Caddesi, and head to the waterfront around the construction work. This tiny white mosque, with a single dome and minaret, was designed by Sinan for Şemsi Paşa in 1580, its *medrese* turned into a public library in 1953. Local fishermen and promenaders gather along the pier, especially at weekends, admiring the view of Istanbul's European side. 🕐 *15 min. Sahil Yolu.*

Mimar Sinan Çarşısı.

Kız Kulesi, wrapped in legend and movie kudos.

9 ★ **kids Mistanbul.** Try for a waterfront table for your coffee and all-day Turkish breakfast, or menemen. This peaceful spot is popular with courting couples and stylish Üsküdar folk. *10 Şemsi Paşa Cad.* ☎ *0216 334 6676. Turkish breakfast 10 TL.*

10 ★ **kids Kız Kulesi (Maiden's, or Leander's, Tower).** From the cafe, it's a pleasant waterfront walk to the shuttle boat to this iconic tower (10-min journey). Used as a lighthouse for centuries, legend has it that a sultan built the tower to protect his daughter from a deadly serpent's bite, as predicted by a soothsayer. But to no avail, as the snake arrived in a basket of fruit and she died in her father's arms. The tower featured in the 1999 James Bond movie *The World is Not Enough.* It's a fun little trip, with a viewing point on the upper gallery (crowded at weekends). Bypass the pricey restaurant in favor of local places to eat. 🕐 *1 hr (exc journey). www.kizkulesi.com.tr. Return ticket 5 TL. Ferries depart daily 9am–6:45pm.*

11 ★ **kids Beylerbeyı Sarayı (Beylerbeyı Palace).** It's a 4km (2½ miles) walk or bus ride north to the waterfront palace, located just beyond the Bosphorus Bridge. This late-19th-century palace was built by Sarkis Balyan for Sultan Abdülaziz when the Ottoman Empire was in decline. Relax in the lush grounds with the strange-shaped Harem Yali Köşkü pavilion, then take a tour inside. I love the Blue Hall, with one of the world's largest *Harike* (luxurious silk) carpets, and Arabic poems inscribed on the ceilings. Look out also for chairs made by Sultan Abdulhamid, imprisoned here for 6 years until his death. 🕐 *1 hr. Abdullah Aga Cad.* ☎ *0216 321 9320/21. www.millisaraylar.gov.tr. Admission inc guided tour 8 TL adult, 3 TL children 12–17 years. Open Tues–Wed and Fri–Sun, Oct–Feb 9:30am–4pm, Mar–Sept 9:30am–5pm. Bus: 15 from Üsküdar pier.*

Eminönü to **Sultanahmet**

1 Yeni Camii
2 Mısır Çarşısı
3 Yeni Camii Parkı
4 Hatice Turhan Valide Sultan Türbesi
5 Sirkeci PTT & Müzesi
6 Sirkeci Garı & Müzesi
7 Konyalı

8 Soğukçeşme Sokak
9 Caferağa Medresesi
10 Haseki Hürrem Hamamı
11 At Meydanı
12 Küçük Ayasofya Camii
13 Kennedy Caddesi

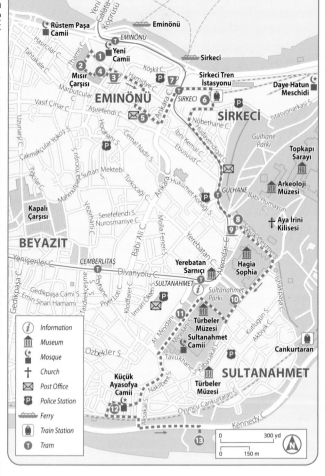

Enter the heart of the Old City, home to many of the city's best palaces, museums, and mosques. This walk lets you experience off-the-beaten-track beauty rather than grandeur, reflecting everyday life, past and present. Begin at one of my favorite Istanbul neighborhoods. START: **Tram or bus to Eminönü.**

1 ★★ kids **Yeni Camii (New Mosque).** Although this mosque is a massive landmark, its cupola and minarets dominating the Old City's skyline, it's off the tourist trail. Ascend the broad steps, past warbling pigeons and enter the courtyard centered on a marble ablutions fountain. Blue and turquoise tiles, and a multi-domed ceiling, dominate its interior. Commissioned by Valide Safiye Sultan, mother of Mehmet III, work began in 1597 forcing out many residents from the Jewish neighborhood. Plagued with leaks, funding problems, embezzlement, and the death of the sultan, construction was finally completed in 1663. As with all mosques, avoid prayer time. ⊕ *20 min. Eminönü Meydanı. Open daily dawn–dusk.*

2 ★★ kids **Mısır Çarşısı (Egyptian, or Spice, Bazaar).** You may have already loaded up with *lokum* (Turkish delight), olives, and textiles (*Best in One Day*, p 9). Try **Hasırcılar Caddesi** for the best (and cheapest) dried fruit and *pül biber* (dried-pepper flakes). Now explore the bazaar's more eclectic section. Facing the main entrance (north side), head left and wind around the outdoor stalls selling plant seeds (mainly vegetables and herbs) and continue to walk around the outside. Listen out for the cheep of budgies and look out for jars of leeches, said to have myriad health benefits including curing rheumatic and arthritic problems. ⊕ *30–60 min. Eminönü. Open Mon–Sat 9am–7pm.*

3 ★ kids **Yeni Camii Parkı.** This outdoor tea garden covers a huge area between the mosque, tomb, and market. Find a spare seat for a glass of tea and wonderful people-watching. *Yeni Camii Parkı.*

4 ★ **Hatice Turhan Valide Sultan Türbesi (Tomb of Hatice Turhan).** It might sound morbid, but I find sultans' tombs fascinating, with their snippets of information about the palace families. (There may be summaries in English.) Here, the tomb of Hatice Turhan and her children make eye-popping reading. She was probably of Russian descent, captured by Tatars, and entered the harem aged 12. Taken under the wing of Sultan Ibrahim's

Preparing for prayers at Yeni Camii.

mother, Kösem Valide Sultan, she was "presented" as a concubine to her son, and gave birth to Mehmet IV. A prominent, ambitious concubine, Hatice Turhan was hugely influential, and saw Yeni Camii and Mısır Çarşısı to completion. Kösem Sultan, however, was murdered in a palace power struggle. Exit the tomb and turn right down Bankacılar Sokak. ⏱ *20 min. Eminönü. Open Tues–Sun 9:30am–4:30pm.*

⑤ ★ kids Sirkeci PTT & Müzesi (Sirkeci Central Post Office & Museum). Join Büyük Posthane Cad, and on the right you'll see the imposing **Sirkeci PTT,** the late-19th-century main post office. You can even buy stamps here while admiring the main hall's colored glass ceiling. Next door, the **PTT Museum,** part of the original post office, has Morse code machines, Ottoman stamps, and vast leather mailbags used by mailmen making deliveries on horseback. Unfortunately, there are few captions in English. As you exit, turn right and look across the road to **Vlora Han,** a sturdy merchants' building with sculpted stone roses on the outside. ⏱ *30 min. PTT Müzesi, Büyük Posthane Cad. Free.*

Mon–Fri 9am–noon and 1:30–4pm. Tram: Sirkeci.

⑥ ★★ kids Sirkeci Garı & Müzesi (Sirkeci Station & Museum). Although I usually enter through the main passenger entrance if boarding a train, it's far better to approach this historic station through the more attractive Sirkeci Istasyon Caddesi entrance. The station was completed in 1890, and the first trains rumbled through shortly after. This is a rare occasion when the cliché "Where East meets West" fits; it was the final station for the fabled Orient Express between the Ottoman Empire and Europe. For visitors arriving from Berlin, Vienna, and Paris, this was their first glimpse of Constantinople. Go through the Orient Express restaurant, where travelers dined before heading west, to the **Railway Museum,** with exhibits from the iconic train, including the front cab and silver cutlery. There are few English captions, but look out for the tile stove used to heat the waiting hall in 1890, and the original 1930 weighing machine (pop on the scale—it's still working!). Exit the main entrance and walk across the

Sirkeci's historic station houses the Railway Museum.

Elegant baths built for Roxelana, wife of Süleyman I.

tram tracks. ⏱ *30 min. Museum: Sirkeci Istasyon Cad.* ☎ *0212 520 6575. www.tcdd.gov.tr. Free. Open Tues–Sat 9am–5pm.*

7 ★★ **kids Konyalı.** Istanbul's famous pastry house has syrupy cakes and *su boreği* (a pasta-type layered cheese snack). Its walls are lined with signed endorsements from luminaries such as Mohammed Ali and Queen Elizabeth II. *5 Mimar Kemalettin Cad.* ☎ *0212 527 1935. Tea and su boreği 6 TL.*

8 ★★ **Soğukçeşme Sokak.** Follow the tram track sweeping up the hill, past the entrance to Gülhane Park and turn left up the cobbled Soğukçeşme Sokak. Twee and fake, or a good re-creation? Opinions are divided about this row of pastel-colored wooden-fronted houses behind Hagia Sophia, built in 1984. The Turkish Touring and Automobile Foundation (TTOK) tore down the existing 300-year-old dilapidated houses, occupied by local employees, and were recreated as accurately as possible, although with more pastel blues and pinks than the original.

Most were turned into **Ayasofya Pensionlar,** guesthouses (*Best Lodging*, p 136). If you need a break, try **Caferağa Medresesi** opposite (**9**). The ornate **Ahmet Çeşme,** Sultan Ahmet III's fountain by Topkapı Palace's Imperial Gate, is at the top. On your right is **Hagia Sophia,** which is also the entrance to the complex of 17th-century **tombs** of Sultan Selim II and his family, Mustafa and Ahmed Ağa. Inside the complex, the oldest mausoleum was converted from a 6th-century baptistery, used to store oils for the mosque after Conquest of Istanbul (admission free; open Tues–Sun 9am–5pm). Exit the tombs and turn right; on the left is the **Archeological Park,** a newly excavated area in the grounds of the Four Seasons Hotel (p 137). ⏱ *30 min.*

9 ★★ **kids Caferağa Medresesi.** Craft shops now fill the original medrese built by Sinan (Best Shopping, p 90), plus there's a tiny cafe in a gorgeous courtyard cooking homely traditional dishes. Open Tues–Sun. *Caferiye Sok.* ☎ *0212 513 3601. Tea and soup 7 TL.*

Mimar Sinan watches over visitors to Caferağa Medresesi.

⑩ ★★ kids Haseki Hürrem Hamamı (Baths of Roxelana). Built for Roxelana (Haseki Hürrem), Süleyman I's cunning wife, architect Sinan designed this elegant double-domed *hamam* in 1556 for worshippers at Ayasofya mosque (the Ottoman name for Hagia Sophia). In use until 1910 as a *hamam*, it was used recently as a government-run carpet shop. After major restoration back to its original use, it reopened in mid-2011 as a luxury (pricey) *hamam*. It's a perfect chance to see the original marble floors, the hexagonal marble massage slabs, and domed hall with tiny skylight. *2/4 Bab-ı Hümayun Cad.* ☎ *0212 517 3535. www.ayasofyahurremsultan hamami.com. Hamam open daily 7am–midnight. Tram: Sultanahmet.*

⑪ ★★ kids At Meydanı (Hippodrome). This Byzantine-era chariot-racing track (p 44) is interspersed with three ancient monuments in a row. The granite **Egyptian Obelisk** dates back to 1500 B.C. and was taken from Luxor. Intertwined serpents form the 5th century B.C. **Serpentine Column,** the heads since knocked off (one is in the Archaeology Museum (p 14); and the bronze covering the **Column of Porphyrogenitus** (named after a 10th-century emperor) was melted down by the Crusaders to make coins, and is now dilapidated. Fast forward a few centuries to the **fountain,** presented by Kaiser Wilhelm II to Sultan Abdülhamid after his visit to the city in 1898. The gold-ceilinged, eight-columned covered fountain, built in traditional German architectural style, still has cool water flowing from its taps. ⏲ *30 min. At Meydanı. Tram: Sultanahmet.*

⑫ ★ Küçük Ayasofya Camii (Küçük Ayasofya Mosque). From the southern end of At Meydani, walk down Tavukhane Sokak, and turn right onto Nakilbent Sokak; Küçük Ayasofya Caddesi then brings you to the run-down yet charming residential area, a world away from Sultanahmet's monuments. Follow this to the mosque, known as Küçük (little) Ayasofya but originally the

Cool down at Kaiser Wilhelm's fountain in the Hippodrome.

Church of SS Sergius and Bacchus, built by Emperor Justinian. Converted to a mosque in the late 15th century, its mosaics and frescoes are long gone, but the Greek inscription on the marble frieze inside names Justinian and his wife as founders. Renovations in 2007 have, in my opinion, led to an overdone interior, with marble-effect paint on the pillars trying to look authentic. Walk up to the balcony to find the tiny section of original stone walls preserved behind glass, and an area of flooring on the first floor. I love the **çaybahçe**, the quaint tea-garden in the leafy courtyard, once part of the old *medrese,* today with minuscule artists' studios making traditional crafts, including calligraphy and ceramics. ⏱ *20–40 min. Mosque open dawn–dusk, çaybahçe open daily 10:30am–6:30pm.*

Peaceful courtyard at newly-restored Küçük Ayasofya.

⑬ ★★ kids Kennedy Caddesi. Head back along Küçük Ayasofya Caddesi, and turn right onto Aksalak Sokak, under the railway bridge, then cross busy Kennedy Caddesi. You'll see a stretch of park and a waterfront, where fishermen gather and gaze out to the Sea of Marmara. This is a little like the fishermen gathering on Galata Bridge but, judging by the number of

beer bottles and deckchairs, I get the feeling this is more of a recreational fishing trip. Children will love the nearby playground, and there's the occasional handcart selling barbecued *mısır* (sweetcorn). From here, you can walk back up to Sultanahmet, or around the main road for a longer walk (or bus ride) to Eminönü. ⏱ *15–30 min. Kennedy Cad.*

New Transport vs Old Treasures

In 2004, construction began for Marmaray, the new high-speed rail link under the Bosphorus from Europe to Asia. Two years later, progress was halted and court battles ensued, after archeological treasures were unearthed: A maze of dams and jetties, sunken ships, and huge forged iron anchors indicated that this was the original 5th-century port of Constantinople. Historians were delighted; developers less so, as it meant mammoth delays and alterations—the project is now due for completion in 2013.

Fener & **Balat**

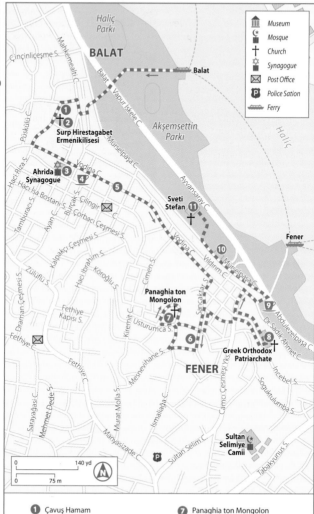

	Museum
	Mosque
†	Church
	Synagogue
✉	Post Office
P	Police Sation
	Ferry

BALAT

Balat

Haliç Parkı

Akşemsettin Parkı

Surp Hirestagabet Ermenikilisesi

Ahrida Synagogue

Sveti Stefan

Fener

Panaghia ton Mongolon

Greek Orthodox Patriarchate

FENER

Sultan Selimiye Camii

0	140 yd
0	75 m

1 Çavuş Hamam

2 Surp Hirestagabet Ermenikilisesi

3 Ahrida Synagogue

4 Börekci

5 Vodina Caddesi

6 Özel Fener Rum Lisesi

7 Panaghia ton Mongolon

8 Greek Orthodox Patriarchate

9 Tarihi Haliç Işkembecisi

10 Kadin Eserleri Kütüphanesi

11 Sveti Stefan

Hugging the Golden Horn, these neighborhoods were home to Istanbul's Sephardic Jews, Greeks, and Armenians over the last 2 centuries. Now, it's mainly migrants from rural Turkey. Discover tucked-away gems revealing the city's multicultural history.

START: **Bus 99A to Balat, opposite Balat Iskele (pier); or walk along the waterfront.**

① ★ Çavuş Hamam. Cross the road by the striped Yusuf Sucaadin Ambari Camii, and head straight on. Turn left onto Kasaplar Sokak, and right up Çavuş Hamam Sokak. You can take a quick peak inside, but this *hamam* is interesting for its history rather than its architecture. When Jews first lived in Balat from the 15th century, they asked Süleyman I to build a *hamam* specially for them, to be used as a *mikvah,* for women's monthly ritual bathing. Permission was granted, and Sinan built two special *hamams*—this being the only one remaining. ⏱ *10 min. Hamam 15 TL. Men 7am–11pm, women 9am–6pm.*

② ★ Surp Hirestagabet Ermenikilisesi (Holy Angels Armenian Church). Turn left, and left again onto Hacı Isa Mektabi Sokak to this historic church, dating back to Byzantine times. The Armenian community took it over in the 17th century and restored it in 1835, from when it survived three fires—a miracle in itself. The sacred spring in the basement is still in full flow, and is a huge appeal for today's visitors. Also known as Mary of Wonders, every year on September 16 worshippers from all faiths come from all over Turkey for all-night prayers, believing that the sacred waters have miraculous powers for just one congregant. ⏱ *20 min. 2 Kamiş Sokaği. Thurs and Sun 10am–2pm.*

③ ★★ Ahrida Synagogue. From the church turn left down Hacı Isa Mektabi Sokak and onto *Kurkcuçeşme Sok.* You'll soon see the deep-red exterior of Turkey's oldest Sephardic synagogue, established in 1430 by Macedonians. Inside, the most eye-catching piece is the *Bimah,* the central raised platform from where Torah readings take place. Some say it's shaped like a galleon, the symbol of Sephardic Jews who sailed here from the Spanish Inquisition, or perhaps the shape of Noah's Ark, representing freedom. Around 100 congregants attend services every Saturday (the Jewish Sabbath). With high security since a 2004 bomb attack on an Istanbul synagogue, anyone wishing to visit must email for permission at least 3 days in advance (see website below). Bring your passport for ID. *9 Kurkcuçeşme Sok, Balat. www. musevicemaati.com. By appointment only, Mon–Fri 9:30am–noon.*

Ahrida Synagogue's exterior, hidden away in Fener.

Old Greek house perched on the corner of Balat market.

4 ★ kids **Börekci.** Join the locals and have a snack in one of the traditional teahouses and börek (savory pastries) parlors. *Vodina Cad. Tea and* börek *3 TL.*

5 ★ **Vodina Caddesi.** Continue along busy Vodina Caddesi, laden with Fener's ramshackle charm, notably the old top-heavy Greek house at the corner. This was the area of the old Çifit Çarşısı, Jewish Market. Newly restored buildings stand beside original buildings with Byzantine arched roofs. Nip left down Çiçekli Bostan Sokak to **Balart** (36 Hizırçavus Köprü Sok) selling miniature models of Balat houses by local artist Beyhan Gürsoy. Rejoin Vodina Caddesi. 🕑 *30 min. Most shops open daily, 9am–7pm.*

6 ★★ **Özel Fener Rum Lisesi (Greek School).** Turn right up the steep, cobbled Sancaktar Sokak, and halfway up you'll see this immense neo-Gothic red-brick monolith. Strings of washing lines above the street, crowned by the school, is one of my favorite Istanbul scenes. Originally named Great Patriarchal School of the Nation, today fewer than 50 students

attend. Founded in 1556 as one of the Ottoman capital's most important Greek educational institutions, it was built in 1881 with bricks brought from France. Turn the corner, keeping the school on your right to reach **6**. 🕑 *10 min. Sancaktar Yokuşu.*

7 ★★ **Panaghia ton Mongolon (St. Mary of the Mongols).** Turn right three times and you'll come to this little church tucked behind high walls. This is the only Byzantine church that never converted to a mosque, thanks to a decree by Mehmet II. Maria, a Christian, married the Mongolian Khan (leader) in the 13th century to improve relations between the two nations. Widowed after 15 years, she returned to Constantinople and founded the monastery, where she spent her remaining years. Ring the bell for the caretaker, who can show you its compact interior (tip appreciated), laden with icons and shrines. He may reveal the underground passageway that led all the way to Hagia Sophia (p 7). Retrace your steps and descend the hill, turning right at Baki Dede Sokak and onto Yıldırım Sokak. 🕑 *15 min. Tevkii Cafer Mektebi Sok.*

8 ★ **Greek Orthodox Patriarchate.** Enter the high-walled courtyard to **St. George's Church's** neo-classical marble entrance. This has been head of the Patriarchate since moving from the Church of the Pammakaristos (p 42) in 1586. Look out for the two mosaic fragments of the Virgin Mary and John the Baptist saved from there, and the Column of Flagellation to which Christ was bound and flogged. Many of the treasures—including lecterns inlaid with mother-of-pearl—were brought from other regions. Like many Greek churches, it's a combination of ostentation and serenity, a wall of gold icons, contrasting with dark

The famous Greek school in Balat.

wooden pews and incense. ⏱ *30 min. 35 Sadrazam Ali Paşa Cad. www.ec-patr.org. Open daily 9am–4:30pm.*

9 ★★ **kids** **Tarihi Haliç Işkembecisi.** Famed for its *işkember* (roast beef intestines) and *kokorec* (intestine soup) this 24-hour restaurant is filled with Atatürk memorabilia, topped by a fabulous terrace. *117 Abdulezelpasa Cad.* ☎ *0212 534 9414. Kokorec 7 TL.*

10 ★ **Kadin Eserleri Kütüphanesi (Women's Library & Information Center).** Architect and poet Cengiz Bektas renovated this gorgeous little once-derelict building, turning it into Turkey's only women's library founded in 1990 by academics and journalists. Shelves groan with books and periodicals on myriad topics relating to women dating back to 1867. ⏱ *15 min. Fener Vapur Iskelesi Karşısı.* ☎ *0212 523 7408. www.kadineserleri.org. Open Mon–Fri 10am–6pm.*

11 ★★ **Sveti Stefan (St. Stephen of the Bulgars).** Hard to believe that this dazzling white church was created from cast-iron, from a flat-pack, one of the world's few surviving iron buildings. Constructed by Hovsep Aznavour in 1898, 500 tons of metal plaques were shipped from Vienna via the Black Sea, then assembled in double-quick time. Inside, the iron pillars and six majestic bells in the 40m-high (13 ft.) belfry were all made in Russia. Built when 30,000 Bulgarians lived in Constantinople, this was a significant part of the Bulgarians' struggle for independence. From here, catch a bus to Eminönü or Taksim, or walk back along the waterfront. ⏱ *20 min. Mürsel Paşa Cad. Open daily 8am–5pm.*

Feast on intestine soup at Tarihi Haliç Işkembecisi.

Beyazit's **Bazaars & Mosques**

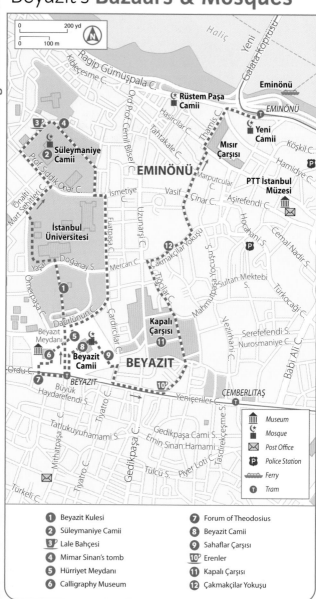

0		200 yd
0	100 m	

Haliç

Yeni Galata Köprüsü

Ragip Gümüşpala C.

Köleçeşme C.

Ord. Prof. Cemil Bilsel C.

Hasırcılar C.

Tahtakale C.

Thamis C.

① Rüstem Paşa Camii

Eminönü

EMINÖNÜ

① Yeni Camii

Mısır Çarşısı

Köşkil C.

Hamidye C.

Süleymaniye Camii

Prof. Sıddık Onar C.

İsmetiye C.

Onalti Mart Şehitleri C.

Yaşar

Fuatpaşa C.

Uzunçarşı C.

EMINÖNÜ

Marpuçcular C.

Vasif

Çınar C.

Aşirefendi C.

PTT İstanbul Müzesi

Hocahanı C.

Cemal Nadir S.

İstanbul Üniversitesi

Doğanay S.

Mercan C.

⑫ Çakmakçılar Yokuşu

Tığcılar C.

Mahmutpaşa Yokuşu

Sultan Mektebi S.

Türkocağı C.

Ömerpaşa C.

Dağıtının C.

①

Çardıcılar C.

⑪ Kapalı Çarşısı

Vezirhanı C.

Şerefefendi S.

Nurosmaniye C.

Babı Ali C.

Beyazıt Meydanı

⑤

⑥

⑧

Beyazit Camii

⑨

BEYAZIT

Ordu C.

⑦

Büyük Haydarefendi S.

BEYAZIT

Yeniçeriler C.

⑩

ÇEMBERLİTAŞ

Tiyatro C.

Tatlukuyuhamamı S.

Mithatpaşa C.

Tiyatro C.

Gedikpaşa C.

Gedikpaşa Cami S.

Emin Sinan Hamamı

Tülcü S.

Piyer Loti C.

Tasdirekçeşme S.

Türkeli C.

🏛	Museum
✦	Mosque
■	
✉	Post Office
🅿	Police Station
🚢	Ferry
T	Tram

①	Beyazit Kulesi	**⑦**	Forum of Theodosius
②	Süleymaniye Camii	**⑧**	Beyazit Camii
③	Lale Bahçesi	**⑨**	Sahaflar Çarşısı
④	Mimar Sinan's tomb	**⑩**	Erenler
⑤	Hürriyet Meydanı	**⑪**	Kapalı Çarşısı
⑥	Calligraphy Museum	**⑫**	Çakmakçılar Yokuşu

Dominated by two major landmarks, Kapalı Çarşısı (Grand Bazaar) and Süleymaniye Camii, historic Beyazit has been a center of commerce for centuries. From Eminönü, you pass a busy working area filled with *hans* (workshops) and the sounds of hammering and chiseling, contrasting to the ethereal mood of the vast Süleymaniye mosque. START: **Tram or walk to Beyazit.**

❶ ★ kids Beyazit Kulesi (Beyazit Tower).

From the tram stop, enter the dominating, ornate gateway to **Istanbul University.** Inside its gardens, Mahmud II built this firewatch tower in 1749 to prevent frequent fires destroying wooden buildings. Made from wood itself, the tower predictably burnt down in 1756, replaced by another (wooden!) tower in 1826—which also burnt down. Thankfully, the practical architect Senekerim Balyan (*Art & Architecture Highlights*, p 173) built this stone tower in Ottoman baroque style in 1828, to which three floors were added. It has since been used for navigation and meteorological purposes, now redundant. Sadly it's impossible to ascend its 250 wooden steps without tortuous bureaucracy, so instead admire its tiered exterior with balconies. ⏱ *10 min.*

❷ ★★★ Süleymaniye Camii.

Walk through the university's grounds to Mimar Sinan's greatest creation in the city, perched atop the highest of Istanbul's seven hills. After you've enjoyed its newly renovated serene interior and huge ornate domes, visit the tomb of Süleyman I and his wife Roxelana and the rose gardens. Outside, in so-called "addicts alley" where opium and hashish were once sold from cafes, traders now specialize in equally pleasurable *kuru fasulye* (white beans), a good brunch choice. Look out for the "Süleymaniye Kütüphanesi" sign and take a peek; this was once part of the mosque's *medrese* (religious school), now a library for students.

Close by, the old hospital and asylum is a fully functioning women's hospital; it's great that most of Sinan's *külliye* is in use today. ⏱ *1 hr. See p 8 for details.*

❸ ★★ kids Lale Bahçesi.

A good choice for tea, *nargile* (tobacco water-pipe), and even a burger, this sunken tea garden was part of the old imaret (kitchen) that once fed the city's poor. It's popular with local students and religious courting couples. *12 Şifahane Sok, Süleymaniye Camii Yani. Tea and nargile 8 TL.*

❹ ★ Mimar Sinan's tomb.

Sinan's modest tomb, which he designed, lies just outside the mosque's main walls and precisely where the architect wanted to be,

Beyazit Kulesi.

Süleymaniye Camii, Mimar Sinan's favorite creation.

close to his favorite Istanbul creation. From the street you can catch a glimpse of the white tomb built from *kufeki* stone, with its marble sarcophagus. The complex also has the tomb of architect Ali Talat Bey (1869–1922). ⏱ *10 min. Corner of Mimar Sinan Cad and Fetva Yokuşu Sok.*

5 ★★ **Hürriyet Meydanı (Freedom Square).** Walk down Mimar Sinan Caddesi, a lovely little street dotted with metalworker shops, hammering out copper and chrome household goods. Turn right onto Fuatpaşa Caddesi to rejoin the Hürriyet Meydanı, the Old City's largest public square, better known today as Beyazit Meydanı. Built in A.D. 393 by Emperor Theodosius as Forum Tauri (Forum of the Bull), it once contained a triumphal arch in the center decorated by bronze bull heads (**7**). Usually the square is peaceful, lined with simple cafe carts selling *simit* (sesame bread), and headscarfed women selling seeds to feed the annoying pigeons.

(You might see a student demonstration, especially on Fridays, watched by van loads of armed riot police; if so, don't hang around!) ⏱ *15 min.*

6 ★★ **Calligraphy Museum.** Lying at the western edge of the square, this museum was once the *medrese* of the simple, stone Beyazit Mosque, later used as a library. Usually deserted, exhibits range from 14th-century Qur'ans with intricate gold calligraphy to huge 19th-century *tuğras* (signatures) of sultans, albeit some woodworm-infested. Forbidden in Islam to depict the human form, calligraphy was the art form of the Ottomans. Strange to think that Sultan Abdülhamid's late-19th-century *tuğra* was created in the same year as Van Gogh's finest paintings. Check out the peaceful central courtyard—if open. Closed at time of writing; reopening in 2012. ⏱ *30 min. Hürriyet Meydanı.* ☎ *0212 527 5851. Admission 5 TL. Open Tues–Sat 9am–4pm. Tram: Beyazit.*

7 ★★ **Forum of Theodosius.** Nip across busy Ordu Caddesi to what's left of the triumphal arch, built by Theodosius the Great, once part of Beyazit Squarewith a vaulted roof and three passageways. I love this rather ramshackle pile of stones, discovered between 1948 and 1961. It includes columns with peacock-feather emblems, which may resemble tears. It's a small reminder that this was the fabled road which led to Thrace. ⏱ *15 min. Ordu Cad.*

8 ★ **Beyazit Camii (Beyazit Mosque).** Built from 1501 to 1506, this was the city's oldest imperial mosque, inspired by **Hagia Sophia** (p 7), with a 17m-diameter (56 ft.) dome and galleries overlooking the central prayer area. Today it's likely to be full at lunchtimes with market traders. Like all imperial mosques, this was part of a *külliye* comprising *hamam, medrese* (**2**), and kitchen. Its serene courtyard houses the limestone tomb of Beyazit II (1447–1512) at the back of the gardens, plus that of his daughter and Grand Vezir Koca Reşit Paşa (1800–58), the distinguished leader of the 19th-century Tanzimat (Reform) movement (*A Brief History*, p 170). Close by is the city's oldest-surviving primary school, restored and now the Hakki Tarik Us Research Library, with a digitized archive of Ottoman periodicals. 🕐 *20 min. Hürriyet Meydanı. Open daily dawn–dusk. Tram: Beyazit.*

9 ★ **Sahaflar Çarşısı (Booksellers Bazaar).** Before the arrival of printing machines in 1729, the printed book was seen as a corrupting European influence, so only hand-written manuscripts were sold here. Today, the picturesque courtyard market specializes in textbooks for local students, with some stalls selling photographic books on Istanbul, calligraphy, and miniatures. At the center, look out for the bust of Ibrahim Muteferrika, who printed the first books in Turkish in 1732. Outside, you'll probably see sellers of *tespi* (prayer beads) and collectors' items, including foreign banknotes. On a recent visit, I was offered old Iraqi banknotes with Saddam Hussain's portrait, for 5 TL. Bargain! If you need some respite before hitting the Grand Bazaar, turn left at the tram tracks and enter the grounds of Çorlulu Ali Paşa mosque. 🕐 *20 min. Sahaflar Çarşısı Sok. Open daily 9am–8pm. Tram: Beyazit.*

10 ★★★ **kids Erenler.** If you need a sit-down with a glass of tea and fruity *nargile* (tobacco waterpipe), this gorgeous leafy courtyard adjacent to the mosque is one of my

Lale Bahçesi, once part of the mosque kitchen.

favorites, packed with backgammon-playing locals and—thankfully—local prices. *36 Çorlulu Alipaşa Medressesi, Yeniçerileri Cad.* ☎ *0212 511 8853. Tea and nargile 5 TL.*

11 ★★★ **kids Kapalı Çarşısı (Covered, or Grand, Bazaar).** From Erenler, you can walk up Bileyciler Sokak, past wholesale silver shops, and enter the Grand Bazaar through Kurkculer Kapisi (gate 2). Keep your eye on the signs or enjoy getting lost! If you're shopping for anything specific, don't buy at the first place you see, especially if it's a big buy; take a business card and shop around. The market retains elements of its centuries-old trading practices (although 16th-century merchants bothered less with the false charm), but TV screens suspended from the ceilings and cappuccinos in stylish cafes bring it firmly into the 21st century. If you need an escape from the inside,

Beyazit Camii, Istanbul's oldest-remaining imperial mosque.

explore the surrounding streets which still retain an air of authentic trading. ⏲ *Anything from 1 hr. See p 8 for details.*

⑫ ★★ kids **Çakmakçilar Yokuşu.** Exit from Mercan Kapisi (gate 16) and turn right down the busy Çakmakçilar Yokusu Sokak (look to the left to see Beyazit Tower). You're now on the street with two of the most famous old *hans*, usually three levels of tiny workshops built around a courtyard, also used for storage. Downhill on

the left is the entrance of **Büyük Valide Han** built by Valide Sultan Kösem just before her death in 1651, with a vast courtyard surrounded by a double-tiered arcade housing Cem Evi, a Shiite mosque. Further down the street on the opposite side is **Büyük Yeni Han,** built in 1764 by Mustafa III. At the bottom of the street, turn left and head down toward Yeni Camii and Eminönü's transport hub. ⏲ *40 min. Hans open Mon–Sat 9:30am–6:30pm. Tram: Beyazit.* ●

Shopping Best Bets

Best for Vintage Wedding Dresses
★★ By Retro, *Suriye Pasajı, off Istiklal Cad (p 86)*

Best Rummage for Designer Seconds
★★★ Beyoğlu Iş Merkezi, *187 Istiklal Cad (p 89)*

Best for Kookie Kitchenware
★ Karinca, *Tünel Meydanı (p 88)*

Best Arty Glassware
★★ Paşabahçe, *150A Istiklal Cad (p 88)*

Best Luxury Ottomania
★★ Sevan Bıçakcı, *3/1A Şair Nedim Cad (p 89)*

Best for Tasty Turkish Coffee
★★ Kurukahveci Mehmet Efendi, *66 Tahmis Sokak (p 87)*

Best for Silk Central Asian Gowns
★★★ Ali Textile, *32/4–5 Çorlulu Ali Paşa Medrese, Yeniçeriler Cad (p 85)*

Best for Second-Hand Accordions
★★ Gözde Musik, *6B Galipdede Cad (p 84)*

Best Hand-Made Costume Jewelry
★★★ Chris Kami, *116/1A Hangecidi Sokak (p 88)*

Adorn your table with fabrics from Galeri Hediye.

Best for Traditional Greek Music
★★ Karakedi Plak Evi, *behind 85 Istiklal Cad (p 85)*

Best for Endless Choice of Carpets
★★★ Kapalı Çarşısı (Grand Bazaar), *Beyazit (p 90)*

Best for Satisfying a Sweet Tooth
★★ Hafız Mustafa, *84–86 Hamidiye Cad (p 87)*

Best for Wannabe Interior Designers
★★ A La Turca, *4 Faikpaşa Yokuşu (p 84)*

Best for Gaziantep Pistachios
★★★ Mısır Çarşısı (Spice Market), *Eminönü (p 90)*

Best Sunny Sunday Market
★★ Ortaköy Craft Market, *Ortaköy Meydanı (p 90)*

Best Hassle-Free Treasure Trove ★★★ Dösim G.E.S., *2/1 Şeyhülislam Hayriefendi Cad (p 85)*

Best Chunky Platform Shoes
★★ Beta, *22A Cevahir AVM, Büyükdere Cad (p 86)*

Best Postcards of Old Istanbul
★★ Levant Koleksiyon, *64B Meşrutiyet Cad (p 84)*

Best Clothes for Street-Smart Guys
★★ Kiğılı, *34 Istiklal Cad (p 87)*

Best for Traditional Anatolian Fabrics
★★ Galeri Hediye, *72 Mısır Çarşısı (p 85)*

Best for Souvenirs for Designer Friends
★★ Armaggan, *8 Bostan Sok, off Abdi Ipekçi Cad (p 87)*

Old City Shopping

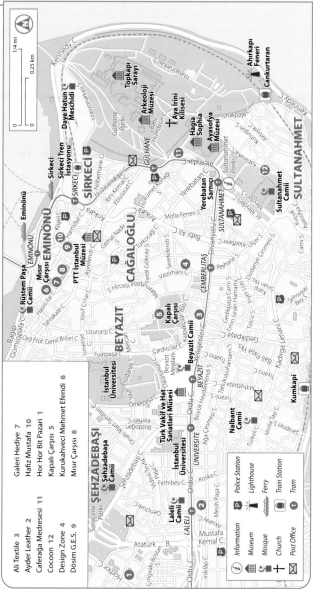

Ali Textile **3**
Ayder Leather **2**
Caferağa Medresesi **11**
Cocoon **12**
Design Zone **4**
Dösim G.E.S. **9**

Galeri Hediye **7**
Hafız Mustafa **10**
Hor Hor Bit Pazarı **1**
Kapalı Çarşısı **5**
Kurukahveci Mehmet Efendi **6**
Mısır Çarşısı **8**

Chapter opener: Make the perfect Turkish coffee in a copper cezve from Mısır Çarşısı.

Beyoğlu Shopping

A La Turca **16**
Bahar Korçan **1**
Beyoğlu İş Merkezi **9**
By Retro **5**
Chris Kami **10**
Denizler Kitabevi **6**
Dolapdere Bazaar **11**
Golden Rose **15**

Gözde Musik **2**
Haremlique **20**
Homer Kitabevi **12**
Istanbul Kitapçısı **8**
Istiklal Kitabevi **19**
Kanyon **21**
Karakedi Plak Evi **17**
Kare Deri **13**

Karinca **3**
Kiğılı **18**
Levant Koleksiyon **4**
Mor **14**
Ortaköy Craft Market **20**
Paşabahçe **7**
Sevan Bıçakcı **20**

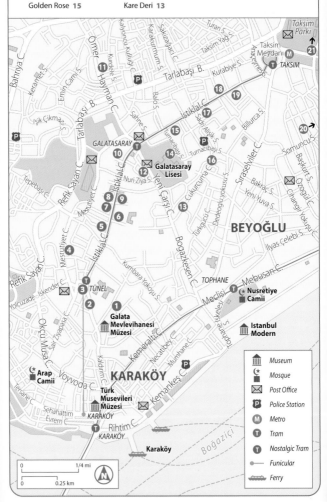

Nişantaşı Shopping

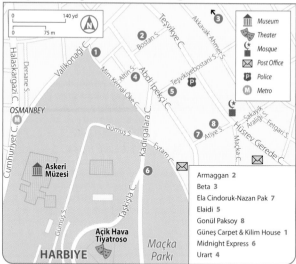

Armaggan 2
Beta 3
Ela Cindoruk-Nazan Pak 7
Elaidi 5
Gonül Paksoy 8
Güneş Carpet & Kilim House 1
Midnight Express 6
Urart 4

Grand Bazaar Shopping

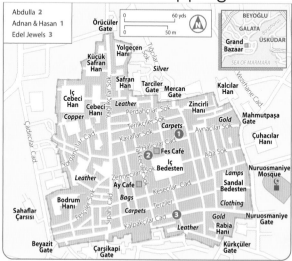

Abdulla 2
Adnan & Hasan 1
Edel Jewels 3

Istanbul **Shopping A to Z**

Antiques & Vintage

★★ A La Turca ÇUKURCUMA
Chic showroom over four floors with European and Turkish treasures, from *kilims* (rugs) to early 1900s' pottery, metal milk churns, and gilded mirrors. Oozing good taste. *4 Faikpaşa Yokuşu.* ☎ *0212 245 2933. www. alaturcahouse.com. AE, DC, MC, V. Bus: Taksim, then walk. Map p 82.*

★ Hor Hor Bit Pazari AKSARAY
Tucked away in a working-class neighborhood, this six-floor arcade has over 200 stores specializing in early-20th-century French and Ottoman antiques. Look for furniture and chandeliers, or candlesticks for easier transportation. *13 Kiriktulumba Sok, off Horhor Cad. MC, V. Tram: Aksaray. Map p 81.*

★★ Levant Koleksiyon BEYOĞLU
New location for this treasure trove of old maps, engravings, and postcards of old Istanbul scenes. With the city's ever-changing face, this gives a real hint of its past. *64B Meş rutiyet Cad.* ☎ *0212 293 4394. www.levantkoleksiyon.com. MC, V. Bus: Taksim. Map p 82.*

Learn the saz or accordion from Gözde Musik.

Books & Music

★ Denizler Kitabevi BEYOĞLU
Specializing in everything nautical, the books will delight old sailors, and 5 centuries of Istanbul maps, posters, and old prints will look good on anyone's wall. *199 Istiklal Cad.* ☎ *0212 249 8893. www. denizlerkitabevi.com. MC, V. Bus: Taksim. Map p 82.*

★★ Gözde Musik TÜNEL   On a street full of music shops, swamped with the sounds of electric guitars and *ney* (bamboo flute), explore this tiny shop with *baglamas* (lutes) hanging from the ceiling and second-hand accordions. *6B Galipdede Cad.* ☎ *0212 251 4364. MC, V. Tunnel: Tünel. Map p 82.*

★★ kids Homer Kitabevi GALATASARAY   A charming bookstore full of English- and European-language books, specializing in international history, art, and architecture. There's a children's section on the lower level. *12A Yeni Çarsi Cad.* ☎ *0212 249 5902. www.homer books.com. MC, V. Bus/metro: Taksim, then walk. Map p 82.*

★ Istanbul Kitapçısı BEYOĞLU
Although staff sometimes seem uninterested, this municipality-run bookstore has a good selection of English-language books on Istanbul and Turkey, plus CDs and local maps. *146 Istiklal Cad.* ☎ *0212 292 7692. www.istanbulkitapcisi.com. MC, V. Bus: Taksim, then walk. Map p 82.*

★★ Istiklal Kitabevi BEYOĞLU
Like many bookstores on Istiklal, this doubles as a music store and cafe. It has a decent English section, and the area's main ticket outlet, Biletix (p 127). *55A Istiklal Cad.* ☎ *0212 292 9518. AE, MC, V. Bus/metro: Taksim. Map p 82.*

★★ **Karakedi Plak Evi** BEYOĞLU
A tiny backstreet stall, which has been on this spot since 1964; the boss, Hasan, is happy to play you specialist Rum (ethnic Greek) and old Jewish traditional music, available on CD, cassette, and vinyl. *Behind 85 Istiklal Cad.* ☎ *0212 243 2498. Cash only. Bus/Metro to Taksim. Map p 82.*

Carpets, Kilims & Fabrics
★ **Adnan & Hasan** BEYAZIT
A novelty in the bazaar's carpet shops: Prices are fixed and clearly displayed. Laid-back owners love their selection of carpets and *kilims* from Turkey, the Caucuses, and Afghanistan, and have a great international following. *89–92 Halıcılar Cad, Kapalıçarşısı.* ☎ *0212 527 9887. www.adnanandhasan. com. AE, DC, MC, V. Tram/bus: Beyazit. Map p 83.*

★★★ **Ali Textile** BEYAZIT
The affable Ali has doubled his shop size in this courtyard lined with carpet-repair workshops. Ali sells bags and cushion-covers made from carpets, plus *kilims* and traditional Central Asian coats, all very affordable. Fixed price and friendly. *32/4–5 Çorlulu Ali Paşa Medrese, Yeniçeriler Cad.* ☎ *0535 367 5333. MC, V. Tram: Beyazit. Map p 81.*

★★★ kids **Cocoon** SULTANAHMET
Hand-made felt accessories come in bright colors, all from traditional Central Asian designs, plus Turkmen and Persian *kilims,* and a huge range of textiles. Seref and Gokhan are the knowledgeable owners. Great for gifts. *93 Arasta Bazaar.* ☎ *0212 638 6450. www.cocoontr. com. AE, MC, V. Tram: Sultanahmet. Map p 81.*

★★★ **Dösim G.E.S.** EMINÖNÜ
This immense government-run emporium has carpets, leather bags, painted ceramics, and glassware (all modern replicas of old

Central Asian traditional gown at Ali Textile.

designs), at very reasonable, fixed prices. What it lacks in atmosphere it more than compensates in choice and value. *2/1 Şeyhülislam Hayriefendi Cad.* ☎ *0212 526 6813. www. ges.gov.tr. MC, V. Tram/bus: Eminönü. Map p 81.*

★★ **Galeri Hediye** EMINÖNÜ
This textile store sells unusual and traditional fabrics using Anatolian designs, usually multicolored ornate stripes. Check out the *kumaş,* a colorful heavy cotton design sold by the meter that makes wonderful tablecloths and throws. *72 Mısır Çarşısı.*

Cocoon fun flowers in felt.

Shopping Zones

The Grand Bazaar and Beyazit area has everything from carpets to glassware, plus cheap jeans and leather jackets. **Sultanahmet** caters for the tourists, with souvenirs galore, and earthy **Eminönü** has traditional markets around the **Spice Market.** Trawl **Çukurcuma's** streets for antique furniture and quaint contemporary arts. In **Beyoğlu,** Turkish fashion stores and lively bookstores cram **Istiklal Caddesi,** and its continuation **Galip Dede Caddesi** is the place for musicians. *Fashionistas* flock to **Nişantaşi's** boutiques for Turkish and foreign designers.

☎ *0212 511 0506. MV, V. Tram: Eminönü. Map p 81.*

★★ Güneş Carpet & Kilim House NIŞANTAŞI

A woman in this male-dominated business, Güneş Öztarakçı, has been selling carpets for 35 years, with an astounding collection in her "carpet museum." An expert, without the high-pressure sales pitch. *5 Mimar Kemal Öke Cad.* ☎ *0212 225 1954. www.gunes carpet.com. AE, DC, MC, V. Minibus: Nişantaşı/Teşvikiye. Map p 83.*

Clothes & Accessories

★ kids Ayder Leather LALELI

You're likely to find huge bargains in leather jackets here, albeit not the height of fashion. This is the neighborhood for rock-bottom prices, cheaper than the Grand Bazaar. Huge selection in a whole range of styles and colors. *Green Center, 21 Laleli Cad.* ☎ *0212 638 2274. MC, V. Tram: Laleli. Map p 81.*

★★ Bahar Korçan GALATA

Istanbul designer Korçan shows off her one-off pieces in her new Galata showroom. She usually mixes fabrics like patchwork coats and appliquéd fish-tail skirts, with obvious inspiration from Ottoman designs. *9 Serdar-i Ekrem Sok.* ☎ *0212 243*

7320. www.baharkorcan.org. MC, V. Bus: Taksim. Map p 82.

★★ Beta ŞIŞLI

My favorite shoe shop specializes in chunky shoes and boots, often in bright colors with flower motifs. Men's designs are more conventional! On the pricey side; check out their seasonal sales. (City-wide branches.) *22A Cevahir AVM, Büyükdere Cad.* ☎ *0212 380 0893. www.betashoes.com. MC, V. Bus/metro: Şişli. Map p 83.*

★★ By Retro BEYOĞLU

This treasure trove crams in second-hand clothes from the 1920s to the present day, from Turkey and Europe. Most were used on movie sets, so it's the place to browse for vintage 1950s' wedding dresses, military costumes, and hippy hats. *Suriye Pasajı, off Istiklal Cad.* ☎ *0212 245 6420. MC, V. Bus/funicular: Taksim. Map p 82.*

★ Elaidi NIŞANTAŞI

Local designer Mehtap Elaidi puts a twist on conventional styles, like crisp tailored shirts with balloon sleeves, or fitted skirts with a fish tail. Check out the small collection of striking, simple jewelry. *Ayde Apartment, 11/1 Bostan Sok.* ☎ *0212 236 3783. www.elaidi.net. MC, V. Minibus: Nişantaşı/Teşvikiye. Map p 83.*

★★ Gonül Paksoy NIŞANTAŞI
Using the very best fabrics, Paksoy's designs mean luxurious clothing and accessories. Using silks, linen, and wool, naturally dyed in mulberry and brown tones, all her pieces are unique, from exquisite hand-made shoes to simple, elegant jackets. *6A Atiye Sokak.* ☎ *0212 261 9081. AE, DC, MC, V. Minibus: Nişantaşı/Teşvikiye. Map p 83.*

★★ Kiğılı BEYOĞLU   A hard one to pronounce, Kiğılı *(keelu)* has top men's clothes over two floors, from fine cotton shirts to the best woolen suits and silk ties, using top European designs. *34 Istiklal Cad.* ☎ *0212 245 0011. www.kigili.com. tr. MC, V. Bus/funicular: Taksim. Map p 82.*

★ Midnight Express NIŞANTAŞI
Tucked-away boutique from Istanbul's husband-and-wife team Banu Bora (fashion) and Tayfun Mumcu (architect), now a small chain. Luxury meets bohemian for womenswear, using soft silks and crushed gold, plus sequined bags. The name is an ironic nod to the U.S. movie. *8/3 Açık Hava Apt, Kadırgalar Cad.* ☎ *0212 215 1968. www.midnight express.com.tr. MC, V. Minibus: Nişantaşı/Teşvikiye. Map p 83.*

Food

★★ Hafız Mustafa SIRKECI   Sample some of Turkey's best *lokum* (Turkish delight), here since 1864, or satisfy a sweet tooth with pastries and fruity boiled sweets. Escape to the simple cafe upstairs for a glass of tea. *84–86 Hamidiye Cad.* ☎ *0212 513 3610. www.hafizmustafa.com. MC, V. Tram: Sirkeci. Map p 81.*

★★ Kurukahveci Mehmet Efendi EMINÖNÜ   The granddaddy of coffee, Mehmet Efendi has roasted beans since 1871. The perennially popular family store outside the Spice Market still roasts and grinds beans in all varieties; a good place for packs of Turkish coffee ("Turks' gift to the world,' as they point out). *66 Tahmis Sokak.* ☎ *0212 511 4262. www.mehmetefendi.com. MC, V. Tram: Sirkeci. Map p 81.*

Homewear & Handicrafts
★★ Abdulla BEYAZIT   Gorgeous hand-made fragranced olive-oil soaps in wooden presentation boxes, natural loofahs, and hand-spun wool shawls make this a popular choice for quality gifts. *62 Halıcılar Cad, Kapalı Çarşısı.* ☎ *0212 527 3684. www.abdulla.com. MC, V. Tram/bus: Beyazit. Map p 83.*

★★ Armaggan NIŞANTAŞI
This seven-floor store sells its own-label designer goodies with a strong Turkish slant. Look out for vases with Ottoman carvings and hand-woven silks printed with organic dyes. *8 Bostan Sok, off Abdi Ipekçi Cad.* ☎ *0212 291 6296. www. armaggan.com. AE, MC, V. Minibus: Nişantaşı/Teşvikiye. Map p 83.*

★ Haremlique AKARETLER
Duvets designed with Ottoman scenes, colored organic bathrobes, and limited-edition fabrics will bring a touch of glamor to your bathroom

A plethora of theatrical vintage gear at By Retro.

or bedroom. Monogrammed towels make a lovely gift. *11 Şair Nedim Bey Cad.* ☎ *0212 236 3843. www. haremlique.com. MC, V, AE. Bus: Beşiktaş. Map p 82.*

★ **Karinca** TÜNEL These bold, original, and humorous items, including graters shaped like women's dresses, clocks created from kitchen utensils, and elephant-trunk funnels, will brighten up any home. Novel gift ideas. *Tünel Meydanı.* ☎ *0212 252 8843. www.karinca design.com. MC, V. Funicular: Tünel. Map p 82.*

★★ **Paşabahçe** BEYOĞLU Creating household glassware since 1935, Paşabahçe's showroom is a few notches above the rest with exquisite tableware, ceramics, contemporary vases, and candlesticks. Check out their hand-painted coffee cups downstairs. *150A Istiklal Cad.* ☎ *0212 244 0544. www.pasabahce. com.tr. AE, MC. V. Bus: Taksim, then walk. Map p 82.*

★★ **Urart** NIŞANTAŞI A dazzling display of creations, some of them in the Archaeology Museum (p 14). Ancient pieces are recreated from silver, gold, or marble. Look out for a miniature version of a Topkapı

Find quality gifts at Abdulla.

Palace pillar and prehistoric Hittite relics, recreated as gold jewelry. *18 Abdi Ipekçi Cad.* ☎ *0212 246 7194. AE, DC, MC, V. Minibus: Nişantaşı/ Teşvikiye. Map p 83.*

Jewelry

★★★ **Chris Kami** BEYOĞLU Kami hand-makes rings, necklaces, and bracelets, weaving and bending wire with polished stones. No precious materials here, so everything is affordable. My favorite Istanbul jeweler! *116/1A Hangecidi Sokak, Hazzo Pulo Pasajı, off Istiklal Cad.* ☎ *0212 292 6819. MC, V. Bus/ metro: Taksim. Map p 82.*

★★ **Design Zone** NURUOS-MANIYE Özlem Tuna specializes in contemporary jewelry design and home accessories, such as chunky gold pendants, stylized tulips, and delicate ceramics. This, her flagship gallery/store, also stocks works by other Turkish designers. *Alibaba Türbe Sok 21–4.* ☎ *0212 527 9285. www.designzone.com.tr. AE, MC, V. Tram: Beyazit. Map p 81.*

★ **Edel Jewels** BEYAZIT The Grand Bazaar's (p 90) outlet for top designer Cemil Ipekçi, whose collection includes rose gold and diamonds set on oxidized silver, all in simple and elegant designs. *73 Kalpakçilar Cad, Kapalıçarşısı.* ☎ *0212 527 9797. www.edeljewels. com. AE, DC, MC, V. Tram/bus: Beyazit. Map p 83.*

★★ **Ela Cindoruk-Nazan Pak** NIŞANTAŞI Young designers Cindoruk and Pak showcase their exquisite jewelry in unusual forms and materials, including paper and resin. Also collections from other young designers. *14 Atiye Sokak, off Abdi Ipekçi Cad.* ☎ *0212 232 2664. www.elacindoruknazanpak. com. MC, V. Minibus: Nişantaşı/ Teşvikiye. Map p 83.*

What Time?

Opening hours vary, depending on the neighborhood, but are usually 10am to 7pm, and many stores on Istiklal Caddesi—especially books and music—are open until 11pm on Friday and Saturday. Most stores city-wide open on Sunday, except for small privately run places. The Grand Bazaar and Spice Market is also closed Sunday. Istanbul's ever-increasing malls—adored by locals at weekends—usually close about 9 or 10pm.

★ **Golden Rose** BEYOĞLU The perfect store if you need a top-up of nail-polish, traveling-size perfume (excellent, cheap copies of the real thing!) and every type of toiletry and cosmetics. The Turkish-brand items are cheap, and good quality. *163B Istiklal Cad. MC, V. Bus/funicular: Taksim. Map p 82.*

★★ **Kare Deri** ÇUKURCUMA You might see Dilek Göker here, hand-stitching soft calf leather and goatskin leather bags in a rainbow of colors. They're all their own designs, from triangular, envelope-slim purses to huge shoulder bags. They'll even custom-make items in your chosen color. *19C Çukurcuma Cad. ☎ 0212 252 2206. www.parsomen.com. MC, V. Bus: Taksim, then walk. Map p 82.*

★★ **Mor** ÇUKURCUMA Gorgeous chunky jewelry including rings, necklaces, and bold strips of hand-twisted silver, by local designers Nurettin Ayan and Zeynep Güven. *16/1 Sarayhan, Turnacıbaşı Sok. ☎ 0212 292 8817. MC, V. Bus: Taksim, then walk. Map p 82.*

★★ **Sevan Bıçakcı** AKARETLER Superb one-off pieces by a master jewelry designer means sculpted Ottoman-inspired rings the size of golf balls, using traditional and unique techniques like micro-mosaics and miniature paintings. *3/1A*

Şair Nedim Cad. ☎ 0212 236 9199. www.sevanbicakci.com. AE, DC, MC, V. Bus: Beşiktaş/Tram: Kabataş. Map p 82.

Markets & Malls

★★★ kids **Beyoğlu Iş Merkezi** BEYOĞLU In a three-floor scruffy mall, trawl through stalls of 90% rubbish to find gems at a fraction of the original price, perhaps Pink gents' shirts or Miss Sixty jeans. *Terzi* (tailors) downstairs make fast alterations for a couple of liras. Great for a wardrobe revamp. *187 Istiklal Cad. Most stalls cash only. Bus: Taksim, then walk. Map p 82.*

Edel Jewels' elegant designs.

★ **Caferağa Medresesi** SULTA-NAHMET Located in an old *medrese*, artisans in tiny workshops surrounding the courtyard run courses including hand-painted ceramics and Ottoman calligraphy. They also sell their handicrafts. *Caferağa Sokak, 1 Soğukkuyu Çikmazi.* ☎ *0212 513 3601. Some stalls take credit cards. Tram: Sultanahmet. Map p 81.*

★ **Dolapdere Bazaar** TARLIBAŞI Sunday street market where locals shop for the best and cheapest fruit, veg, cheeses, and honey, plus headscarves, stripy socks, and bed linen. Forget souvenirs; this gypsy area is wonderful for people-watching. *Note:* Guard your valuables VERY well! *From Omer Hayyam Cad. Cash only. Bus: Tepebaşı (Tarlıbaşı Cad), then walk. Map p 82.*

★ **Kanyon** LEVENT Istanbul's most architecturally stunning mall houses upmarket boutiques, brasseries, and movie halls, curving around a clever use of courtyards and terraces. Look out for **Remzi Kitabevi** (books), **Harvey Nichols** (designer fashion), **Vakko** (fashion), and **Paşabahçe Bütik** (homewear). *Büyükdere Cad.* ☎ *0212 353 5300. www.kanyon.com.tr. AE, MC, V. Metro: Taksim to Levent. Map p 82.*

★★★ **Kapalı Çarşısı (Grand Bazaar)** BEYAZIT The grande dame of markets, this is a great historical shopping destination. It has Istanbul's best selection of carpets, leather, painted ceramics, and gold, for a souvenir-rich shopping experience. (See p 8 for more details.) *Beyazit. www.kapalicarsi.org.tr. Some stores accept credit cards. Tram/bus: Beyazit. Map p 81.*

★★★ **Mısır Çarşısı (Spice, or Egyptian, Bazaar)** EMINÖNÜ An ancient Istanbul spice market, now veering toward souvenirs and jewelry stores. A good selection of spices, dried fruit, and *lokum* (Turkish delight), with more choices at the stalls outside where the locals shop. (See p 9 for more details.) *Eminönü. Some stores accept credit cards. Tram/bus: Eminönü. Map p 81.*

★★ **Ortaköy Craft Market** ORTAKÖY Fun weekend market on cobbled streets with jewelry and accessories, busy in summer. Browse the waterfront stalls with good-natured vendors (*Best in 3 Days*, p 21). *Ortaköy Meydanı. Some stores accept credit cards. Bus/ferry: Ortaköy. Map p 82.* ●

Clued Up on Carpets

How much do carpets cost? Anything between $100 and $10,000. If you know what you want and what it should cost, the Grand Bazaar is a good starting point, with many stores competing for business. For novices, I recommend fixed-price stores with no hard-sell, to indicate what your money can buy. Try the government-run **Dösim G.E.S.** (p 85) with prices of new carpets and kilims clearly marked, starting from $80. If local "friends," tour guides, or hotel staff take you to a store, their commission—anything from 20–50%—will be added to your price; best go alone.

5 The Best of the **Outdoors**

Gülhane **Park**

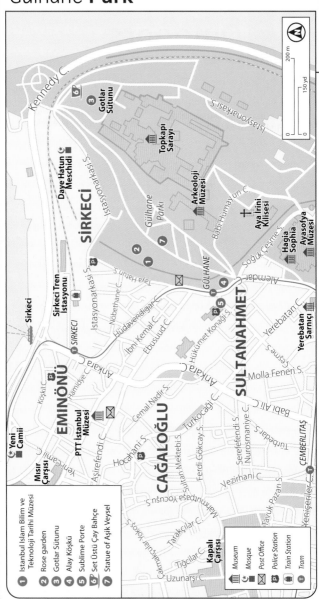

Kennedy C.

Gotlar Sütunu
❸

İstasyonarkası S.

Topkapı Sarayı

Daye Hatun Meschidi ■

İstasyonarkası S.

Gülhane Parkı

Arkeoloji Müzesi

Babıhümayun C.

Aya İrini Kilisesi

SİRKECİ

❷
❼
❶

Ⓟ

Hagia Sophia

Ayasofya Müzesi ✝

Sirkeci Tren İstasyonu

Taya Hatun S.

GÜLHANE

❹

Soğuk Çeşme S.

Alemdar

İstasyonarkası S.

Sirkeci

Ⓣ SİRKECİ

Nöbethane C.

İstasyonarkası S.

İstasyonarkası C.

Hüdavendigar C.

Ⓟ❺
Ⓣ

Yerebatan C.

Yerebatan Sarnıcı ■

İbni Kemal C.

Ebussuud C.

Hükümet Konağı S.

SULTANAHMET

Çeşme S.

Yeni Camii ℃

Ankara C.

Molla Feneri S.

Hamidye C.

Ankara C.

Mısır Çarşısı

Köşkü C.

Ⓟ

Yeni Camii C.

EMİNÖNÜ

PTT İstanbul Müzesi ■ ⊠

Aşirefendi C.

Hocahanı S.

Ⓟ

Cemal Nadir S.

ÇAĞALOĞLU

Sultan Mektebi S.

Türkocağı C.

Ferdi Gökçay S.

Babıali C.

Türbedar S.

Nurosmaniye C.

Şerefendi S.

ÇEMBERLİTAŞ

Ⓣ

Yeniçeriler C.

Vezirhani C.

Mahmutpaşa Yocuşu S.

Tavuk Pazarı S.

Çakmakçılar Yokoş S.

Tarakçılar C.

Tığcılar C.

Kapalı Çarşısı

Uzunçarşı C.

Previous page: Take a horsedrawn carriage through the park.

❶ İstanbul İslam Bilim ve Teknoloji Tarihi Müzesi
❷ Rose garden
❸ Gotlar Sütunu
❹ Alay Köşkü
❺ Sublime Porte
❻ Set Üstü Çay Bahçe
❼ Statue of Aşık Veysel

■ Museum
℃ Mosque
■ Post Office
⊠ Police Station
Ⓟ Train Station
Ⓣ Tram

200 m
150 yd

Nestled in the original first courtyard of Topkapı Palace, Istanbul's oldest park is also, at 66 hectares (163 acres), the city center's largest. Used in Byzantine times as a barracks and a military warehouse, it became the sultans' imperial garden and an important public meeting place. Today it's a respite from the city, a locals' favorite for weekend walks and picnics. START: **Tram to Gülhane.**

1 ★★ kids **Istanbul Islam Bilim ve Teknoloji Tarihi Müzesi (Istanbul Museum of the History of Science & Technology in Islam).** Located on the left side of the park, this museum, opened in 2008 by Turkish historian Fuat Sezgin, tells the story of Islamic scientists and astrologers from the 9th to 16th centuries. With instruments and other objects recreated by a German university, it demonstrated how these great men were at the forefront of early intellectual discoveries. Exhibits cover the first astrological instruments in the Islamic world, dating back to the 9th century, and include spherical astrolabes, the precursors to the sextant which were used to measure celestial bodies and as navigation aids. At the main entrance, don't miss the recreation of a globe made by 14th-century Caliph al-Ma'mun with Baghdad at the center of the known world. It was interesting to learn about the first pioneers of calculus (it brought back memories of school math exams) and even

the math of music, where the 13th century saw divisions of the octave into 17 unequal degrees. There's even a 14th-century distillation apparatus for making rose-petal extract. If you've seen your fair share of mosques, it's interesting to look at the models and the explanation of the science of the first skyscrapers—in other words, minarets! ⏱ *1 hr. Gülhane Park.* ☎ *0212 528 8065. Admission 5 TL, children under 7 years free. Open Wed–Mon, 9am–4:30pm. Tram: Gülhane.*

2 ★ **Rose garden.** *Gülhane* is the Persian for 'house of roses' so it's no coincidence that recent improvements include a newly planted rose garden outside the museum. This historic park was originally made into a rose garden to allow the flowers' scent to waft over to the palace and now, thanks to the smartening up or removal of several ugly buildings, the flowers stand out so much better. A new curved wooden sculpture, like a latticed dome, is a graceful addition outside the museum. Includes some plants

Newly created ornamental bridge adds to the park's new look.

Escape the crowds.

from Northern Cyprus and a miniature of Galata Tower (a favorite photo point, see p 10).

③ ★ Gotlar Sütunu (Goth's Column). No, nothing to do with dressing in black. On the eastern edge of the park, look through the trees to this 15m-high (49 ft.) granite monolith, surmounted by a Corinthian capital, dating back to the third century—one of Istanbul's oldest monuments. Although its history is uncertain, it probably derived its name from the Latin inscription at its base: "Fortune is restored to us because of victory over the Goths," commemorating a 3rd-century Roman victory. For such an historic

Goth's Column celebrating a Roman victory.

landmark, it's a shame there's no sign to explain its history (a complaint I have for many Istanbul spaces). Close by are more historic remains, probably belonging to an early Byzantine structure. A squat column of stones is topped with a relief of a cross; behind a fenced-off area lie the remains of a series of small rooms and an irregular colonnade.

④ ★ Alay Köşkü. Translated as Procession Pavilion, this was where the sultans would sneakily watch official processions opposite, especially the comings and goings outside the ornate Sublime Porte entrance (**⑤**). In the case of Ibrahim I, sultan between 1640 and 1648 and nicknamed Ibrahim the Mad because of his eccentricities and excesses, rumor has it that the pavilion was a perfect vantage point to aim his crossbow from and threaten unsuspecting bystanders. These days, the building sports a smart yellow-and-white-painted facade with arched windows, approached by a steep path. With offices inside, it's not possible to get much farther than the main doorway.

⑤ ★ Sublime Porte. You might have passed this typically ornate rococo gateway when traveling up on the tram from Eminönü to Sultanahmet. On the right-hand side, its curvaceous roof dipping over the monogrammed marble gate of 1843

Gülhane Park's Facelift

Since opening to the public in 1912, the park has seen significant events. On September 1 1928, Atatürk showed the Latin alphabet in a special ceremony to the public for the first time (previously Arabic script was used). The last decade has seen some of the most radical changes in the park. Gone are the scruffy zoo (which was Istanbul's oldest, founded in 1955), aquarium, and a plethora of vendors and barbecues; its recent facelift sees an ornamental bridge, fountain, laid-out paths, museum, and ongoing renovations to the old barracks. Thankfully, some things don't change; it's still filled with families at weekends and courting couples on sneaky weekday afternoons.

is hard to miss. Translated from the French to *Bab-i Ali*, this was the gateway to the political hub of the Ottoman Empire, its buildings containing the principal state departments, and later the official residence of the grand viziers (high-ranking political advisors). Today, the superb rococo gate with armed police outside leads to the *vilayet*, the more pedestrian-sounding provincial government departments.

Rococo gate of the Sublime Porte.

6 ★★ kids **Set Üstü Çay Bahçe.** Locals love to dwell here for samovars of tea, so it's especially busy on summer evenings and weekends. Perched high at the northeastern edge of the park overlooking Seraglio Point, with dramatic views of the Sea of Marmara and over to Asia, kids will love the burgers or over-stuffed jacket potatoes (*kumpir*; 10 TL). Pricier than it used to be, but worth it.

7 ★ **Statue of Aşik Veysel.** With surprisingly few statues and monuments in such an historic park, my favorite is a charming sculpture of musician Aşik Veysel (1894–1973), playing the *saz* (traditional stringed instrument). His life was marked with drama and sadness. Born in a field near Sivas as his mother returned from milking the cows, he contracted smallpox and went blind as a child; his parents and his baby son died, and later his wife ran off with his brother's servant. The superb *saz* player found his niche writing folk songs about the inevitability of death. Popular in Turkey as a poet and musician, he became the official state poet in 1965, died of leukemia in 1973, and is still revered today.

Palatial Park Life

Perhaps it's no coincidence that Istanbul's primary parks had a strong connection with Ottoman life. Gülhane Park, originally an area in the lower town of the ancient Greek city of Byzantium, was incorporated into Topkapı Palace as a rose garden for the sultans to stroll. Similarly, Yıldız Park (p 21), a forest in Byzantine times, was part of the Yıldız Palace complex and sultans' hunting ground—especially loved by Abdul Hamid II. The city's largest is the pine-filled Emirgan Park, near Sakıp Sabancı Museum (p 33) in the northern district of Sarıyer, named after Persian prince Emir Gune Han. Although not attached to any Ottoman palace, this eventually belonged to Khedevi Ismail, who built noble wooden pavilions (*köşk*), used today for Istanbul's tea-drinking public.

New York rock musician Joe Satriani was so inspired by his *saz* playing on a trip to Istanbul that he dedicated the track "Aşik Veysel" on his 2008 album *Professor Satchafunkilus and the Musterion of Rock* to him.

Close by, and a world away, is Turkey's oldest **statue of Atatürk,** cast in bronze by Austrian sculptor Heinrich Krippel in 1928. Want to know what the time is? Within the flowerbeds close to the path are two hands of a clock, which actually tell the time accurately! ●

Dining Best Bets

Best for Orient Express Glamor
★★ Agatha *52 Meşrutiyet Cad (p 101)*

Best Asian-Side Dining
★★★ Çiya *43, 44, and 48B Güneşlibahçe Sok (p 103)*

Best Taste of India
★ Dubb *10 Incili Çavuş Sok (p 103)*

Best Family-Run Meyhane
★★ Sofyalı 9 *9 Sofyalı Sok (p 108)*

Best Cozy Home-Cooking
★★ Hala *26 Çukurlu Çeşme Sok (p 104)*

Best Sushi with Style
★★ Vogue *13/F, 48 BJK Plaza (p 109)*

Best Sultanahmet Seafood
★★ Balıkçı Sabahattin *1 Cankurtaran Cad (p 102)*

Best-Value Tünel Meal
★★ Lokanta Helvetia *12 General Yazgan Sok (p 105)*

Best Wannabe Michelin Star
★★ Mimolett *55 Sıraselviler Cad (p 106)*

Best Dining by the Sea
★★ Feriye Lokantası *40 Çırağan Cad (p 104)*

Best Homely Bistro
★★ Dai Pera *54 Yeni Çarşı Cad (p 103)*

Best Dramatic Views
★★★ Topaz *50 İnönü Cad (p 109)*

Best for Liver Lovers
★★★ Canım Ciğerim *162 Istiklal Cad (p 102)*

Best Istanbul Photographs
★★ Kafe Ara *8 Tosbağa Sok, off Yeniçarşı Cad (p 104)*

Lavash *bread, fresh from the oven at Şar (p 108). Previous page: Banyan.*

Old City Dining

Asitane **1**
Bab-i Hayat **3**
Balıkçı Sabahattin **9**
Çapari Arif **10**
Dubb **6**
Hamdi Et Lokantası **2**
Rumeli **5**
Şar **7**
Seasons **8**
Sirkeci Balıkçısı **4**

Beyoğlu Dining

Museum		
Theater		
Mosque		
Ferry		
Metro		
Tram		
Nostalgic Tram		
Funicular		

Agatha **20**	Hala **8**	Melekler **6**
Boncuk **9**	Hünkar **1**	Mikla **22**
Borsa **2**	Istanbul Culinary	Mimolett **7**
Canım Ciğerim **14**	Institute **12**	Moreish **21**
Cezayir **15**	Kafe Ara **11**	Nu Teras **19**
Çiya **26**	Leb-i Derya **23**	Otantik **10**
Dai Pera **17**	Lokanta **13**	Sofyalı 9 **24**
Doğa Balık **16**	Lokanta Helvetia **25**	Topaz **4**
Haci Baba **5**	Mekan **18**	Vogue **3**

Bosphorus Dining

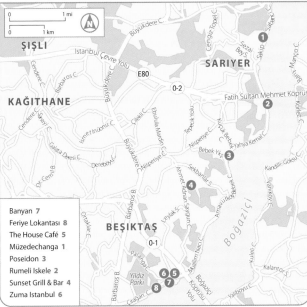

ŞİŞLİ

SARIYER

KAĞITHANE

BEŞİKTAŞ

Banyan **7**
Feriye Lokantası **8**
The House Café **5**
Müzedechanga **1**
Poseidon **3**
Rumeli Iskele **2**
Sunset Grill & Bar **4**
Zuma Istanbul **6**

Istanbul Dining **A to Z**

★★ **Agatha** TEPEBAŞI *INTERNA-TIONAL* In the gorgeously reno-vated Pera Palace Hotel, their flagship fine-dining restaurant inter-twines cuisines from France, Italy, and Turkey—three of the countries on the fabled Orient Express route. Elegant dining room, with the open kitchen on show. *52 Meşrutiyet Cad.* ☎ *0212 377 4000. www.perapalace. com. Entrees 25–40 TL. AE, MC, V. Breakfast, lunch, & dinner daily. Bus: Taksim. Map p 100.*

★★ **Asitane** EDIRNEKAPI *OTTOMAN* Find out how the sultans dined with menus based on palace archives. Try their specialty baked melon stuffed with lamb, veal, and pista-chios, reflecting Arab and

Bab-i Hayat, a restored warehouse in the Spice Market.

Mediterranean fusion. Located next to the Kariye Museum (p 20), its gar-den is lovely in summer. *6 Kariye*

Camii Sok. ☎ *0212 534 8414. www. asitanerestaurant.com. Entrees 20–35 TL. AE, MC, V. Lunch & dinner daily. Bus: 87. Map p 99.*

★★ kids **Bab-i Hayat** EMINÖNÜ *TURKISH* A good-value feed in the area, this cavernous restaurant was renovated in 2007 from the Spice Market's former warehouse. Feast on *hunka begendil kabab* (lamb stew with eggplant puree). Kids will enjoy the lunch buffet selection. *39/47 Misir Çarşısı.* ☎ *0212 520 7878. www.babihayat.com. Entrees 10–15 TL. V. Breakfast, lunch, & dinner daily. Tram: Sultanahmet. Map p 99.*

★★ **Balıkcı Sabahattin** SULTANAHMET *SEAFOOD* This family-run restaurant in a traditional house has dark wooden floors, *kilims*, and a fabulous fish menu popular with well-heeled Istanbullus. From octopus salad move on to fresh fish of the day. Tables spill out onto the peaceful courtyard in summer. Reservations recommended. *1 Cankurtaran Cad.* ☎ *0212 458 1824. www. balikcisabahattin.com. Entrees 30–50 TL. MC, V. Lunch & dinner daily. Tram to Sultanahmet or train to Cankurtaran. Map p 99.*

Banyan's stylish terrace.

★ **Banyan** ORTAKÖY *ASIAN FUSION* A huge open terrace overlooking the Bosphorus and a stylish dining room make Banyan especially popular in summer. Its fresh Asian fusion food includes sake-marinated fillet mignon and king prawns with lemongrass risotto, plus fruity cocktails. Stylish and fun. *3 Salhane Sok, Muallim Naci Cad.* ☎ *0212 259 9060. www.banyan restaurant.com. Entrees 31–50 TL. AE, MC, V. Lunch & dinner daily. Bus: Ortaköy. Map p 101.*

★★ **Boncuk** BEYOĞLU *ARMENIAN/ TURKISH* One of many *meyhanes* (traditional restaurants) on noisy Nevizade Sokak, this has distinctive Armenian flavors as well as favorite Turkish *mezes*. Perennially popular, try the (noisy) street-level tables or slightly quieter terrace, and check with the waiters for the freshest fish of the day. *19 Nevizade Sok.* ☎ *0212 243 1219. Entrees 15–20 TL. MC, V. Bus/funicular: Taksim. Map p 100.*

★ **Borsa** HARBIYE *TURKISH* Highly rated by elite Turks for its quality of traditional meat (and some fish) dishes, this place is a real draw if you get a table on its huge open terrace. Handy for many hotels and adjoining the congress center, it's popular for business lunches. *Lütfi Kırdar Uluslararası Kongre ve Sergi Sarayı.* ☎ *0212 232 4201. www. borsarestaurants.com. Entrees 20–40 TL. MC, V. Lunch & dinner daily. Bus: Taksim, then walk. Map p 100.*

★★★ **Canım Ciğerim** BEYOĞLU *KEBABS* New, larger location, including a roof terrace, for this liver-lovers' fave. Tiny cubes of liver or chicken are skewered, barbecued, and served with mounds of fresh salad and bread. Friendly and cheap. *162 Istiklal Cad.* ☎ *0212 243 1005. www.asmalicanimcigerim. com. Entrees 8–18 TL. Cash only. Lunch & dinner daily. Tunnel: Tünel. Map p 100.*

★★ **Çapari Arif** KUMKAPI *FISH* In the historic enclave downhill from Sultanahmet, the cobbled streets are filled with traditional *meyhanes* specializing in fish, and this is one of its best. This once very "touristy" area has calmed down in recent years and is very popular with locals. Lively musicians play at your table—dancing optional! Try the calamari starters and delicious fish kebabs. *47 Çapariz Sok.* ☎ *0212 517 2271. Entrees 15–25 TL. MC, V. Lunch & dinner daily. Tram: Beyazit, then walk. Map p 99.*

★★ **kids Cezayir** GALATASARAY *MODERN TURKISH* Housed in a 100-year-old Italian school, it's now a popular, laid-back restaurant, with a stylish foliage-filled garden terrace in summer. Traditional dishes are given a contemporary feel, like sea bass stew with fennel, and smoked salmon with dried rose petals. *16 Hayriye Cad.* ☎ *0212 245 9980. www.cezayir-istanbul.com. Entrees 16–35 TL. AE, DC, MC, V. Breakfast, lunch, & dinner daily. Bus/metro: Taksim. Map p 100.*

★★★ **Çiya** KADIKÖY *KEBAB* A busy dining street on the Asian side has three branches of this wonderful restaurant. Their kebab restaurant is a bargain and always busy, serving a selection of fresh sizzling meats from around Turkey (maybe cooked with sour cherries and whole garlic cloves), plus a buffet for appetizers. Try all three to find your favorite. *43, 44, and 48B Güneş libahçe Sok.* ☎ *0216 336 3013. www.ciya.com.tr. Entrees 10–20 TL. MC, V. Lunch & dinner daily. Boat: Kadıköy. Map p 100.*

★★ **Dai Pera** CIHANGIR *TURKISH* It's a labor of love for owner-chef Arzu, influenced by her Armenian mom's traditional recipes, with homely cooking from outstanding Turkish brunch to meatballs

Freshest of seafood at Doğa Balık.

wrapped in eggplant. Narrow yet cozy dining space, with fresh flowers and funky art. *54 Yeni Çarşı Cad.* ☎ *0212 252 8099. www.dai restaurant.com. Entrees 15–25 TL. MC, V. Breakfast, lunch, & dinner daily. Bus/metro: Taksim, then walk. Map p 100.*

★★★ **Doğa Balık** CIHANGIR *TURKISH* A real hit with locals, this terrace seafood restaurant does grilled fish in season, plus a fantastic range of greens (rarely seen in Turkish restaurants!) like sorrel, endives, and spinach root salad. *7/F Hotel Villa Zurich, 46 Arkarsu Yokusu.* ☎ *0212 243 3656. www.dogabalik.com.tr. Entrees 20–40 TL. MC, V. Lunch & dinner daily. Bus/metro: Taksim, then walk. Map p 100.*

★ **Dubb** SULTANAHMET *INDIAN* At the city's best Indian restaurant, feast on mixed kebabs, vegetarian dishes, and tandoori sea bream. Or taste several dishes on the set menu. Indian art lines the ochre walls, and the terrace overlooking Hagia Sophia is fabulous for summer evenings. *10 Incili Çavuş Sok, off Divan Yolu.* ☎ *0212 513 7308. www.dubbindian.com. Entrees 15–22 TL, set meal 31 TL. AE, MC, V. Lunch & dinner daily. Tram: Sultanahmet. Map p 99.*

★★ **Feriye Lokantası** ORTAKÖY *OTTOMAN/TURKISH* This waterfront venue with outdoor tables serves traditional Ottoman dishes with a contemporary twist, such as roasted-pomegranate-glazed duck or octopus with cinnamon. A great choice for a romantic treat, with views of Ortaköy's mosque and Bosphorus Bridge. Reservations highly recommended. *40 Çırağan Cad.* ☎ *0212 227 2216. www.feriye.com. Entrees 25–40 TL. AE, DC, MC, V. Lunch & dinner daily. Bus: Ortaköy. Map p 101.*

★ kids **Haci Baba** TAKSIM *TURKISH* Originally the living quarters for adjacent Aya Triada Church (p 47), with the original fountain that spouted wine for booze-loving priests, the restaurant has been going since 1921. Try traditional Ottoman dishes like lamb shank with eggplant; friendly staff help you choose. *39 Istiklal Cad.* ☎ *0212 244 1886. www.hacibabarest.com. Entrees 18–25 TL. AE, MC, V. Daily 11am–1am. Bus/metro: Taksim. Map p 100.*

★★ kids **Hala** BEYOĞLU *GÖZLEME* My favorite place for home cooking, this cozy spot offers a cheap, filling lunch or dinner on *gözleme* (stuffed pancakes with meat, spinach, or potatoes). The good veggie choice includes *hingal* (potato-filled ravioli in garlic sauce), plus hearty soups. *26 Çukurlu Çeşme Sok, off Büyük Parmakkapı Sok.* ☎ *0212 293 7531. Entrees 4–10 TL. MC, V. Lunch & dinner daily. Bus: Taksim. Map p 100.*

★ **Hamdi Et Lokantası** EMINÖNÜ *TURKISH* Spread over four floors, Hamdi has a fabulous selection of southeast Turkish kebabs, including house specialties *erikli kebap* (minced sucking lamb), and *testi kebap* stew for groups of 10. Book a table with an unbeatable Bosphorus view. *17 Kalçın Sok, Tahmis Cad.*

☎ *0212 528 0390. www.hamdi restorant.com.tr. Entrees 12–20 TL. MC, V. Lunch & dinner daily. Tram: Eminönü. Map p 99.*

★★ kids **The House Café** ORTAKÖY *BISTRO/EUROPEAN* This is my favorite of their several outlets, with a chic, informal dining area and vast waterfront terrace. Think stylish comfort food (eggs Benedict), innovative pizzas, and a decent children's menu. Trendy locals love after-work cocktails—delicious! *1 Salhane Sok.* ☎ *0212 227 2699. www.thehousecafe.com. Entrees 20–30 TL. AE, MC, V. Breakfast, lunch, & dinner daily. Bus/Boat: Ortaköy. Map p 101.*

★ **Hünkar** NIŞANTAŞI *TURKISH* This is where stylish Nişantaşı meets an earthy *lokanta* (simple restaurant). Popular dishes include traditional lamb shank with smoked eggplant puree and *köfte* (meatballs); staff will happily advise. The large dining room spills out onto a tiny patio. *21 Mimar Kemal Öke Cad.* ☎ *0212 225 4665. Entrees 16–21 TL. MC, V. Lunch & dinner daily. Minibus: Nişantaşı. Map p 100.*

★★ kids **Istanbul Culinary Institute** TEPEBAŞI *CONTEMPORARY TURKISH* This stylish apprentice-run restaurant recreates Ottoman cuisine with a contemporary twist. A daily-changing lunch menu might include zucchini fritters with dill sauce. Good value. *59 Meş rutiyet Cad.* ☎ *0212 251 2214. www.istanbulculinary.com. Entrees 12–18 TL. MC, V. Breakfast & lunch (to 6pm) Mon–Sat. Bus: Tepebaşı. Map p 100.*

★★ kids **Kafe Ara** GALATASARAY *BISTRO* A huge attraction are the photos by Istanbul's Ara Güler adorning its walls. Buzzing with cultured locals feasting on pasta and *köfte*, it's a great people-watching spot especially from patio tables. *8*

The funky bar at Lokanta.

Tosbağa Sok, off Yeniçarşı Cad.
☎ *0212 245 4105. Entrees 10–20 TL.*
MC, V. Breakfast, lunch, & dinner
daily. Bus/tram: Taksim, then walk.
Map p 100.

★★ Leb-i Derya (Richmond)
BEYOĞLU *TURKISH/INTERNATIONAL*
On the sixth floor of a glass-fronted
building, this stylish restaurant
boasts panoramic views and is
famed for its 40-spiced beef fillet,
plus international dishes
like lime and ginger chicken. Try
their fresh fruit cocktails, served by
young, and improbably trendy, staff.
Sister restaurant to Leb-i Derya
(*Nightlife*, p 111). *6/F Richmond
Hotel, 227 Istiklal Cad.* ☎ *0212 243
4375. www.lebiderya.com. Entrees
25–45 TL. MC, V. Lunch & dinner
daily. Map p 100.*

★ Lokanta TEPEBAŞI *EUROPEAN*
Housed in the tranquil French Pasaj
known as Nu Pera, this winter-only
restaurant (see *Nu Teras*, p 107 for
summer) has a contemporary yet
cozy interior. Try the *moules marin-
ières* and braised lamb shank, and
watch the bar lights subtly change
color. (No, you haven't been drinking too much.) Relaxed and stylish
with friendly service, this becomes a
club at weekends. *149/1 Meşrutiyet
Cad.* ☎ *0212 245 6070. www.lokanta*

*daneve.com. Entrees 22–35 TL. AE,
MC, V. Lunch & dinner Mon–Sat.
Open mid-May–early Oct. Bus:
Tepebaşı. Map 100.*

★★ kids Lokanta Helvetia TÜNEL
TURKISH Cozy, with exposed brick
walls and wooden tables, this serves
hearty, cheap home-made dishes.
Vegetarians will love the delicious
mixed hot and cold dishes like potato
with lentils or roast peppers in oil;
carnivores can feast on chicken and
lamb dishes. A good choice for a
quick fill-up in stylish, fun Tünel. *12
General Yazgan Sok.* ☎ *0212 245
8780. Entrees 10–15 TL. No credit
cards. Lunch & dinner daily. Tunnel:
Tünel. Map p 100.*

★ Mekan TEPEBAŞI *MODERN
EUROPEAN* Mekan manages to be
cozy and hip at the same time; a
good-value restaurant with a charming brick-walled interior opening
onto a small terrace. Service is
friendly; cuisine is Turkish with
Armenian influences, such as grilled
vegetables with halloumi and
chicken shish with tomatoes. *3 Eski
Çiçekçi Sokak, off Istiklal Cad.* ☎ *0212
252 6052. www.mekanrestaurant.
com. Entrees 10–20 TL. MC, V. Lunch &
dinner daily. Bus: Taksim, then walk.
Map p 100.*

★★★ **kids Melekler** TAKSIM *OCAKBAŞI* A no-frills barbecue joint with a few pavement tables where the Antakya-born owner cooks up fresh grilled kebabs. Try spicy *urfa* and milder *adana* (lamb) kebab, or good old chicken wings, with piles of salad and fresh bread. *113 Ipek Sok, off Küçük Parmakkapi Sok.* ☎ *0212 243 0585. Entrees 5–10 TL. No credit cards. Lunch & dinner daily. Bus/ metro/funicular: Taksim. Map p 100.*

★★ **Mikla** TEPEBAŞI *TURKISH/ SCANDINAVIAN* On the top floor of the Marmara Pera hotel, the tiny terrace with Golden Horn views has to be one of Istanbul's most romantic, chic settings. Feast on superb fusion cuisine, with meat dishes its specialty. End with after-dinner cocktails by the pool to the in-house DJ's soothing sounds. The late-night bar is popular with wealthy 30-somethings at weekends. Reservations recommended. *167 Meşrutiyet Cad.* ☎ *0212 293 5656. www.mikla restaurant.com. Entrees 35–50 TL.*

AE, MC, V. Dinner Mon–Sat. Bus: Tepebaşı. Map p 100.

★★ **Mimolett** BEYOĞLU *MEDITER-RANEAN* Istanbul's closest thing to a Michelin star, this boutique restaurant, with opulent decor, was opened in late 2009 by esteemed chef Murat Bozok. Boasting the very finest Mediterranean cuisine, try delights such as duck confit with foie gras, and ossobuco. The place for a real treat; reservations essential. *55 Sıraselviler Cad.* ☎ *0212 245 9858. www. mimolett.com.tr. Entrees 40–75 TL. AE, DC, MC, V. Dinner Mon–Sat. Bus/ tram: Taksim. Map p 100.*

★ **Moreish** TEPEBAŞI *MODERN EUROPEAN* Opened in 2007, its owner-chef Esra Muslu creates experimental dishes such as foie gras crème brulée, and hummus lamb shank in red wine. Stylish urban decor with white walls and a splash of contemporary art; DJs from Nu Teras (p 107) at weekends. *67 Meşrutiyet Cad.* ☎ *0212 245 6070. www.moreishrestaurant.com. Entrees 20–40 TL. MC, V. Dinner Mon–Sat. Bus: Tepebaşı. Map p 100.*

Afyet Olsen!

In recent years Istanbul has improved its quality and quantity of world cuisines from Japanese to French in leaps and bounds. That said, you'll also sample many varieties of Turkish dishes. Especially in *meyhanes* (tavern-style restaurants), meat and fish meals usually kick off with *meze* (hot or cold starters): try *börek* (savory pastries), *patlıcan soslu* (smoked eggplant puree), *dolma* (stuffed vegetables), or *ezme salatası* (spicy pepper dip). Fresh fish (waiters will advise on the freshest) is usually grilled or fried. Kebabs from around the country include *patlıcan kebap* (cubed meat grilled with eggplant), *İskender kebap* (lamb on pitta bread with yogurt and tomato sauce), and many varieties of *köfte* (meatballs). As a vegetarian, I love *imam bayıldı* (stuffed eggplant with tomato and onions), and *zeytinyağlı* (seasonal vegetables cooked slowly in olive oil). Accompany with *rakı* (local aniseed liquor), and end with baklava and fresh fruit. Most people will wish you *"afyet olsen,"* the local equivalent of bon appétit.

★★ **Müzedechanga** EMIRGAN *TURKISH/MEDITERRANEAN* Oozing style, with open kitchen and huge windows, the huge terrace is a major draw at this museum restaurant. Light lunchtime dishes, then it's all gourmet food for dinner (think grilled lamb loin with quince sauce) changing seasonally. It's been a hit since opening in 2005. *Sakıp Sabancı Müzesi, Atlı Köşk, 22 Sakıp Sabancı Cad.* ☎ *0212 323 0901. www. changa-istanbul.com. Entrees 22–49 TL. AE, DC, MC, V. Lunch & dinner Tues–Sun. Bus: Emirgan. Map p 101.*

★ **Nu Teras** TEPEBAŞI *MEDITERRA-NEAN* The summer months see **Lokanta** (p 104) decamp to this rooftop restaurant. Enjoy eye-popping Bosphorus views with great Mediterranean dishes prepared in the open kitchen, including wood-fired pizzas. *67 Meşrutiyet Cad.* ☎ *0212 245 6070. www.nupera. com.tr. Entrees 22–35 TL. AE, MC, V. Dinner daily. Open mid-May–late Sept. Bus: Tepebaşı. Map p 101.*

★ **kids** **Otantik** BEYOĞLU *TURK-ISH* It's far from fancy, wherein lies the charm. Local Anatolian dishes in this homely restaurant spread over four floors—think lots of *kilims*, woman making pancakes in the window, huge menu of soups and casseroles, and modest prices. *170 Istiklal Cad.* ☎ *0212 293 8451. www.otantikay.com. Entrees 8–20 TL. MC, V. Lunch & dinner daily. Bus: Taksim. Map p 100.*

★ **kids** **Poseidon** BEBEK *FISH* Treat yourselves on the waterfront in Istanbul's posh neighborhood to fresh fish, usually simply grilled or fried. Kick off with grilled calamari and go for anything in season; check for portion prices with the waiters. *58 Cevdetpaşa Cad.* ☎ *0212 287 9531. www.poseidon bebek.com. Entrees 38–60 TL. AE,*

Once a printing house, now Rumeli cafe.

DC, MC, V. Lunch & dinner daily. Bus: Bebek. Map p 101.

★ **Rumeli** SULTANAHMET *BRASSE-RIE* Spread over four tiny floors with brick and terracotta walls, this friendly restaurant has Ottoman dishes like chicken with rice, raisins, and pine nuts, and international choices, including risotto. A print house until renovated in 1994, now it's the place for snug, candlelit winter evenings; summers see everyone trying for the tiny terrace. *8 Ticarethabe Sok, off Divan Yolu.* ☎ *0212 512 0008. Entrees 15–25 TL. MC, V. Lunch & dinner daily. Tram: Sultanahmet. Map p 99.*

★ **Rumeli Iskele** RUMELI HISARI *FISH* Fish is always pricey in Istanbul, good fish even more so. But this perennially popular restaurant is loved by well-heeled locals, for rich *mezes*, simple fried fish or hearty *bugulama* (fish stew). Book a waterfront table for a touch of romance. *1 Yahya Kemal Cad.* ☎ *0212 263 2997. Entrees 40–75 TL. AE, MC, V. Lunch & dinner daily. Bus: 25. Map p 101.*

★ **kids** **Şar** BEYAZIT *TURKISH* A cut above the usual *lokanta*, especially in the Old City, this is a decent choice for an inexpensive dinner, close to the Grand Bazaar. Pick from the front counter—staff will always help out. Shish kebabs, vegetables slow-cooked in olive oil, and *kiremitte balık* (fish casserole), all served with a huge basket of warm *lavash* bread. *43 Gedikpaşa Cad.* ☎ *0212 516 8794. www.sar restaurant.com. Entrees 8–15 TL. MC, V. Lunch & dinner daily. Tram: Beyazit. Map p 99.*

★ **kids** **Seasons** SULTANAHMET *TURKISH* Even if you can't afford a night here, enjoy a romantic (but pricey) dinner in the garden's glass-walled gazebo. It might lack local atmosphere, but the quality of seasonal dishes is good. Typical choices include thyme-roast chicken or fresh seafood pasta; there's also a good children's menu. *1 Tevkifhane Sok.* ☎ *0212 402 3000. www.fourseasons. com/istanbul. Entrees 30–48 TL. AE, DC, MC, V. Breakfast, lunch, & dinner daily. Tram: Sultanahmet. Map p 99.*

★★ **Sirkeci Balıkcısı** SIRKECI *SEAFOOD* This fish restaurant keeps prices lower than most but doesn't lack quality. On a quiet side street, with outdoor tables and rooftop terrace in summer, the assorted fish platter is a good way to begin. Then choose from freshly caught fish, served grilled, fried, or steamed. Simple and delicious, with good service. *5 Taya Hatun Sok.* ☎ *0212 528 4344. www.sirkecibalikcisi.com. Entrees 20–30 TL. MC, V. Lunch & dinner daily. Tram: Sirkeci. Map p 99.*

★★ **Sofyalı 9** ASMALIMESCIT *TURKISH* One of my favorite *meyhanes*, this family-run place has a charming host, mustard-walled interior, and small terrace with outdoor heaters. Relatively quiet in a busy area, enjoy *mezes* like my favorite *semizotu* (purslane in garlicky yogurt) and *dolma* (peppers stuffed with meat) washed down with local Efes beer. *9 Sofyalı Sok, off Asmalımescit.* ☎ *0212 245 0362. www.sofyali.com.tr. Entrees 35–50 TL. MC, V. Lunch & dinner Mon–Sat. Bus: Tepebaşı. Map p 100.*

★★ **Sunset Grill & Bar** ULUS *INTERNATIONAL* With a stunning hilltop location, Sunset is perennially popular, with superb dishes including sushi, sea bass, and T-bone

A cheap eat at Şar.

Sunset Grill & Bar

steak. The menu caters for locals wanting modern European, and visitors preferring traditional Ottoman cuisine. The decked terrace is perfect on summer evenings; daytimes see businessmen shoulder to shoulder with ladies who lunch. *2 Yol Sok, Adnan Saygun Cad, Ulus Park.* ☎ *0212 287 0358. www.sunsetgrill bar.com. Entrees 50–80 TL. AE, DC, MC, V. Lunch Mon–Sat, dinner daily. Taxi. Map p 101.*

★★★ **Topaz** GÜMÜŞSUYU *MEDITERRANEAN* Opened in late 2007, this sleek, stylish restaurant has cuisine favoring contemporary Turkish/Med dishes, and fantastic service. Splash out on the six-course degustation Ottoman menu, and book a table by the floor-to-ceiling windows for staggering Bosphorus views. *50 Inönü Cad.* ☎ *0212 249 1001. www. topazistanbul.com. Entrees 30–50 TL. 6-course menu 95–110 TL. AE, DC, MC, V. Lunch & dinner daily. Bus/ metro: Taksim, then walk. Map p 100.*

★★ **Vogue** AKARETLER *SUSHI/ INTERNATIONAL* With Bosphorus views from a rooftop terrace, this is where the beautiful people dine on top sushi. Settle on the terrace's soft white seats (indoors in winter) with contemporary cuisine, like braised zucchini rolls and hot chestnut cake. Sunday buffet brunch is a highlight. Reservations essential; open late. *13/F, 48 BJK Plaza, A-Blok, Spor Cad.* ☎ *0212 227 2545. www. voguerestaurant.com. Entrees 30–60 TL. AE, DC, MC, V. Lunch & dinner daily. Bus: Beşiktaş. Map p 100.*

★★ **Zuma Istanbul** ORTAKÖY *JAPANESE* This top-notch restaurant imported from London fits well into Ortaköy's hip dining scene—this is one for a splurge. Try the tasting menu or special miso-marinated black cod. The first floor opens onto a terrace, with sushi bar and Japanese robata grill, and is all earthy wood tones and sleek sofas. Dress to impress; reservations essential. *7 Salhane Sok.* ☎ *0212 236 2296. www.zumarestaurant. com. Entrees 25–60 TL. AE, DC, MC, V. Lunch & dinner daily. Bus: Ortaköy. Map p 101.* ●

Food & Drinks Basics

Breakfast	kahvaltı	kah-valtuh
Lunch	öğle yemeği	ur-leh yeme-i
Dinner	akşam yemeği	aksham yeme-i
Beer	bira	bira
Soft drinks	meşrubatlar	mesh-rubat-lar
Mineral water	su	su
Starters (assorted)	mezeler	meh-zeh-ler
Red/white wine	kırmızı/beyaz şarap	kurmu-zu/beyaz sharap
Dessert	tatlı	tat-lu
Fish	balık	baluk
Eggplant	patlıcan	pat-lu-jan
Chicken	tavuk	tavuk
Meat	et	et
Eggs	yumurta	yumurta
Beans	fasulye	fasul-yeh
Bread	ekmek	ekmek
White cheese	peynir	peynir
Anchovy	hamsi	hamsi
Fried	tava	tava
Grilled	izgara	izgara
Tomato	domates	do-mah-tes
Savory pastries	börek	burek
Meatballs	köfte	kuf-teh
Vegetables w/olive oil	zeytinyağlı	zeytin-yarluh
Turkish coffee	Türk kahve	Turk kar-veh
Tea	çay	chay
Juice	suyu	su-yu
(Lentil) soup	(mercimek) çorba	(mer-ji-mek) chorba
Rice	pilav	pilav
Salad	salata	salata
The check, please	Hesap, lütfen	hesap, lutfen

Nightlife Best Bets

Magical courtyard at K.V.

Best **Fairy-Lights**
★★ K.V., *10 Tünel Geçidi (p 115)*

Best **Leafy Courtyard**
★★ Cezayir, *16 Hayriye Cad (p 116)*

Best for a **Mature Wine & Cheese Evening**
★★ Corvus Wine & Bite, *5 Şair Nedim Cad (p 114)*

Best Longstanding **Gay Nightclub**
★★ Tek Yon, *63 Sıraselviler Cad (p 120)*

Best for **Cutting-Edge Music**
★★ Dogzstar, *3/F 3 Kartal Sok (p 118)*

Best for **Watching the Water**
★★★ Dersaadet, *Yeni Galata Koprüsü (p 116)*

Best **Terrace for Sipping Cocktails**
★★ 360Istanbul, *9/F 163 Istiklal Cad (p 119)*

Best **Waterfront Boogie**
★★ Angelique, *5 Salhane Sok (p 118)*

Best **Tünel Hideaway**
★★★ Badehane, *5 General Yazgan Sok (p 114)*

Best **Theatrical Decor**
★★ 5.Kat, *5/F 7 Soğancı Sok (p 114)*

Best for a **No-Nonsense Beer**
★★ Aslanım, *22 Nevizade Sok (p 114)*

Best for **Old City Nargile**
★ Café Meşale, *45 Arasta Bazaar (p 116)*

Best for **Village Style**
★ Lucca *51, Cevdetpaşa Cad (p 118)*

Previous page: View onto busy Nevizade mayhanes galore.

Beyoğlu Nightlife

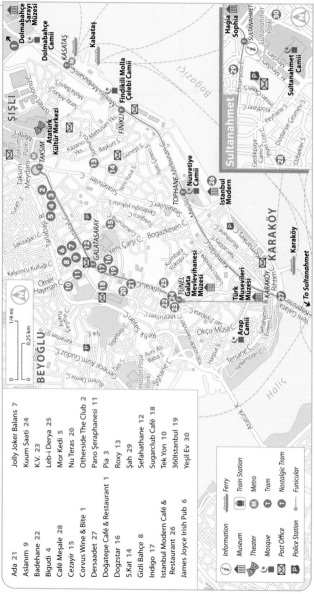

Ada 21
Aslanım 9
Badehane 22
Bigudi 4
Café Meşale 28
Cezayir 15
Corvus Wine & Bite 1
Dersaadet 27
Doğatepe Café & Restaurant 1
Dogzstar 16
5.Kat 14
Gizli Bahçe 8
Indigo 17
Istanbul Modern Café &
Restaurant 26
James Joyce Irish Pub 6

Jolly Joker Balans 7
Kuum Saati 24
K.V. 23
Leb-i Derya 25
Mor Kedi 5
Nu Teras 20
Otherside The Club 2
Pano Şeraphanesi 11
Pia 3
Roxy 13
Şah 29
Sefahathane 12
Sugarclub Café 18
Tek Yon 10
360Istanbul 19
Yeşil Ev 30

ℹ	Information
🏛	Museum
🎭	Theater
☪	Mosque
✉	Post Office
🅿	Police Station

⛴	Ferry
🚆	Train Station
Ⓜ	Metro
Ⓣ	Tram
Ⓣ	Nostalgic Tram
⋯	Funicular

Ortaköy Nightlife

Map legend:
- (Mosque)
- † Church
- ✉ Post Office
- ℗ Police Station
- ⛴ Ferry

Şair Necati S.
Portakal Yokuşu C.
Aydınlık S.
Dereboyu C.
Portakal Yokuşu C.

0-1

Defterdar
Ibrahimpaşa Camii

Çevirmeci C.
Taşbasamak S.
Aladoğan S.

ORTAKÖY

Muallim Naci C.
Boğaziçi Köprüsü Yolu

3 4

Çarşıağası S.
Muallim Naci C.

℗

⛴ Ortaköy

Çırağan C.

1 2

✉

Büyükmecidiye
Camii

Boğaziçi

0 — 240 yd
0 — 120 m

5

Angelique 1
The House Café 2
Lucca 5
Reina 4
Supper Club 3

Istanbul Nightlife A to Z

Bars

★★ **Aslanım** BEYOĞLU In busy Nevizade, this bustling bar/cafe crams tables onto the pavement terrace for crowd-watching. It has an informal, studenty vibe, friendly atmosphere, and decent snack menu. *22 Nevizade Sok, off Balık Pazarı.* ☎ *0212 249 3897. www. aslanimrestaurant.com. Bus/metro: Taksim. Map p 113.*

★★★ **Badehane** TÜNEL Tucked away in a bohemian Tünel alleyway, street tables fill up on summer evenings with beer-drinking young locals. Inside, it's a good-natured squeeze, especially for live gypsy clarinet music from legendary Selim Sesler every Wednesday

(10pm–1:30am). *5 General Yazgan Sok.* ☎ *0212 249 0550. Tunnel: Tünel. Map p 113.*

★★ **Corvus Wine & Bite** AKARETLER Located on this stylish street (*Arty Istanbul, p 28*), come here for a mature evening of fine Turkish wines. Owned by the eponymous vineyard company, it serves a civilized glass of their finest labels, accompanied by small tapas plates and Turkish cheeses. *5 Şair Nedim Cad.* ☎ *0212 260 5470. www.wine andbite.com. Bus: Beşiktaş. Map p 113.*

★★ **5.Kat** CIHANGIR One of Istanbul's first venues to capitalize on its Bosphorus view, locals love Beşinci Kat's ("5th floor") terrace for summer.

Inside, it's all deep red walls and chandeliers in an arty, gay-friendly bar, with actress-owner Yasemin Alkaya watching over the fun. Decent food served all day. Open to 3am at weekends. *5/F 7 Soğancı Sok.* ☎ *0212 293 3774. www.5kat.com. Bus: Taksim, then walk. Map p 113.*

★ **Gizli Bahçe** BEYOĞLU   Not the place for a quiet drink after 9pm, when the jazz-funk reaches a deafening pitch, especially at weekends. Homely rather than chic, come for an early-evening beer, sinking into a mismatched armchair on the terrace, before dinner at a nearby *meyhane*. *15 Nevizade Sok.* ☎ *0212 249 2192. Bus/metro: Taksim. Map p 113.*

★ **James Joyce Irish Pub** BEYO-ĞLU   If you're itching to watch a Manchester United match on TV, eat an Irish breakfast, and drink Guinness while being surrounded by "Oirish" paraphernalia, join young expats and locals at Istanbul's first Irish pub. The terrace is busy in summer, with nightly live music in winter. *26 Balo Sok, off Istiklal Cad.* ☎ *0212 244 7970. www.theirish centre.com. Metro/bus: Taksim. Map p 113.*

★★ **K.V.** TÜNEL   In an ornate 19th-century courtyard, K.V. (pronounced "keh-veh") has outdoor tables among plants and fairy lights for a romantic

Gizli Bahçe, just like a comfortable living room.

touch. When chilly, step into the tiny high-ceilinged restaurant with huge chandeliers and pink neon lighting. It's popular, so getting a table at weekends can be difficult, especially when there's live jazz. *10 Tünel Geçidi, off General Yazgan Sok.* ☎ *0212 251 4338. www.kv.com.tr. Tunnel: Tünel. Map p 113.*

★★ **Pano Şeraphanesi** GALA-TASARAY   Also a lively restaurant, this traditional Greek wine house has good deals on own-label wines in a city with pricey alcohol. Perch at high tables with a plate of cheeses

No Smoking?

Most Turks smoke like chimneys, so a trip to a bar, cafe, or club usually comes with cigarette fumes. So what changed when the smoking ban hit Turkey in 2009? Nothing much! Some venues adhere strictly, but many turn a blind eye and—allegedly—know the right people to pay off. Still, you can always partake of a *nargile* (tobacco waterpipe) usually at outdoor tables with tea and backgammon, not always with alcohol. Your best bets for this are the Fuat Uzkinay Sokak and Imam Adnan Sokak streets off Istiklal Caddesi, and near Istanbul Modern (p 17), behind Tophane mosque.

Get away from the crowds at Yeşil Ev's garden.

or meats with your drink, or sit outside in summer at pavement tables. *Hamalbaşı Cad.* ☎ *0212 292 6664. www.panosarap.com. Bus/metro: Taksim, then 10-min walk. Map p 113.*

★ **Şah** SULTANAHMET   One of the Old City's few authentic bars, it's a gathering place in summer with a mixture of tourists and locals. There are separate stone-walled partitions with rugs and stools off the courtyard, plus adjacent cafe and restaurant. DJs play European hits nightly. *9 Incili Çavuş Çıkmaz Yolu.* ☎ *0212 519 5807. www.sahbar.com. Tram: Sultanahmet. Map p 113.*

★ **Sefahathane** BEYOĞLU Tucked away down Atlas Pasaj by the cinema, this tiny bar-cafe has rock music, photos on the walls, and a laidback boho atmosphere, refreshingly unpretentious. Come for beers and fancy cocktails. *Atlas Pasajı, Istiklal Cad.* ☎ *0212 251 2245. www.sefahathane.com.tr. Bus/metro: Taksim. Map p 113.*

★ **Yeşil Ev** SULTANAHMET   In the grounds of this rebuilt Ottoman house, now a guest house (*Lodging*, p 131), the leafy garden is a peaceful escape from sightseeing and crowds. A perfect way to start your evening

with a glass of wine (not open late). *5 Kabasakal Cad.* ☎ *0212 517 6785. www.istanbulyesilev.com. Tram: Sultanahmet. Map p 113.*

Cafe-Bars & Restaurant Bars

★ **Ada** BEYOĞLU   Inside this huge bookstore, the cavernous cafe covers most of the first floor. Good for an early-evening glass of wine while listening to their excellent music from around the world, or a coffee while browsing through books. Open until about 10pm every evening. *158A Istiklal Cad.* ☎ *0212 251 6682. www.adakitapcafe.com. Bus/ metro: Taksim. Map p 113.*

★ **Café Meşale** SULTANAHMET It might be a tourist trap, but this sunken courtyard can be a pleasure in the evenings, when locals gather over tea, *sheesha,* and regular live events. Or just come down to play backgammon! *45 Arasta Bazaar.* ☎ *0212 518 9562. Tram: Sultanahmet. Map p 113.*

★★ **Cezayir** GALATASARAY   This restaurant (*Dining*, p 97) is loved for its garden terrace in summer, and plant-filled indoor bar and stylish upstairs. It's a real hit with Istanbul's 30-something nightbirds, especially for its weekend DJs. *16 Hayriye Cad.* ☎ *0212 245 9980. www.cezayir- istanbul.com. Bus/metro: Taksim. Map p 113.*

★★★ **Dersaadet** KARAKÖY There is nothing overly stylish about this cheerful cafe-bar, at the northern end of Galata bridge. This is the place to kick back with a tea, backgammon, beer, or *nargile* (tobacco waterpipe), watching boats cruise the Bosphorus or, catering for all tastes, enjoying live music and soccer on the TV. *Yeni Galata Köprüsü, Altı Karaköy.* ☎ *0212 292 7001. Tram: Karaköy. Map p 113.*

Making Friends?

While Istanbul is generally safe, with hospitable locals, here are a few hints for first-time visitors. Avoid the scam of a single white male tourist invited by a friendly chap on the street to "a great bar," resulting in ladies at his table and a colossal bar check. In some gay clubs, bear in mind that things aren't always as they seem; women may really be men and some men are rent boys (homosexuality is legal in Turkey but rarely tolerated outside Istanbul). A newcomer might find gay clubs alarming, with transvestites and transsexuals galore. The bars and clubs listed here are "safe," where a lone tourist from abroad won't feel out of place. Finally, like everywhere in the world, look after your wallet!

★ **Doğatepe Café & Restaurant** HISARÜSTÜ This cafe-bar is worth the 20-minute bus ride from Taksim on summer nights for a terrace seat and views over Rumeli Hisarı (p 39) and the majestic Bosphorus bridge. Open daily till 2am. *4–6 Duatepe Parkı, Nispetiye Cad, Rumeli Hisarüstü.* ☎ *0212 257 4391. www.dogatepe.com.tr. Bus: 599C from Taksim. Map p 113.*

Fight for the best seats in the house at Leb-i Derya.

★★ **The House Café** ORTAKÖY A popular restaurant (*Dining*, p 97), the outdoor deck comes alive on summer evenings. Bar staff create fruity cocktails, or you can sip a cold beer while watching the colored lights on the bridge. The wooden-floored interior is also inviting. *1 Salhane Sok.* ☎ *0212 227 2699. www. thehousecafe.com.tr. AE, MC, V. Bus/boat: Ortaköy. Map p 114.*

★★ **Istanbul Modern Café & Restaurant** TOPHANE Attached to the museum (p 17) with a tiny Bosphorus-facing terrace, this is a restaurant by day and popular bar in the evenings. Very stylish. *4 Antrepo, Liman Işletmeleri Sahası, Meclis-i Mebusan Cad.* ☎ *0212 292 2612. www.istanbulmodern.org. Tram: Fındıklı. Map p 113.*

★★ **Kuum Saati** TÜNEL Bars in Tünel Square seem to come and go regularly. This one has several small sections, all brick-walled, lined with old photographs, and with a homely feel. Come for no-nonsense beer, wine, and snacks. *1 General Yazgan Sok, off Tünel Meydanı.* ☎ *0212 245 7273. Bus: Taksim. Map p 113.*

★★ Leb-i Derya GALATASARAY
Also a restaurant, and little brother to Leb-i Derya Richmond (p 105), its tiny rooftop terrace attracts young, well-heeled professionals. Find a seat outside, or take in lounge music, liqueur-laced tea, and carefully concocted cocktails. *7/F 57 Kumbaraci Yokuşu.* ☎ *0212 293 4989. www.lebiderya.com. Bus: Taksim, then 10-min walk. Map p 113.*

★ Lucca BEBEK
This bistro bar is favored by trendy Bebek locals, who love its brasserie-style cuisine and contemporary art gallery. It's one for people-watching and checking out the beautiful people dancing to house DJ music. *51 Cevdetpaşa Cad.* ☎ *0212 257 1255. www.luccastyle. com. Bus: Bebek. Map p 114.*

★ Pia BEYOĞLU
Wooden floors, minimal decor, creaky stairs, and a gorgeous upper floor, with window seats overlooking the street. This popular cafe-bar is suitable for lone women for an undisturbed drink. There's a daily menu chalked up on the blackboard, from breakfast to pasta dishes. *4A Bekar Sok, off Istiklal Cad.* ☎ *0212 252 7100. Bus: Taksim. Map p 113.*

Clubs & DJ Bars

★★ Angelique ORTAKÖY
One of Istanbul's best-loved summer clubs with a Bosphorus-facing terrace. Weekends are for members only, but you can phone ahead to join the week-night guest-list, then dress to impress with a wealthy young crowd partying to Turkish and European pop. International cuisine including sushi is on the club's menu. *Free entry. 5 Salhane Sok, Muallim Naci Cad.* ☎ *0212 327 2844. www. istanbuldoors.com. Bus/boat: Ortaköy. Map p 114.*

★★ Dogzstar GALATASARAY
A friendly little club with a mixed crowd, its three tiny floors fill up after midnight at weekends. House DJs mix edgy sounds, from post-punk and drum-and-bass to electro-rock. Pop downstairs to see a live band, usually unconventional. *3/F 3 Kartal Sok.* ☎ *0212 244 9147. www. dogzstar.com. Closed Sun and Mon. Bus/metro: Taksim. Map p 113.*

★ Indigo GALATASARAY
Electronic techno acts and DJs regularly perform in this club, loved for its great lighting, sound system and laser shows. Hard-core clubbers seek solace in the vast, dark space. Buy advance tickets for popular acts. *1–4 Arkasu Sok, off Istiklal Cad.* ☎ *0212 244 8567. www.living indigo.com. Cover charge. Bus: Taksim. Map 113.*

Pricey Tipple

Istanbul is now recognized as a world-class city for nightlife, on a par with London and New York. Unfortunately, it's matched by similar prices for alcohol, thanks to excessive government taxation. Gone are the days when a beer cost a dollar! Costs can be reduced by sticking to local drinks; Efes beer is great (bottled or draught), and Turkish wines have improved enormously over recent years—try a Kavaklidere. Avoid domestic vodka and gin, and rakı (their famous aniseed liquor) should be treated with caution: stick to drinking it with dinner.

Drink Balans' very own brew.

★★ **Jolly Joker Balans** BEYOĞLU
This microbrewery has a bit of
everything: Huge brewing paraphernalia, snack food, and live soccer on
the TV. At the back the club has DJ
nights with techno, dance, or house
(cover charge varies) or live local
bands (p 125). *22 Balo Sok, off
Istiklal Cad.* ☎ *0212 293 5690.
www.jollyjokerbalans.com. Metro:
Taksim. Map p 113.*

★ **Nu Teras** TEPEBAŞI   After pizza
or pasta (*Dining*, p 97) the party
starts, when this summer restaurant
transforms into a casually fashion-
able club at weekends (mid-May–
early Oct). Enjoy Bosphorus views
and dance to house DJ sounds—
even better after a vodka hazelnut
shot. *149/1 Meşrutiyet Cad.* ☎ *0212
245 6070. www.nupera.com.tr. Bus:
Tepebaşı. Map p 113.*

★ **Reina** ORTAKÖY   Local celebs
(and wannabes) flock to be seen at
this vast entertainment complex.
You might get in early in the week—
after making reservations—for
drinks and music on the terrace bar.
Black-suited doormen are choosy;
think brash clothing rather than
tasteful glamor. During winter, the
terrace is heated. Steep cover
charge (varies) and drinks prices.

44 Muallim Naci Cad. ☎ *0212 259
5919. www.reina.com.tr. Boat/bus:
Ortaköy. Map p 114.*

★ **Roxy** CIHANGIR   A busy club,
the live rock and pop bands most
nights attract a casual bunch of
20-somethings in its cavernous interior. Yan Gastro bar has decent food.
5 Aslanyatagi Sok, Siraselviler Cad.
☎ *0212 249 1283. www.roxy.com.
tr. Cover charge. Bus/metro: Taksim.
Map p 113.*

★ **Supper Club** ORTAKÖY   Part of
the European chain, trendy young
locals lounge on white sofas to dine
on a four-course dinner by candle-
light, followed by live entertainment. Come for drinks, a dance on
the decking to deep house, or
recline to late-night chill-out music,
bathed in lighting that changes
color. *65 Muallim Naci Cad.* ☎ *0212
2611 988. www.supperclub.com.
Closed Sun and Mon. Bus: Ortaköy.
Map p 114.*

★★ **360Istanbul** BEYOĞLU   At
the top of Mısır Apartment (p 31)
this terrace bar-club-restaurant is a
real hit with *fashionistas*. Glass walls
mean enjoying the views even when
it's too chilly for the terrace; at
weekends excellent house DJs light
up the dance floor into the small

hours. Line your stomach with international cuisine before sampling top cocktails. *9/F 163 Istiklal Cad.* ☎ *0212 251 1042. www.360istanbul.com. Bus: Taksim. Map p 113.*

Gay Nightlife

★★ **Bigudi** TAKSIM Istanbul's first lesbian bar has changed venues several times since opening in 2007, and opens only at weekends. A women-only terrace club, plus a cafe-bar downstairs open to all, things get busy after midnight. *5 Mis Sok, off Istiklal Cad.* ☎ *0535 509 0922. www.bigudiproject.net. Bus: Taksim. Map 113.*

★★ **Mor Kedi** TAKSIM A homely cafe for gays and lesbians, Mor Kedi also a drop-in center, friendly coffee bar, and information point rolled into one. It's all about armchairs, board games, and newspapers, rather than a cruisey pick-up joint. If you're new in town and want the low-down, this is a good start. *3/F 7 Imam Adnan Sok, off Istiklal Cad.* ☎ *0212 244 2592. www.cafemorkedi.com. Bus/ metro: Taksim. Map p 113.*

★ **Otherside The Club** TAKSIM Originally a gay restaurant and then cozy cafe, local gay guys love this club on the fourth floor of an apartment block, with kitsch decor and serious dance action on a tiny dance floor to popular European dance tracks. Regular karaoke nights. *Zambak Sok 2/5, off Istiklal Cad.* ☎ *0212 292 8852. www.othersideistanbul. com. Bus/metro: Taksim. Map p 113.*

★ **Sugarclub Café** BEYOĞLU A little like **Mor Kedi,** this is a good daytime spot to get up-to-date info from local gay guys about Istanbul's nightlife. A simple cafe and bar, it has DJs on summer weekends with crowds spilling out onto the courtyard. *3 Sakasalim Çıkmazı, off Istiklal Cad.* ☎ *0212 245 0096. www.sugar-cafe.com. Bus: Taksim. Map p 113.*

★★ **Tek Yon** BEYOĞLU Istanbul's most popular gay club, previously for local "bears," now attracts a mixed crowd; gay and straight women are welcome, but perhaps not at weekends when things get busy. Loud Turkish and Euro pop is the norm, with plenty of space for a chat upstairs, until everyone packs onto the dance floor. Don't arrive before midnight! *63 Sıraselviler Cad.* ☎ *0535 233 0654. www.clubtekyon. com. Bus: Taksim. Map p 113.* ●

White-sofa style at Supper Club.

Arts & Entertainment Best Bets

Best for Eclectic DJs & Fusion Bands
★★★ Babylon, *3 Şeybender Sok* (p 127)

Best Strike Action
★★ Bab Bowling Café, *24 Yeşilcam Sok* (p 129)

Best Venue for an Orchestra
★★ Hagia Eirene, *Topkapı Sarayı* (p 126)

Best Experimental Dance
★★ garajistanbul, *11A Kaymakam Reşat Bey Sok* (p 126)

Best for a Cozy Jazz Night
★★ Nublu, *4 Jurnal Sok* (p 128)

Best Goal Celebrations
★★★ Beşiktaş FC, *İnönü Stadium* (p 129)

Best Music for a Summer Night
★★ Cemil Topuzlu Açikhava Tiyatrosu, *Harbiye* (p 125)

Best Place for a Flutter
★ Veliefendi, *Veliefendi Hipodromu* (p 129)

Best Funky New Club
★★ Ghetto, *10 Kalyoncu Kulluk Cad* (p 128)

Best Spiritual Experience
★★★ Whirling Dervish Ceremony, *c/o Les Arts Turcs 3/F 37 Incili Çavuş Sok* (p 126)

Best Night at the Opera
★★ Süreyya Opera House, *29 Bahariye Cad* (p 126)

Best Art & Jazz Experience
★★ Tamirane, *Eski Silahtarağa Elektrik Santralı* (p 128)

Best for Local Chamber Music
★★ Akbank Sanat, *1 Zambak Sok* (p 125)

Have a flutter at Veliefendi racetrack. Previous page: A concert at Hagia Eirene.

Beyoğlu Arts & Entertainment

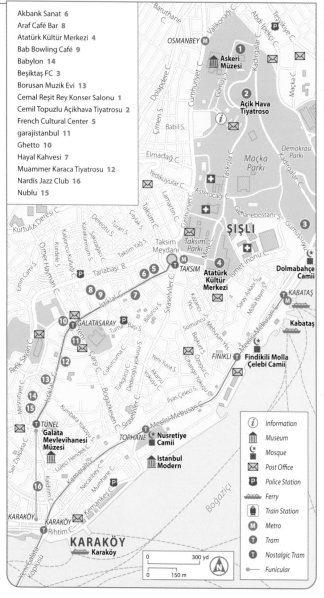

Akbank Sanat **6**
Araf Café Bar **8**
Atatürk Kültür Merkezi **4**
Bab Bowling Café **9**
Babylon **14**
Beşiktaş FC **3**
Borusan Muzik Evi **13**
Cemal Reşit Rey Konser Salonu **1**
Cemil Topuzlu Açikhava Tiyatrosu **2**
French Cultural Center **5**
garajistanbul **11**
Ghetto **10**
Hayal Kahvesi **7**
Muammer Karaca Tiyatrosu **12**
Nardis Jazz Club **16**
Nublu **15**

i Information
🏛 Museum
☪ Mosque
✉ Post Office
Ⓟ Police Station
⛴ Ferry
🚃 Train Station
Ⓜ Metro
Ⓣ Tram
Ⓣ Nostalgic Tram
• Funicular

0   300 yd
0   150 m

Greater Istanbul A&E

Fenerbahçe FC 7
Galatasaray FC 1
Hagia Eirene 5
Istanbul Jazz Center (JC's) 6
Süreyya Opera House 8
Tamirane 2
Veliefendi 3
Whirling Dervish Ceremony 4

0   1½ mi
0   1.5 km

Arts & Entertainment **A to Z**

Live Music Venues

Dance, Music & Theater
★★ Akbank Sanat BEYOĞLU
This privately sponsored cultural center has a small theater, cinema, and even its own chamber orchestra (a good example of the benefits of banks sponsoring the arts). Hosting regular local dance groups, concerts, and films, and a prominent venue in the city's arts festivals (*Savvy Traveler*, p 159), its monthly program is displayed in the window. *1 Zambak Sok, off Istiklal Cad.* ☎ *0212 252 3500. www.akbanksanat.com. Tickets from 15 TL. Map p 123.*

★★ Atatürk Kültür Merkezi
TAKSIM   This Taksim Square landmark is a multi-purpose arts and cultural center, its main concert hall seating 1,300 plus a second concert hall, chamber theater, and cinema. Closed for major refurbishment at the time of writing—although its future isn't clear. *Taksim Meydanı. www.idobale.com. Metro/bus: Taksim. Map p 123.*

★ Borusan Muzik Evi BEYOĞLU
Established in 2009, this newly renovated six-story building houses many forms of the arts, from contemporary art galleries to concert hall, modern dance, and rehearsal space for the Borusan Philharmonic Orchestra. Its program is usually listed on the window outside. *Orhan Adli Apaydin Sok, off Istiklal Cad.* ☎ *0212 336 3280. www.borusanmuzikevi.com. Bus: Taksim. Map p 123.*

★★ Cemal Reşit Rey Konser Salonu
HARBIYE   This huge theater is home to its own symphony orchestra, with a regular and varied program including classical, jazz, and world music, plus occasional traveling ballet and modern dance companies. Closed during summer. *Darülbedayi Cad, Harbiye.* ☎ *0212 232 9830. www.crrks.org. Bus: Harbiye. Map p 123.*

★★ Cemil Topuzlu Açikhava Tiyatrosu (Cemil Topuzlu Open Air Theater)
HARBIYE   This fantastic open-air venue is loved in summer, when it hosts performances as diverse as Balkan genius Goran Bregovic, and the feel-good *Abba The Show*. Most concerts are mid-July to early August. *Harbiye. www.biletix.com. Box office* ☎ *0212 296 2404. Tickets from 20 TL. Metro: Osmanbey. Map p 123.*

★ French Cultural Center
TAKSIM   Located inside the gorgeous grounds of the French consulate, this small theater is a venue for Istanbul's theater and film festivals (*Savvy Traveler*, p 159). Look on the noticeboard outside for events. *Istiklal Cad.* ☎ *0212 393 8111. www.infist.org. Tickets from 15 TL. Bus/Metro: Taksim. Map p 123.*

Atatürk Kültür Merkezi shortly before refurbishment.

★★ **garajistanbul** GALATASARAY
A venue for contemporary performing arts, this space was created in a parking lot basement—an unlikely venue for such a vibrant arts group. Launched by a group of local artists in 2007, it's quickly made a name for itself, hosting performances from visiting avant-garde dance and theater troupes, and producing works by in-house writers through their production company GarajistanbulPro. English surtitles if the performance is in Turkish. *11A Kaymakam Reşat Bey Sok, off Yeni Çarşı Cad.* ☎ *0212 244 4499. www.garajistanbul.com. Tickets approx 10–35 TL. Bus: Taksim. Map p 123.*

★★ **Hagia Eirene** SULTANAHMET
The famous Byzantine church in the grounds of Topkapı Palace (p 24) is rarely open—in fact your main chance is for concerts during June's Istanbul Music Festival. These will usually be the opening and closing nights, but take any opportunity to go, even just to appreciate the venue, which means booking well in advance. *Topkapı Sarayı. www.iksv. org. Tickets from 20 TL. Tram: Gülhane. Map p 124.*

★ **Muammer Karaca Tiyatrosu**
BEYOĞLU Although most theater performances are in Turkish, you'll find occasional folk dancing and sema (the Whirling Dervish ceremony) here, on stage in this tucked-away venue. Look for listings in the local press or Biletix. *Muammer Karaca Sok, off Istiklal Cad.* ☎ *0212 252 4456. Bus/metro Taksim, then walk. Map p 123.*

★★ **Süreyya Opera House**
KADIKÖY While Ataturk Kültür Merkezi continues its infuriatingly protracted period of closure (supposedly for restoration), this is the venue for regular Istanbul State Opera and Ballet performances. Built in the 1920s on the model of the great European theaters, with art deco influences, it had a huge renovation in 2006. *29 Bahariye Cad.* ☎ *0216 346 1531. www. sureyyaoperasi.org. Tickets from 20 TL. Boat: Kadıköy. Map p 124.*

★★★ **Whirling Dervish Ceremony** Galatasaray Mevlevihanesi hosts weekly *sema* ceremonies performed for visitors by the Dervishes, every Sunday evening. After closing for major refurbishment, it reopened in June 2011; please check for performances, prices, dates, and times (p 51). Alternatively, for a more authentic experience, take a peek inside a "working" dervish lodge: **Les Arts Turcs.** This

Try to experience a concert at Hagia Eirene.

What's On?

Listings of theater, dance, movies, concerts, and sporting events appear in the monthly English edition of *Time Out Istanbul*. The English-language daily newspaper *Hürriyet Daily News* (www.hurriyetdaily news.com) also has basic listings. Buy advance tickets for concerts, plays, or sports events at **www.biletix.com**—also at the **Biletix** outlet at Istiklal Kitabevi, 55A Istiklal Caddesi. The website has good day-to-day listings of what's on. Most cultural festivals (p 160) are organized by the excellent **Istanbul Kültür Sanat Vakfi** (Istanbul Foundation for Culture and Arts); check **www.iksv.org** for dates and listings. Look out for flyers appearing on the walls of Istiklal Caddesi advertising concerts. **Movie halls,** especially around Istiklal Caddesi and multiplexes in shopping malls, show recent Hollywood releases. Check they are subtitled into Turkish, rather than dubbed (ask: *'Orijinal dilde mı?'*).

wonderful cultural organization offers tours, courses, and information, and organizes small groups to experience this spiritual ceremony. White-robed dervishes spin slowly to attain spiritual enlightenment, a somber ceremony which can last several hours. Dress respectfully (women should wear headscarves); no photographs allowed. Highly recommended. *For Galatasaray Mevlevihanesi see p 51. Les Arts Turcs, 3/F 37 Incili Çavuş Sok.* ☎ *0212 527 6859. www. lesartsturcs.com. Tram: Sultanahmet. Map p 124.*

Catch the Whirling Dervish sema ceremony.

hear gypsy clarinetist Selim Sesler (every Tues). *32 Balo Sok, off Istiklal Cad.* ☎ *0212 244 8301. www.araf.com.tr. Bus: Taksim. Map p 123.*

★★★ Babylon

GALATA One of the best music venues in the city, this relatively small venue started out as more of a club, but found its niche as a great live music venue. Most of the acts are international, incorporating a range of music genres from nu-jazz and Latin to Balkan gypsy-techno fusion. Guest international DJs give the place a more "clubby" feel. Buy tickets in advance for popular acts from the box office or online. *3 Şeybender Sok, off Asmalımescit.* ☎ *0212 292 7368. www.babylon.com.tr. Tickets from 25 TL. Bus/metro Taksim, then 15-min walk. Map p 123.*

Rock & Jazz

★ Araf Café Bar BEYOĞLU

Slightly down-market and popular with English teachers and students, this cozy bar has an excellent selection of live "alternative world music" most nights. It's another venue to

Ticket prices

Where entry prices are not given, this is because prices vary according to the event. At some venues entry can be free (generally early in the week), whereas major acts can command high ticket prices. Please check for individual events.

★★ **Ghetto** GALATASARAY This little club in an old bakery hosts live bands, especially roots, progressive, and rock, from Turkey and abroad. Recent international artists include Tricky. A narrow balcony overlooks the stage and crowd. Look out for their monthly program in local book and music shops. *10 Kalyoncu Kulluk Cad.* ☎ *0212 251 7501. www. ghettoist.com. Bus/metro: Taksim. Map p 123.*

★★ **Hayal Kahvesi** BEYOĞLU A real local favorite, this venue has live bands most nights, usually Turkish rock and pop acts. The atmosphere is laid-back and grungy, rather than anything too flash, with the program posted outside. *11C Büyükparmık-kapi Sok.* ☎ *0212 244 2558. www. hayalkahvesibeyoglu.com. Metro/ bus: Taksim. Map p 123.*

★★ **Istanbul Jazz Center (JC's)** ORTAKÖY Live jazz nightly at this sophisticated club in Ortaköy, open during winter months only. Boasting an international line-up with stars from the U.S.A., Europe, and South America, with top-quality Yamaha piano and acoustics, there is also a good restaurant serving European food, and a pleasant courtyard. *10 Salhane Sok, off Çırağan Cad.* ☎ *0212 327 5050. www.istanbuljazz. com. Tickets from 40 TL. Bus to Ortaköy. Map p 124.*

★★ **Nardis Jazz Club** GALATA Live music from Turkish and international acts every night in this stone-walled cozy den draws in the jazz fans. The venue was created for local musicians and their friends by husband-and-wife owners Önder (musician) and Zuhal Focan. Food and drink are pricey, but the small round tables and tiny balcony make it a friendly joint. *14 Galata Kulesi Sok.* ☎ *0212 244 6327. www.nardis jazz.com. Most tickets from 25 TL. Bus/metro Taksim. Map p 123.*

★★ **Nublu** TÜNEL This cozy cafe-bar, little brother to the club Baby-lon (p 127), was previously known as Babylon Lounge. It's now a relaxed jazz club, with live music from local and overseas bands, jam sessions, DJs, and occasional after-parties. There's also a record market first Sunday of every month (1–6pm). *4 Jurnal Sok, off Asmalımescit.* ☎ *0212 245 3800. www.babylon. com.tr. Closed Sun and Mon. Tram/ tunnel: Tünel. Map p 123.*

★★ **Tamirane** EYÜP This funky cafe and music venue is part of the santralistanbul site (p 32), and has regular daytime and evening performances. You could time your visit to the gallery to see afternoon jazz sessions with Sunday brunch, or Indie music. There are DJ sessions on Saturday afternoons and usually international acts on Friday and Saturday evenings. Check the website for listings. *Eski Silahtarağa Elektrik Santralı, Kazım Karabekir Cad 2/8, Eyüp.* ☎ *0212 311 7309. www. tamirane.com. Tickets from 10 TL. Bus: Eyüp. Map p 124.*

Sport

Bowling

★★ kids Bab Bowling Café
BEYOĞLU   Visitors of all ages love this six-lane 10-pin bowling alley complete with bar, snack food, glitter ball, and disco music. Pool tables and soccer on the big screen make this a fun, sporty night out. *24 Yeş ilcam Sok.* ☎ *0212 251 1595. www. babbowling.com.tr. Bowling from 10 TL. 10am–midnight. Bus/metro: Taksim. Map p 123.*

Horseracing

★ kids Veliefendi BAKIRKÖY
This historic racecourse is headquarters of the Turkish Jockey Club. Although Atatürk promoted this noble sport, most people are more interested in the betting than any particular equine finesse (thankfully, rules at betting counters are pretty easy to understand). There's usually one weekend and one midweek race meeting. International jockeys and horses participate in the most lucrative race meeting of the year, the Topkapı Trophy in September. There's a decent selection of cafes, bars, and a picnic area. Check the website or the *Hürriyet Daily News*

Teaching them young at Inönü stadium with Beşiktaş supporters.

for race schedules. *Türkiye Jokey Kulübü, Veliefendi Hipodromu, Bakırkoy.* ☎ *0212 444 0855. www. tjk.org. Entry 2–10 TL. Tram to Zeytinburnu, then minibus or taxi.*

Soccer (Football) Clubs

★★★ Beşiktaş FC GÜMÜŞSUYU
The most accessible ground—a 10-minute downhill walk from Taksim Square—with a stunning view of the Bosphorus and Dolmabahçe Palace (p 20) for a pleasant distraction. Beşiktaş's last league victory was

Go for a strike at Bab Bowling.

Soccer—a National Obsession

Between late August and early May, it's hard to avoid the soccer season, especially as Turkey's top league, the Super Lig's usual top three teams are all from Istanbul: Beşiktaş, Fenerbahçe, and Galatasaray. If you're a sports fan I recommend going to a match, although given the intense passion and rivalry of supporters it's advisable to avoid a local derby. If possible, experience the wonderful İnönü Stadium to see Beşiktaş—and I'm not even trying to disguise my allegiance here; they were my team of choice when living in Istanbul in 1998 and I cheered them on at home games. Many women and families attend matches (a greater proportion than in my native England), especially in my favorite Yeni Açık section of the stadium. This stand also has the advantage of the best views—beyond the pitch you can also see the Bosphorus and Dolmabahçe Palace's clock tower.

2003, and they have yet to make inroads into European trophies. You will find a healthy number of women and families in the crowd. *İnönü Stadium.* ☎ *0212 310 1000. www.bjk. com.tr. Tickets from 30 TL. Bus/ metro: Taksim, then walk. Map p 123.*

★ **Fenerbahçe FC** KADIKÖY
Over on the Asian side, this spectacular stadium, one of Europe's finest, is home to the Canaries, Turkey's most successful club, with 18 league titles. They also won the 2010/11 Turkish Super league, narrowly pipping Trabzonspor to the post. Their kit shops are modestly called Feneriums. *Şükrü Saraçoğlu Stadium, Kızıltoprak.* ☎ *0216 449 5667. www.fenerbahce.org. Tickets*

from 35 TL. Ferry: Kadıköy, then walk. Map p 124.

★ **Galatasaray FC** SEYRANTEPE
Turkey's most famous (and arguably most supported) team, "Com Bom" have won the domestic league 17 times, plus the UEFA Cup in 2000 over Arsenal. The notorious Ali Sami Yen stadium (famed for the banner "Welcome to the hell"), was replaced by the immense, multi-purpose Türk Telecom Arena stadium, which opened in early 2011. It soon broke official world records for the noisiest crowd, in their match against archrivals Fenerbahçe. *Turk Telekom Arena, Seyrantepe.* ☎ *0212 273 2850. www.galatasaray.org. Tickets from 30 TL. Bus: Seyrantepe. Map p 124.* ●

Lodging **Best Bets**

Best **Location for Grand Bazaar**
★★★ Hotel Niles *19 Dibekli Cami Sok (p 139)*

Best **Secret Garden**
★★★ Hotel Empress Zoe *4 Akbıyık Cad (p 138)*

Best for **Famous Guests**
★★★ Pera Palace *52 Meşrutiyet Cad (p 140)*

Best **Waterfront Terrace**
★★ Radisson Blu Bosphorus Hotel *46 Çırağan Cad (p 141)*

Best **Use for an Old Distillery**
★★★ Sumahan on the Water *51 Kuleli Cad (p 141)*

Best **Contemporary Style**
★★★ Witt Istanbul Suites *26 Defterdar Yokuşu (p 142)*

Most **Affordable Jacuzzi**
★★ Tan Hotel *20 Doktor Eminpaşa Sok (p 142)*

Best for **Secluded Romance**
★★ A'jia *27 Çubuklu Cad (p 135)*

Best **Sultanahmet Cheapie**
★★ Peninsula *6 Adliye Sok (p 140)*

Best **Ultra Chic Lobby**
★★★ W Hotel *22 Süleyman Seba Cad (p 142)*

Best **Circular Bed**
★★ Eklektik Guest House *4 Kadribey Çikması (p 137)*

Best **Value for Families**
★★ Galata Residence *2 Felek Sok (p 138)*

Best for **Blue Mosque View**
★★ Mavi Ev *14 Dalbasti Sok (p 140)*

Best **Guest Relations Staff**
★★★ Sirkeci Konak Hotel *5 Taya Hatun Sok (p 141)*

Best for **Business Travelers**
★★ Mövenpick *4 Büyükdere Cad (p 140)* and ★★ Ansen 130 *70 Meşrutiyet Cad (p 135)*

Most **Unusual Exterior**
★★★ Four Seasons Hotel *1 Tevkifhane Sok (p 137)*

Businesslike elegance at Mövenpick Hotel. Previous page: W Hotel.

Old City Lodging

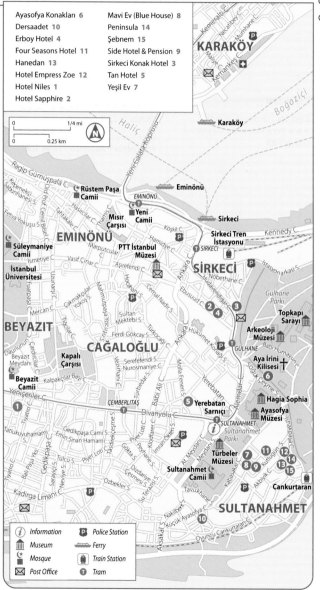

Ayasofya Konakları 6
Dersaadet 10
Erboy Hotel 4
Four Seasons Hotel 11
Hanedan 13
Hotel Empress Zoe 12
Hotel Niles 1
Hotel Sapphire 2

Mavi Ev (Blue House) 8
Peninsula 14
Şebnem 15
Side Hotel & Pension 9
Sirkeci Konak Hotel 3
Tan Hotel 5
Yeşil Ev 7

0   1/4 mi
0   0.25 km

KARAKÖY

Bogaziçi

Haliç

Karaköy

Ragip Gümüşpala C.

★ **Rüstem Paşa Camii**

EMİNÖNÜ

Eminönü

Yeni Camii

Mısır Çarşısı

Sirkeci

Sirkeci Tren İstasyonu

SİRKECİ

Kennedy C.

EMİNÖNÜ

PTT İstanbul Müzesi

Süleymaniye Camii

İstanbul Üniversitesi

SİRKECİ

Gülhane Parkı

Topkapı Sarayı

BEYAZIT

Kapalı Çarşısı

CAĞALOĞLU

Arkeoloji Müzesi

GÜLHANE

Aya İrini Kilisesi †

Beyazit Camii

ÇEMBERLITAŞ

Yerebatan Sarnıcı

SULTANAHMET

Hagia Sophia

Ayasofya Müzesi

Türbeler Müzesi

Sultanahmet Camii

Cankurtaran

SULTANAHMET

ⓘ Information
🏛 Museum
★ Mosque
✉ Post Office

🅿 Police Station
⛴ Ferry
🚉 Train Station
Ⓣ Tram

Beyoğlu Lodging

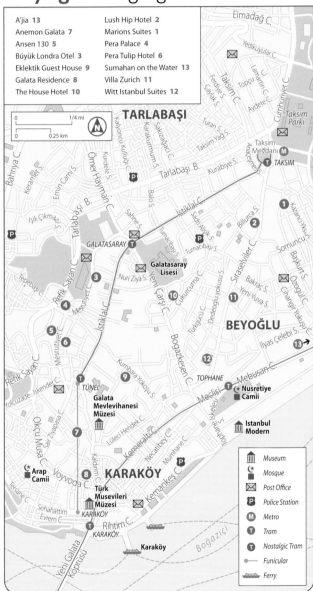

A'jia **13**
Anemon Galata **7**
Ansen 130 **5**
Büyük Londra Otel **3**
Eklektik Guest House **9**
Galata Residence **8**
The House Hotel **10**

Lush Hip Hotel **2**
Marions Suites **1**
Pera Palace **4**
Pera Tulip Hotel **6**
Sumahan on the Water **13**
Villa Zurich **11**
Witt Istanbul Suites **12**

Bosphorus Lodging

Çirağan Palace Kempinski **2**

Four Seasons Hotel-
Istanbul at the Bosphorus **3**

Mövenpick **5**

Radisson Blu Bosphorus Hotel **4**

W Hotel **1**

Istanbul Lodging **A to Z**

★★ **A'jia** KANLICA   In a remote part of the city, this restored Ottoman mansion perches on the Asian side of the Bosphorus. Rooms have stunning sea views, some with a private balcony, and an uncluttered feel with wooden floors and contemporary art. Great dining on the terrace. *Ahmet Rasim Pasha Mansion, 27 Çubuklu Cad.* ☎ *0216 413 9300. www.ajiahotel.com. 16 units. Doubles from 250€. AE, MC, V. Taxi to Kanlica. Map p 134.*

★★ **Anemon Galata** GALATA This luxury "special" hotel, housed in a Grade II listed building, has comfortable rooms with period furniture and sparkling white linens. It's

right next to the famous tower with perfect views from the terrace, and has the recommended Pitti restaurant. *Büyükhendek Cad.* ☎ *0212 293 2343. www.anemonhotels.com. 30 units. Doubles from 175€. MC, V. Taxi from Taksim. Map p 134.*

★★ kids **Ansen 130** TEPEBAŞI Housed in a restored century-old building, good-value chic Zen rooms have kitchenette, sofa, and writing desk. Rooms are spacious, each with a huge plasma TV, Wi-Fi, and power shower, all in contemporary, minimalist style. Check for good online deals. *70 Meşrutiyet Cad.* ☎ *0212 245 8808. www.ansen suites.com. 10 units. Doubles from*

Where to Stay?

Hotels cluster around Sultanahmet and Beyoglu, poles apart in ambience and amenities, so your choice depends on priorities. If you prefer views of the Blue Mosque and vicinity to historical monuments, with perhaps no TV in your room, Sultanahmet is for you. Bring earplugs for neighboring mosques' dawn call-to-prayer, and be prepared for carpet touts and never-ending souvenir shops. If good restaurants, bars, and clubs are important, stay in Beyoğlu, where Istiklal Caddesi and Tünel buzz most of the night—although it can be noisy if your room is near Taksim Square or a nightclub. Work on this logic: it's easier to travel to Sultanahmet during the day than to travel back there after a night out in Beyoğlu.

180€. AE, MC, V. All buses from Taksim. Map p 134.

★ **Ayasofya Konakları** SULTA-NAHMET These nine wooden houses are part of a clever rebuilding project on a cobbled pedestrian street (p 67) behind Hagia Sophia. The 64 rooms have tasteful 19th-century-style decor, including a small Turkish bath in the Pasha Suite. Most rooms are without TV. Breakfast is served on quaint terraces. *Soğukçeşme Sokağı.* ☎ *0212 513 3660. www.ayasofyakonaklari.com. 64 units. Doubles from 170€. MC, V. Tram: Sultanahmet. Map p 133.*

Ayasofya Konakları's recreated tradition.

★ **Büyük Londra Otel** TEPEBAŞI The entrance in this century-old mansion oozes faded decadence, especially the chandeliers and Ottoman nick-nacks. Guest rooms are simpler (than the entrance), but ensure you get one of their renovated rooms. A great location for Beyoğlu's nightlife. Its kudos heightened when featured in two recent Turkish films. *53 Meşrutiyet Cad.* ☎ *0212 245 0670. www.londra hotel.net. 54 units. Doubles from 80€. AE, MC, V. Bus: Tepebaşı. Map p 134.*

★★ **Çirağan Palace Kempinski** BEŞIKTAŞ Splash out on a room in this former Ottoman palace, with outstanding top-notch (and top-dollar) features including the outdoor "infinity" pool (heated in winter) and spa. Lottery winners could try the multi-roomed Grand Sultan Suite (30,000€). *32 Çirağan Cad.* ☎ *0212 326 4646. www.kempinski-istanbul. com. 314 units. Doubles from 360€. AE, DC, MC, V. Bus: Beşiktaş to Ortaköy. Map p 135.*

★★ **kids Dersaadet** SULTANAH-MET This family-run Ottoman-era house in a quiet neighborhood has well-kept rooms and great service.

Some rooms have Bosphorus views—one double has its own *hamam*—and the penthouse suite boasts 180-degree views and Jacuzzi. Breakfast is served on the flower-filled roof terrace. *5 Kapıağası Sok, off Küçük Ayasofya Cad.* ☎ *0212 458 0760. www.hotel dersaadet.com. 17 units. Doubles from 115€. AE, MC, V. Tram: Sultanahmet. Map p 133.*

★★ Eklektik Guest House

GALATA   Hidden away down a quiet street, this gay-friendly guesthouse has seven unique rooms in a converted Ottoman house. Choose from contemporary style in the Black Room, marble shower in the Sultan's Room, or the Red Room's circular bed—pure camp. Breakfast is served at a communal table. *4 Kadribey Çikması, off Serdar-i Ekrem Cad.* ☎ *0212 243 7446. www. eklektikgalata.com. 7 units. Doubles from 95€. No credit cards. Tunnel: Tünel. Map p 134.*

★ Erboy Hotel SIRKECI   Great

value and hospitality at this centrally located three-star with simple, bright rooms and free Wi-Fi in the communal areas. Wonderful Bosphorus views from the roof terrace. *18 Ebussuud Cad.* ☎ *0212 513 3750. www.erboyhotel.com. 108 units. Doubles 74€. MC, V. Tram: Sirkeci. Map p 133.*

★★★ Four Seasons Hotel SUL-

TANAHMET   An Istanbul longstanding favorite, this is Sultanahmet's most luxurious hotel, with worldclass service. Converted from the neo-classic Sultanahmet Prison in 1986 with distinctive ochre watchtower (and prisoners' graffiti in the basement), its high-ceilinged rooms are spacious and luxurious. The hotel also houses the Seasons restaurant (p 108). *1 Tevkifhane Sok.* ☎ *0212 638 8200. www.four seasons.com/istanbul. 65 units.*

Seaview terrace at Dersaadet.

Doubles from 350€. AE, DC, MC, V. Tram: Sultanahmet. Map p 133.

★★ Four Seasons Hotel— Istanbul at the Bosphorus

BEŞIKTAŞ   Making a huge impact since opening in 2008, Istanbul's second Four Seasons is in a refurbished 19th-century Ottoman palace overlooking the water. The contemporary feel is enhanced with mahogany furnishings and handpainted motifs on the ceilings, plus luxury spa and indoor and outdoor pools. *28 Çirağan Cad.* ☎ *0212 381 4000. www.fourseasons.com/ bosphorus. 166 units. Doubles from*

The Four Seasons—fine use for an ex-prison.

Hotel Niles in busy Beyazit.

residence.com. 21 units. Doubles
from 75€. MC, V. Tunnel: Tünel.
Map p 134.

★★ Hanedan SULTANAHMET A
friendly little guesthouse in a quiet
street where no-frills rooms mean
wooden floorboards with simple furniture, and fantastic terrace views of
the Sea of Marmara with your buffet
breakfast. For a little extra, some
large rooms have a sea view. (20%
discount for online booking.) *3
Adliye Sok, off Akbıyık Cad.* ☎ *0212
516 4869. www.hanedanhotel.com.
10 units. Doubles from 65€. MC, V.
Tram: Sultanahmet. Map p 133.*

★★★ Hotel Empress Zoe SULTA-
NAHMET Converted from three
townhouses, this has a vast selection of rooms, from standard double
to duplex with two bedrooms and
kitchen. Cleverly using the original
wood and stone, history is retained
but mod cons are added. The tiny
garden is a peaceful hideaway for
breakfast. *4 Akbıyık Cad.* ☎ *0212
518 2504. www.emzoe.com. 25
units. Doubles from 120€. MC, V.
Tram: Sultanahmet. Map p 133.*

★★★ kids Hotel Niles BEYAZIT
Tucked away near the Grand Bazaar,
this gem of a hotel, loved for its
friendly service, has simple rooms

450€. AE, DC, MC, V. Bus: Beşiktaş.
Map p 135.*

★★ kids Galata Residence
GALATA Once the Camondo family
home (p 57), these apartments are
good value, even the small ones
with simple kitchens. Two-bedroom
apartments have a living room, a
good option for families, although
it's off a steep road. Most of the
original furnishings remain. Watch
out for pricey items in the refrigera-
tors! *2 Felek Sok, off Midilli Sok.*
☎ *0212 292 4841. www.galata*

How Much?

Prices listed are the online rate for high season (roughly mid-
Mar–late Oct), including breakfast and tax, often 10–20% less in low
season. Top hotels often have good deals on their websites or
through online booking agencies, and can be quieter in August, with
fewer business visitors. You can also try phoning the hotel direct to
ask for any special rates, especially out of season; some offer discounts for cash payments. Hotels book up quickly and prices usually
increase for Şeker Bayram (the festival after Ramazan), Christmas,
and major local events—especially the Istanbul Grand Prix (p 160).

with tasteful decor. Room size ranges from small to spacious suites and a duplex—ideal for families—some with private *hamam*. Buffet breakfast is served on the roof terrace, which stays open as a 24-hour cafe-bar. *19 Dibekli Cami Sok, off Ordu Cad. ☎ 0212 517 3239. www. hotelniles.com. 39 units. Doubles from 70€. MC, V. Tram: Beyazit. Map p 133.*

★★ Hotel Sapphire SIRKECI

Fantastic value in a convenient part of town, away from Sultanahmet's carpet shops but near enough to the sights. Simple, light rooms have ornate touches, minibar, and small baths. There are also family-friendly large triple rooms, a large ornate lobby, and friendly and efficient staff. *14 Ibnikemal Cad. ☎ 0212 520 5686. www.hotelsapphire.com. 55 units. Doubles from 80€. MC, V. Tram: Sirkeci. Map p 133.*

★★ The House Hotel GALA-

TASARAY Part of the House Café chain, this 19th-century four-story mansion underwent a stylish renovation and opened as an hotel in 2010. Its 20 suites all retain the original architectural qualities, including graceful high ceilings, Italianate marble, and parquet floors. Hilly neighborhood. *19 Bostanbaşı Cad. ☎ 0212 252 0422. www. thehousehotel.com. 20 units. Doubles from 145€. MC, V. Bus: Taksim, then 10-min walk/taxi. Map p 134.*

★★ Lush Hip Hotel CIHANGIR

Chic decor in this converted apartment block puts this firmly in the "hip hotel" category. Close to Taksim Square (rooms overlooking the street are noisy), rooms come in varying sizes and styles but all are uncluttered and light, with natural tones and different prints of Beyoğlu scenes adorning the walls. *12 Siraselviler Cad. ☎ 0212 243 9595. www.lushhiphotel.com. 35 units. Doubles from 100€. AE, MC, V. Bus: Taksim. Map p 134.*

★ Marions Suites CIHANGIR

Formerly known as Suite Home Cihangir, this is tucked away in a central residential neighborhood. Contemporary suites come in different styles and sizes; huge sofas and kitchenettes are a real bonus, with separate living rooms and balcony in the larger suites. Long-stay business travelers love the small meeting rooms and spa. *12 Başkurt Sok. ☎ 0212 243 3101. 14 units. Doubles*

Hip artwork adorns Lush Hip Hotel.

from 90€. MC, V. Metro/bus: Taksim. Map p 134.

★★ kids Mavi Ev (Blue House)

SULTANAHMET This restored Ottoman house opposite the Blue Mosque is charming, with small, plain rooms and tiny bathrooms, and traditional touches such as brass double beds and wooden floorboards. Ask for a room with views, at no extra cost. *14 Dalbasti Sok. ☎ 0212 638 9010. www.bluehouse.com.tr. 27 units. Doubles from 160€. AE, MC, V. Tram: Sultanahmet. Map p 133.*

★★ Mövenpick

LEVENT A good chain choice for business guests in the heart of the banking district. Contemporary rooms have extra-large desks, Wi-Fi, and the Skyline Club Lounge for all executive-floor guests. The hotel also houses business and banqueting rooms, sauna, and pool. *4 Büyükdere Cad. ☎ 0212 319 2929. www.moevenpick-hotels.com. 249 units. Doubles from 240€. AE, DC, MC, V. Metro: 4. Levent. Map p 135.*

★★ kids Peninsula

SULTANAHMET Converted from an old townhouse on a traffic-free street, rooms are simple, although there's no TV. Standard rooms are small, the basement rooms cheaper, with two interconnecting rooms suitable for families and a good-value larger double. Friendly staff, with superb buffet breakfast on the terrace. A good budget option. *6 Adliye Sok, Akbıyık Cad. ☎ 0212 458 6850. www.hotelpeninsula.com. 12 units. Doubles from 45€. MC, V. Tram: Sultanahmet. Map p 133.*

★★★ Pera Palace

TEPEBAŞI Istanbul's first-ever hotel, built for Orient Express passengers, reopened in late 2010 after major renovation. This luxury hotel, whose guests included Agatha Christie, Atatürk, and Queen Elizabeth II, combines original 19th-century features with an elegant high-tech edge. *52 Meşrutiyet Cad. ☎ 0212 377 4000. www.perapalace.com. 115 units. Doubles from 250€. AE, DC, MC, V. Bus: Tepebaşı. Map p 134.*

★★ kids Pera Tulip Hotel

TEPEBAŞI This compact, friendly hotel enjoys a great Beyoğlu

Special Hotels

Of all the cities in all the world, Istanbul surely boasts some of the most astounding variety of accommodation, from sleek apart-hotels the size of small houses to restored Ottoman mansions with original furnishings. I've avoided listing too many international chain hotels, as I think it's important to enjoy the city's independent hotels with their own character. However, there are two exceptions: The **Four Seasons** (Sultanahmet) (p 137) is famously housed in a former prison, and is set to be doubling in size—once they resolve the issue of the archeological excavations next door, currently being addressed in the courts. Another hugely exciting opening, in late 2012, is the new **Shangri-La.** Joining a cluster of Bosphorus-lining luxury hotels, this is built on the site of a former tobacco factory and, astoundingly, seven of its 14 floors will be underwater!

location, and extras include small business center, meeting rooms, *hamam,* and indoor pool. Chic rooms have lovely touches like bold-patterned cushions and strong colors. Larger executive rooms are worth the extra cost. *103 Meşrutiyet Cad.* ☎ *0212 243 8500. www. peratulip.com. 84 units. Doubles from 100€. AE, DC, MC, V. Bus: All buses from Taksim. Map p 134.*

★★ kids **Radisson Blu Bosphorus Hotel** ORTAKÖY   The waterfront location is a highlight, especially for breakfast on the terrace. Add good business facilities, meeting rooms, and Wi-Fi throughout, plus some rooms with a Bosphorus view. At weekends, ask for a room away from the nearby nightclub if you want to sleep. Be prepared for traffic congestion at weekends. *46 Çırağan Cad.* ☎ *0212 310 1500. www.radissons blu.com/hotel-istanbul. 120 units. Doubles from 250€. AE, MC, V. Bus: Ortaköy. Map p 135.*

★ kids **Şebnem** SULTANAHMET Rooms are simply done with white walls and dark-wood floors, at the pricey end for guesthouses in this area. Rooms with a tiny garden are worth the extra. Breakfast is served on the flower-filled terrace. Free Wi-Fi and use of laptops and obliging staff. *1 Adliye Sok, off Akbıyık Cad.* ☎ *0212 517 6623. www. sebnemhotel.net. 15 units. Doubles from 90€. MC, V. Tram: Sultanahmet. Map p 133.*

★ kids **Side Hotel & Pension** SULTANAHMET   The beauty of Side (pronounced see-deh) is the choice of accommodation, from a simple pension room with shared bathroom (great if you're on a budget) to a small self-catering apartment with a Jacuzzi, all very reasonable especially for families. *Utangaç Sok 20.* ☎ *0212 458 5870. www.sidehotel. com. Doubles from €40, 2-bedroom*

Şebnem's bijoux garden.

apartments from 90€. MC, V. Tram: Sultanahmet. Map p 133.

★★★ kids **Sirkeci Konak Hotel** SIRKECI   This luxury boutique hotel, known for its fantastic guest relations, has been a hit since opening in 2007. Tastefully furnished rooms have dark-wood floors and a writing desk, some have a balcony and there's a private Jacuzzi in the triple deluxe suite. Guests enjoy free afternoon tea in the bar, and use of the small pool and *hamam. 5 Taya Hatun Sok.* ☎ *0212 528 4344. www. sirkecikonak.com. 52 units. Doubles from 184€. AE, MC, V. Tram: Sirkeci. Map p 133.*

★★★ **Sumahan on the Water** ÇENGELKÖY   A village on the Asian side of the Bosphorus is perfect for a romantic hideaway in this boutique hotel renovated from an Ottoman distillery. Rooms are effortlessly elegant and minimalist in light woods, each with huge windows and unbeatable views. Duplex suites have their own terrace; many rooms have a *hamam. 51 Kuleli Cad.* ☎ *0216 422 8000. www.sumahan.com. 18 units. Doubles from 250€. AE, MC, V. Boat/ bus: Çengelköy. Map p 134.*

W Hotel.

★★ kids Tan Hotel SULTANAH-MET   A cut above other hotels in this price bracket, this new hotel in a quiet side-street has large modern rooms, all with fridge, large sofa, and Jacuzzi. Grand suites (with fluffy bathrobes) have a sofa bed and sleep three people. Rooms on higher floors have decent views. *20 Doktor Eminpaşa Sok, Çatalçeşme Meydanı.* ☎ *0212 520 9130. www. tanhotel.com. 20 units. Doubles from 125€. MC, V. Tram: Sultanahmet. Map p 133.*

★★ Villa Zurich CIHANGIR   This friendly hotel in a charming residential neighborhood has newly renovated rooms in tasteful pale blues and creams, many with bath and Jacuzzi. Front-facing rooms have small balconies, with Doğa Balık restaurant (p 103) on the roof terrace. *36 Akarsu Yokuşu Cad.* ☎ *0212 293*

0604. www.hotelvillazurich.com. 45 units. Doubles from 99€. MC, V. Bus/ metro: Taksim. Map p 134.

★★★ W Hotel AKARETLER   Mirrored tables, purple neon, and silver drapes—and that's just the welcome area. Opened in 2008 in the former Dolmabahçe Palace kitchens, this sexy hotel has rooms with a contemporary twist on classic Ottoman style, such as Marmara marble sinks. Fancy extras (think iPod docking stations) and spa, plus hip bar on site. *22 Süleyman Seba Cad.* ☎ *0212 381 2121. www.whotels. com/istanbul. 134 units. Doubles from 280€. AE, DC, MC, V. Bus: Beşiktaş. Map p 135.*

★★★ Witt Istanbul Suites BEŞIKTAŞ   This exquisitely designed boutique hotel has modish suites with a luxury apartment feel. Each 60 sq. m (645 sq. ft.) suite has a kitchenette and huge bathroom, with the Witt's elegant floral motif on walls and furnishings. Sweeping views from the top floor's fitness studio deter any inclination to laziness. *26 Defterdar Yokuşu.* ☎ *0212 393 7900. www.wittistanbul.com. 17 units. Doubles from 170€. AE, MC, V. Bus: Beşiktaş. Map p 134.*

★ Yeşil Ev SULTANAHMET   Rebuilt from an existing Ottoman wooden house, this popular guesthouse has brass beds and antique furniture, although its steep prices mean value for money is debatable. The standard double room is tiny and the bathroom minuscule. Still, its green wooden exterior and garden are charming, and service is good. *5 Kabasakal Cad.* ☎ *0212 517 6786. www.istanbulyesilev.com. 19 units. Doubles from 250€. AE, MC, V. Tram: Sultanahmet. Map p 133.* ●

Princes' Islands

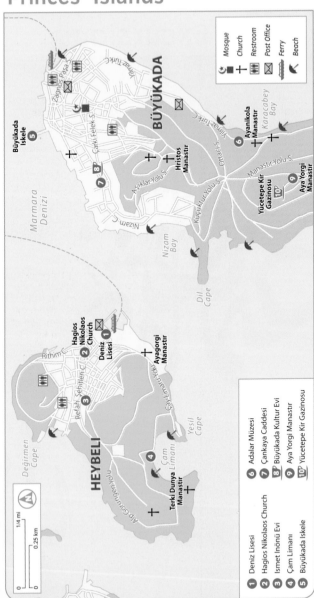

Mosque
Church
Restroom
Post Office
Ferry
Beach

BÜYÜKADA

Zağnos Paşa S.
Yılmaz Türk C.
Çarkı Felek S.
Büyükada Iskele
Karacabey Bay
Yılmaz Türk C.
Ortaçay S.
Ayanikola Manastır
Aşıklar Yolu S.
Hristos Manastır
Kültür Yolu S.
Küçüktur Yolu S.
Manastır Yolu S.
Nizam C.
Yücetepe Kir Gazinosu
Aya Yorgi Manastır
Marmara Denizi
Nizam Bay
Dil Cape

Rithim C.
Hagios Nikolaos Church
Deniz Lisesi
Ayagorgi Manastır
Refah Şehitleri C.
Çam Limanı Yolu
Çam Limanı
Yeşil Cape
Terki Dunya Manastır
Değirmen Cape
Alp Görünen Yolu
HEYBELİ

N

1/4 mi
0.25 km

1. Deniz Lisesi
2. Hagios Nikolaos Church
3. İsmet İnönü Evi
4. Çam Limanı
5. Büyükada İskele
6. Adalar Müzesi
7. Çankaya Caddesi
8. Büyükada Kultur Evi
9. Aya Yorgi Manastır
10. Yücetepe Kir Gazinosu

Previous page: Eski Camii, Erdine.

The jewel-like cluster of nine islands off Istanbul has a colorful history: Summer houses for the elite, a haven for Jewish, Greek, and Armenian minorities, and exile for "White Russians"—now a traffic-free escape for locals. You can't cover all in one day, so enjoy Heybeliada and Büyükada and walk or cycle, or hire a *phaeton* (horse and carriage). Stick to weekdays to avoid the crowds. START: **Heybeliada ferry pier.**

1 ★ Deniz Lisesi (Naval High School). You won't miss the huge waterfront naval school from the ferry pier on Heybeliada (literally "Saddlebag Island," due to its shape). Originally, the Naval War Academy set up in 1852. It's been a high school since 1985, and the white facade makes a striking sight. It's closed to the public, and uniformed cadets on patrol will prevent you taking photographs close up. From the street, you'll catch a glimpse of the Church of the Panaghia Kamariotissa, the last Byzantine church built before the fall of Constantinople in 1453. *Heybeliada Iskele.*

2 ★ Hagios Nikolaos Church. Dominating the village's main square, this Greek Orthodox church, dedicated to St. Nikolaos, patron saint of mariners, celebrated 150

Dramatic approach to Princes' Islands.

years in 2007. It's unlikely to be open outside Sunday services, attended by around 30 locals, although it's worth a try. The interior is adorned with gold, chandeliers, and frescoes, with the tomb of Patriarch Samuel I behind the altar. Opposite, in the square, are several **bicycle hire** shops. If you prefer to travel by **phaeton,** head back to the ferry pier for the rank. *Belediye Meydanı, Ayyildiz Caddesi. Service: Sun 9–11am.*

3 ★★ Ismet Inönü Evi. A 15-minute walk along **Refah Şehitleri Caddesi** brings you to this historic wooden mansion. Now a house museum, this was once a part-time residence of Ismet Inönü, president of the new Republic of Turkey (1938–50). He originally rented the house during poor health in 1924, but bought it in 1934 (with furniture given by Atatürk) and lived there until his death in 1973. The house is perfectly preserved, from his book-filled office to his daughter's cartoon stickers on her closet. I love the photos on the walls, vacation snaps of the family in bathing suits enjoying Heybeliada's beaches. ⏱ *45 min. 59 Refah Şehitleri Cad.* ☎ *0216 351 8449. Admission free. Closed Nov–Mar, open Tues–Sun 10am–5pm.*

4 ★ Çam Limanı (Cam Bay). Depending on how far you want to walk, cycle, or ride, continue along **Refah Şehitleri Caddesi,** until you descend to the small bay of Çam Limanı, a beautiful, almost 1-hour, walk with woods, fields, and

Jumping in from Çam Limanı pier.

occasional glimpses of the sea. (If in doubt, follow the road which the phaetons take.) Although not picturesque golden sands, the bay is a good spot to rest on sun loungers or swim off the wooden pier. From here, go back along **Gemici Kaynagi Sokak** until you pass **Deniz Lisesi** (①) on your right, and the **ferry pier,** from where you sail to **Büyükada.**

⑤ ★ **Büyükada Iskele (Büyükada Quay).** After a 15-minute journey, ferries arrive at **Büyükada's** (Big Island) striking quay, with ornate tiles on the upper front facade of the terminal. Built in 1914, this replaced the wooden quay built in 1899, and was used as the first movie hall on the island in 1950–51. You might be able to pick up a map of the island from the tourist office. If you want to continue on two wheels, head to the bicycle-hire shops on **Çinar Caddesi,** with kids' bikes and tandems also available.

⑥ ★ **Adalar Müzesi (Museum of Princes' Islands).** Opened in late 2010, this little museum shows, through exhibits, locals' accounts, and photographs, how the islands were such a phenomenon; to hold so many different ethnic communities—Armenians, Jews, Greeks, and Russians—in such harmony must have been a world first. History, local geology, day-to-day living, and

political developments provide a fascinating insight. 🕐 *45 min. Adalar Müzesi Hangar, Aya Nikola Mevkii.* ☎ *0216 382 6430. Admission 5 TL. Tues–Sun 10am–5pm.*

⑦ ★ **Çankaya Caddesi.** If you're walking up to **Aya Yorgi Manastır** (St. George's Monastery) a long but rewarding hour's walk, I recommend taking the longer but more picturesque route along Çankaya Caddesi. Lined with grandiose wooden mansions, previous residents included Ottoman diplomats, painters, princes, and lawyers, and Leon Trotsky in Ilyasko Köçk at the end of Hamlacı Sokak. My favorite is the white mansion at **#44,** headquarters of the *Kaymakam* (district governor).

Noble exterior of the Kaymakam's HQ.

Practical Matters

Ferries and sea-buses leave from Kabataş (p 164), with a more frequent service during the summer (mid-June–mid-Sept). Fast ferries take 35 minutes to reach Heybeliada, then 30 minutes onward to Büyükada. Slow ferries take 90 minutes between Kabataş and Büyükada. Ferries have some seating outside (check for sun direction before finding a spot), with simple refreshments served on board. Buy a *jeton* (token) before boarding, or use your *akbil* (p 164); single journeys cost approx 1.75–2.50 TL. It's advisable to avoid the last ferry of the day at weekends, or arrive in very good time at the pier; they're usually overcrowded and you might not even get on otherwise. Check at the ferry pier for times (☎ **0216 444 4436,** www.ido.com.tr/en).

8 ★ **Büyükada Kultur Evi.** With a 50-year-old phaeton in the garden, this mansion has been converted into a cultural center, housing exhibitions and summer concerts. Build up your strength with tea, beer, and snacks on the terrace. *21 Çankaya Cad.* ☎ *0216 382 8620. Coffee and snacks from 10 TL.*

9 ★★ **Aya Yorgi Manastır (St. George Monastery).** You might opt for a phaeton, or bargain for a donkey-ride up this long uphill cobbled path, although I strongly recommend the walk .On the left you'll see pieces of fabric tied onto the bushes, each representing a prayer—usually from women wishing for a child. The bell tower is your first glimpse of the monastery. Pass through the tiny courtyard—where women should cover their head and legs—into the 6th-century monastery's silent, remote interior. On the right is a large glass container filled with hand-written prayers, written by people of all religions who believe that St. George performs miracles. Thousands flock here on April 23 and September 24, when all wishes are thought to come true. Brave the crowds if you want to find out! ⏱ *1 hr. Yüce Tepe. Admission free. Open daily 9:30am–6pm.*

Aya Yorgi Manastır: Worth the climb.

10 ★★★ **Yücetepe Kir Gazinosu.** This simple restaurant adjacent to the monastery is perfect for its hilltop terrace with panoramas of the islands. There's little else but meatballs and perhaps eggplant with yogurt—but add a cool beer and the views and it's unbeatable. *Yüce Tepe.* ☎ *0216 382 1333. Meatballs 10 TL.*

Bursa

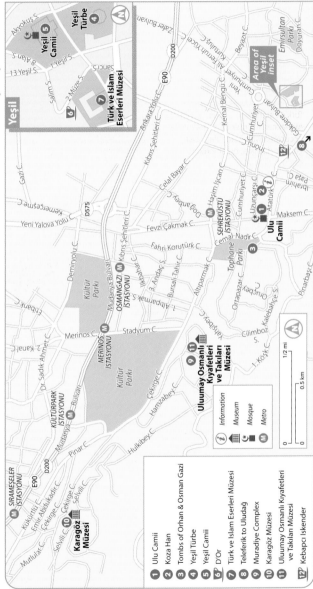

Yeşil

- Akyokuş S.
- Yeşil Türbe ⑤
- Yeşil Camii ④
- 13 Yeşil S.
- 8 Alan S.
- 1 Yeşil S.
- Salim S.
- 2 Müze S.
- Sancı S.
- ⑥
- ⑦ Türk ve Islam Eserleri Müzesi

- Area of Yeşil inset
- Emirsultan Parkı
- Doyuran C.
- Gökdere Bulvarı
- Yeni Ali Fenun Kücel C.
- Cumhuriyet C.
- Kurtuluş C.
- Beyazıt C.
- Zafer Bulvarı
- D200
- E90
- Antakaryolu C.
- Kıbrıs Şehitleri C.
- Kemal Bengü C.
- İnönü C.
- Cumhuriyet C.
- ⑫
- ⑧
- İbrahim Paşa C.
- Gazi C.
- Kemerçeşme C.
- Yeni Yalova Yolu C.
- D575
- Celal Bayar C.
- Doğanbey C.
- Haşim İşcan C.
- Uzunçarşı C.
- ① ② ⓘ
- Atatürk C.
- Maksem C.
- ③
- **Ulu Camii**
- ŞEHREKÜSTÜ İSTASYONU Ⓜ
- Fevzi Çakmak C.
- Cemal Nadir C.
- Fahri Korutürk C.
- Tophane Parkı
- Ortapazar C.
- Oruçbey C.
- Kalebahçe S.
- Pınarbaşı C.
- Altıparmak C.
- 1. Altıparmak S.
- Bursalı Tahir C.
- İlkbahar C.
- 3. Andaç S.
- Yarışbey C.
- Çilimboz S.
- 1. Koşk C.
- 1/2 mi
- 0.5 km
- Demiryolu C.
- Mudanya Bulvarı
- Kıbrıs Şehitleri C.
- OSMANGAZİ İSTASYONU Ⓜ
- Kültür Parkı
- MERİNOS İSTASYONU Ⓜ
- Merinos C.
- Stadyum C.
- Kültür Parkı
- ⑨ ⑪ Uluumay Osmanlı Kiyafetleri ve Takıları Müzesi
- KÜLTÜRPARK İSTASYONU Ⓜ
- Mudanya C.
- Bulvarı
- Çekirge C.
- Hamzabey C.
- Hulkbey C.
- Pınar C.
- Eribank C.
- 2. Kanal C.
- Dr. Sadık Ahmet C.
- SIRAMESELER İSTASYONU Ⓜ
- E90
- D200
- Kükürtlü C.
- Emir Abdulkadir C.
- Çekirge C.
- Selvili C.
- Çekirge C.
- Selvili C.
- Murtula C.
- **Karagöz Müzesi** ⑩

Legend:
- ⓘ Information
- 🏛 Museum
- ☪ Mosque
- Ⓜ Metro

① Ulu Camii
② Koza Han
③ Tombs of Orhan & Osman Gazi
④ Yeşil Türbe
⑤ Yeşil Camii
⑥' D'Or
⑦ Türk ve Islam Eserleri Müzesi
⑧ Teleferik to Uludağ
⑨ Muradiye Complex
⑩ Karagöz Müzesi
⑪ Uluumay Osmanlı Kiyafetleri ve Takıları Müzesi
⑫ Kebapçı İskender

Silk, mineral spas, ski-slopes, and mausoleums: The Ottoman Empire's first capital, Bursa, nestles at the foot of Mount Uludağ. A packed day gives you time to savor ancient and modern delights, from bejeweled sultans' tombs to traditional puppet shows, ending with Bursa's famous *Iskender kebap*. START: **Bus to Ulu Camii.**

① ★★ Ulu Camii (Great Mosque).

The largest Ottoman mosque built before the conquest of Istanbul is typical of early Seljuk Turkish architecture. Built in 1400 by Ali Naccar, its interior is beautifully decorated with bold, black calligraphic designs, outstanding against plain cream walls. I love the 16-sided white marble *şadırvan* (fountain for ritual ablutions) which, unusually, lies inside. Apparently, it was so built because when land for the mosque was purchased, one woman refused to sell and her house was taken by force. As a mosque cannot be built on land not given willingly, the fountain was built on the spot of her house. Uniquely, the mosque has 20 arches—four rows of five—supported by 12 arches. This is said to originate to Sultan Bayezid I's vow to build 20 mosques after winning the Battle of Nicopolis in 1396. But, perhaps realizing the rashness of his promise, he adapted it so that each single dome could "represent" a mosque. ⏱ *30 min. Atatürk Cad. Open dawn–dusk.*

② ★★ Koza Han.

This *caravanserai* (literally meaning Cocoon Inn) is the centerpiece of **Kapalı Carşısı** (Grand Bazaar). An international trading center since the 15th century, the silk market was the location of healthy trade between merchants when Bursa was the final stop on the Silk Road from China. Even today, tiny stores surrounding the cafe-filled courtyard do a thriving business in multicolored silk scarves and clothing (although much is now imported). Enjoy a glass of tea in the courtyard peppered with ancient

Bursa's Great Mosque.

plane trees and watch the world go by. The cocoon auction takes place late June/early July, bringing silk-breeders from around the world to sell their valuable wares. ⏱ *1 hr.*

③ ★★ Tombs of Orhan & Osman Gazi.

The tombs of the Ottoman state's original founders are located inside the tiny **Tophane Park.** After conquering Bursa, Osman Gazi (Osman I) was the founder and first sultan of the empire that was finally established in 1326. It is thought that his deathbed wish, made to his son Orhan, was to be buried "under that silver dome—Bursa will be the city where our throne stands." Almost 7 centuries later, it's fascinating to remember those words when gazing at their ornate tombs. Osman's tomb dazzles with mother-of-pearl casing

Tophane Park's most noticeable landmark is the clock tower.

and embroidered cover and I love its subtly colored mosaic floor, Byzantine remnants from the Monastery of Prophet Elijah. A few meters away, inside a separate structure, is that of his son. Both tombs were constructed in 1863 by Sultan Abdülaziz, replacing earlier ones destroyed by fire and an earthquake. The park's most noticeable landmark is the 35m-high (115 ft.) five-floor clock tower, built as a fire watchtower in 1905. Outside the park, pastel-colored restored Ottoman houses lie around Kale Sokak, near the hisar (castle) entrance.

④ ★★ Yeşil Türbe (Green Tomb).

It's a pleasant walk east from the bazaar area over the Gök Dere river to the Yeşil neighborhood. Marking a change in the architectural style (from Seljuk to Turkish), the hexagonal mausoleum of Sultan Mehmed I (1382–1421) was built by Hacı Ivaz Paşa (who also designed the mosque, ⑤). Its distinctive appearance is thanks to the green–blue tiles cladding the exterior which were added to the tiles from Kütahya after the 1855 earthquake. Enter through the carved wooden doors to the richly tiled interior, with scriptures and brightly colored flower designs echoing the mosque's interior. Of the eight tombs, Mehmed's, on a raised central platform, is of course the most magnificent. Restored in 2008, the building is a distinctive sight, especially among the pretty cypress trees. ⏱ *15 min. Open daily 9am–5pm.*

⑤ ★★ Yeşil Camii (Green Mosque).

Lying opposite Yeşil Türbe, this is one of the main jewels in Bursa's crown. One of many important buildings damaged in the devastating 1855 earthquake, its central doorway is surrounded by intricate carved marble stonework, a typical Timurid feature. For such a famous mosque (one of the finest Ottoman creations), it's surprisingly small but, boy, what detail. Look out for the colorful glazed tiles, the densely decorated *mihrab* (niche pointing to Mecca) and the triangular squinches (known as "Turkish triangles") supporting the dome. Closed for major restoration at the time of research. ⏱ *15 min.*

Getting There & Around

The best way to Bursa is by fast ferry from Yenikapı to Yalova (70 min; 20 TL single), then minibus to Bursa bus terminal (30 min; 10 TL). Bus 38 takes you to the center; ask for Ulu Camii. The best way to get around is by *dolmuş*, a comfortable white shared taxi with the *dolmuş* sign on the roof. Routes are fixed, with journeys costing 1.50–2 TL; make sure you're on the correct road then flag down a cab, and call out your destination to the driver. For an overnight stay, try the quaint **Safran Otel** (Arka Sok 4, off Ortapazar Cad, ☎ 0224 224 7216, www.safranotel.com) in a restored Ottoman house. To submerge in warm mineral pools in the Çekirge district, the 5-star **Marigold Thermal & Spa Hotel** (1 Murat Cad 47, ☎ 0444 4000, www.marigold.com.tr) has luxury facilities.

6 ★ kids **D'Or.** Opened in early 2011, this slick little cafe serves home-made organic dishes, from hearty breakfasts to fried eggplant and delicious home-made baklava. It also sells organic honey, herbs, olive oil, and teas from all over Turkey. *4 Müze Sok.* ☎ *0224 327 9098. Turkish breakfast 10 TL.*

7 ★ **Türk ve Islam Eserleri Müzesi (Museum of Turkish and Islamic Arts).** Housed in the original *medrese* in the mosque complex, the museum's tiny rooms surround the courtyard. You'll see the first coins produced by the Bursa mint after Orhan Gazi's conquest of Bursa in 1477, and 13th-century ceramics. One of my favorites is the calligraphy room, with an enormous, highly decorated 14th-century Qur'an, plus accoutrements such as the original ink sets. ⏱ *40 min. Admission free. Open Tues–Sun 9:30am–5pm.*

8 ★ kids **Teleferik to Uludağ.** Depending on the weather, take a cable-car trip up the mountain, either for skiing and snowboarding (Dec–Apr) or, in the warmer months,

for gorgeous walks in Uludağ National Park. The ski center has decent facilities for a brief stay, or just a day trip, with equipment hire, ski trainers, and hotels. *Cable car departs approx every 30 min*

Orhan Gazi's tomb, Tophane Park.

Healing Waters

Since Roman times, Bursa has been a magnet for those seeking the curative waters of its thermal springs. Today, the Çekirge neighborhood on Bursa's western side has luxury hotels with their own spas, making the most of the warm mineral-rich spring mountain waters flowing from Uludağ. Alternatively, head to a traditional *hamam* such as **Eski Kaplica, Yeni Kaplica,** or **Kukurtlu Kaplica**—believed to cure everything from leprosy to syphilis and obesity.

8am–10pm with halfway stop at Kadıyayla; 10 TL return.

⑨ ★★ Muradiye Complex. This peaceful courtyard complex, built by Murat II (the "Muradiye") in 1426, the last Ottoman Sultan reigning in the city, is one of my favorite Bursa sites. Inside there's a mosque, medrese, hospice, *hamam*, and tombs built for him and his relatives. Inside Murat II's tomb, look up to

Cafe D'Or for organic food.

the hole in the dome allowing rain to fall on his tomb, as he had wished. One of the most striking tombs is that of Şezahde Mustafa and Cem Sultan, having the earliest-known Iznik tiles. 🕐 *1 hr.*

⑩ ★★ kids Karagöz Müzesi. Traditional shadow puppetry, for which Bursa is famed, is honored in this new museum. According to legend, Karagöz dates back to two construction workers, Karagöz and Hacivat, building Orhan Gazi mosque in 1396. They entertained their workmates with comedy routines, causing hilarity—and also time-wasting, which led the enraged sultan to order the beheading of the two men. Two centuries later, the two formed the basis of puppetry "soap opera," humorous stories performed with hand-painted flat puppets typically in mosques and public spaces during the Ramazan fasting month. At the museum, characters from these stories are explained, accompanied by modern-day wooden models. The second exhibition room has 200-year-old hand-painted puppets made with camel skin and traditional musical instruments used in performances. Kids love the puppet shows performed downstairs in the little theater; even though the narration is in Turkish, you can get the gist of its comic value (on weekdays, most of the

The tomb of Şezahde Mustafa in the Muradiye Complex.

audience is giggling local primary school kids). Across the road, don't miss the huge **Karagöz and Haciabat Monumental Grave.** *Tip:* If you want to buy puppets to take home, visit one of Bursa's most famous Karagöz "practitioners": Şinasi Çelikkol at his antique shop in the covered market (12 Eski Aynaliç Çarşı). ⏰ *1 hr. Çekirge Cad.* ☎ *0224 233 8429. Open Tues–Sun 9:30am–5:30pm. Adult 5 TL.*

⑪ ★ kids Uluumay Osmanlı Kıyafetleri ve Takıları Müzesi (Ottoman Folk Costumes and Jewelry Museum). A real labor of love, local septuagenarian Esat Uluumay, once a prize-winning folk dancer, displays his personal collection of Ottoman traditional costume from countries including Iraq and Yemen. Kitschly mounted on rotating pedestals, there's enormous variety in the 400-odd displays. They include silk religious garb from the Armenian Catholic church, an Ottoman judge's outfit, 19th-century bridalwear from Skopje, and folk-dancing outfits from 19th-century Kosovo. His collection of jewelry is astounding—look out for chains that (apparently) inspired Madonna's stylist for her 1992 tour, and filigree headdresses. If Mr Esat is around, he'll gladly give you a tour. ⏰ *1 hr. II Murat Cad, Şair Ahmetpaşa Medresesi.* ☎ *0224 222 7575. Admission 5 TL. Open daily 9am–6pm (Mon 1–6pm).*

⑫ ★★ kids Kebapçı Iskender. This is the most famous place to taste Bursa's specialty kebap, from the direct descendants of its creator: Sliced lamb served on bread, slathered with browned butter. Delicious! *Ünlü Cad 7.* ☎ *221 4615. Iskender kebap 8 TL.*

Edirne

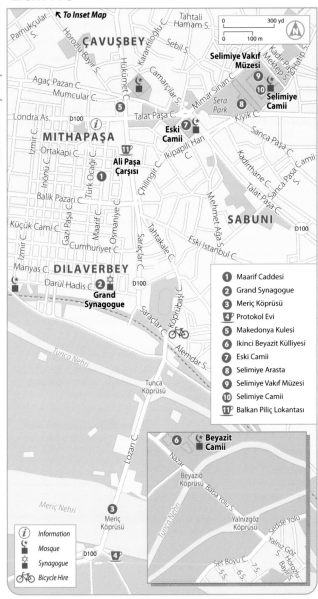

1 Maarif Caddesi
2 Grand Synagogue
3 Meriç Köprüsü
4 Protokol Evi
5 Makedonya Kulesi
6 Ikinci Beyazit Külliyesi
7 Eski Camii
8 Selimiye Arasta
9 Selimiye Vakıf Müzesi
10 Selimiye Camii
11 Balkan Piliç Lokantası

Beyazit Camii

i Information
Mosque
Synagogue
Bicycle Hire

Once the capital of the Ottoman Empire, Edirne sits strategically near the Greek and Bulgarian borders; today, it's best known for the Selimiye Mosque and Kırkpınar oil-wrestling festival. It's one of my favorite Turkish cities—smaller and more relaxed than Istanbul, with most places of interest clustered in the center easily reached on foot. START: **Hürriyet Meydanı.**

1 ★ kids Maarif Caddesi. In the street running south from Hürriyet Meydanı, there's a charming collection of traditional *Türkevi* (Turkish wooden houses) for which the city is renowned. Head down to **Kırkpınar Evi** on the right, a restored house-museum exhibiting the history of Edirne's traditional oil wrestling (p 156). Opening hours are erratic, unfortunately, as there are lovely exhibits of this traditional sporting event, held just outside Edirne's center. If it's closed, peek into the gardens for a taster, with noble statues of past *başpehlivans* (head wrestlers) and *ağa* (wealthy tournament benefactors). 🕐 *45 min (if open).*

2 ★ Grand Synagogue. What's left of Edirne's only synagogue is at the southern end of Maarif Caddesi, once populated with Jews who worked in the bazaar. The building suffered major disrepair when the domed ceiling collapsed. During Edirne's huge fire in 1905, 13 synagogues were destroyed and replaced by this one, but no Jewish community exists today. Turn left around the corner at the bottom of the street to see the main gate to visualize its former glory. At the time of writing, repairs to the building. were underway, due to be completed in early 2013. 🕐 *10 min. Maarif Cad.*

3 ★ Meriç Köprüsü (Meriç Bridge). From the synagogue, it's a 15-minute walk down Karaağaç Yolu to the pretty bridge over the Maritza River. Completed in 1847, the 263m-long (863 ft.) stone bridge with 12 pointed arches has drainage ports to prevent the floods that destroyed the previous wooden bridge. Pop into the tiny marble memorial booth halfway along, used as a viewing point, with its decorative painted ceiling. After your tea break (4), if you don't want to walk back, look out for minibuses to the city center.

Walk over the 19th-century Meriç Köprüsü.

Slippery Sport

Statues of wrestlers dot the city, a nod to Edirne's ancient tradition of Kırkpınar *yağli güreş* (oil wrestling) competition, every year in late June/early July. With roots dating back to the 14th century, when Ottoman troops returned from conquest, modern-day wrestlers compete in heavy leather breeches, their bodies covered in olive oil. The 3-day tournament takes place a few miles outside the center at Kaleiçi, and has traditional music, excitable crowds, and a spirit of genuine humility, tradition, and ceremony. The winner of each level, determined by weight, wins cash prizes, with the heavyweight (*başpehlivan*) also winning a golden belt. The festival is popular, so if you're planning to attend, book your hotel and bus tickets in good time.

Edirne's iconic wrestlers caught in a grapple.

4 ★★ **kids** **Protokol Evi.** Once the police station, this restored house over the bridge is now a charming council-run cafe. Take a table at the terrace's edge for a perfect view of Selimiye Mosque with a glass of tea. *Lozan Cad.* ☎ *0284 2233 282.*

5 ★★★ **kids** **Makedonya Kulesi.** Also known as Saat Kulesi (Clock Tower), this landmark, built in 1894, is now part of an "archeological park" excavated in 2003. The park's main external wall is a mix of Roman, Byzantine, and Ottoman construction, with remains of a 10th-century Byzantine church and fresco, plus late-Roman pottery ovens. Spot fragments of Ottoman human bones embedded in the foliage-covered southern wall, once the cemetery. The Roman wall used no cement, and still has rivets marking where iron bars were used to connect it. If the gate is locked, ask in the cafe opposite for a key. A fantastic discovery. ⏱ *45 min. Mumcular Sok. Admission free. Daily 8:30am–6pm.*

Look out for bones at Makedonya Kulesi.

More astounding when you take into account that this was the 15th century, an era when the world cast out, and burned, the mentally ill. It used progressive therapies such as musicians playing on a stage and a fountain providing soothing sounds. Most interesting is the hospital's revolutionary design, an octagonal ward for high efficiency with few staff, and a sloping floor to catch the fountain's overflow. Check out the exhibition on eye-watering 16th-century Ottoman medical procedures—not for the faint-hearted!
⏱ *90 min. Admission 10 TL, children under 8 years free. Open daily 9am–5pm.*

6 ★★★ Ikinci Beyazit Külliyesi (Beyazit II Complex). It's a little far to walk, so pick up a minibus from opposite the tourist office. North of the city, this *külliye* (mosque complex), comprising originally a mosque, kitchens, hospital, and school, is a real treasure. Highlight is the award-winning **Museum of Health,** in the former psychiatric hospital. Its superb displays reveal the hospital's groundbreaking treatment of its patients, with care and empathy from top-rated doctors.

7 ★★ Eski Camii (Old Mosque). With room for 3,000 worshippers, Edirne's oldest Ottoman monument, completed in 1414 under Mehmet I, has a striking interior dominated by the huge Arabic calligraphy of "Allah" and "Mohammed" on its walls. Built in a perfect square, each of its nine domes—in the style of Ulu Camii in Bursa (p 149)—is 13m (43 ft.) in diameter. Look out for the small piece of stone from Mecca encased in glass, on the wall near the *minbar* (pulpit). Outside on the left is a statue of

Practical Matters

Speedy, comfortable buses run from Istanbul's bus station to Edirne, the 250km (155 miles) taking 2½ hours. Allow extra time for the *servis*, the free shuttle minibus service collecting passengers from various points to the *otogar*; the ticket office will inform you where and when (*Savvy Traveler*, p 159). On arrival at Edirne, jump on a minibus to Hürriyet Meydanı or Selimiye Camii. For a full-day trip, try to depart around 7am, and buy your return ticket to leave late evening. **Edirne Tourist Office,** 17 Hürriyet Meydanı (☎ 0284 213 9208) has helpful staff and maps. If you'd like to cycle, check out the bicycle hire shop **Diramalılar Motorsiklet & Bisiklet** behind the sports stadium (☎ 0543 294 5868).

pehlivans (wrestlers), an Edirne emblem. 🕐 *30 min. Corner of Talatpaşa Aşfaltı and Londra Aşfaltı. Open daily dawn–dusk.*

8 ★ Selimiye Arasta. Like many markets of this era, this was founded as a charitable establishment for the Selimiye Mosque. Its 73-arches layout dates back over five centuries—its fruit-shaped soap and fridge magnets less than that. The piles of cheap shoes are a reminder that part of this market was the "ready-made Shoe-Makers' Bazaar," as recorded by Evlia Celebi, the prolific writer and traveler (1611–82). Merchants in past centuries swore an oath in the mosque that their transactions would be honest. *Selimiye Camii complex. Admission free. Open daily 9am–dusk.*

9 ★★ kids Selimiye Vakıf Müzesi (Selimiye Foundation Museum). Opened in 2007, this smart museum occupies the Dar'ul Kurra *medrese* (religious school) adjacent to **Selimiye Camii** built by Sinan in 1575. It's laid out around a square garden, using individual classrooms for different themes. Most displays specialize in Ottoman crafts such as calligraphy and ornate brassware and if you're a fan of inlaid wood, you'll love the 18th-century wooden Qur'an stands and tables inlaid with mother-of-pearl. Walk around the museum counter-clockwise and you finish at the Qur'an room, with realistic life-size models of a Qur'an class. 🕐 *1 hr. Selimiye Külliyesi, Sarul Kurra Medresi.* ☎ *0284 212 1133. Admission free. Open Tues–Sun 9am–5pm.*

10 ★★★ Selimiye Camii (Selimiye Mosque). Why not save the best till last? Wonder-architect Mimar Sinan did, completing this aged 80 in 1575. He regarded it as his finest creation and symbol of the Ottoman state. (It's also been

Sinan's masterpiece: Selimiye Camii.

nominated for UNESCO World Heritage Status.) Through the main entrance, you pass the impressive statue of the architect, indicating the reverence Edirne held for him. The four pencil-slim minarets are dazzling, each 71m (233 ft.) high with three ornate balconies. In the middle of the courtyard lies the 16-sided *şadırvan* (ablutions fountain, where men wash before praying). Inside, the plain walls mean that your eyes are drawn up to the 40m-high (131 ft.) dome, covered with intricate painted designs in blue and deep red. Take a close look at the ornately carved marble *minbar* with tiled top, plus the gold, exquisite Iznik tiles, and mother-of-pearl used throughout. 🕐 *1 hr. Mimar Sinan Cad. Open daily dawn–dusk; no entry at prayer time.*

11 ★ Balkan Piliç Lokantası. This no-nonsense eatery is handily placed in Edirne's center on a pleasant pedestrianized street. It serves tasty (and cheap) chicken dishes and hearty soups. *Saraçlar Cad 14.* ☎ *0284 225 2155. Main course 10 TL.* ●

Before You Go

Government Tourist Offices

In the U.S.: 821 UN Plaza, New York, NY 10017 (☎ **212 687 2194**); 2525 Massachusetts Avenue, Washington, DC 20008 (☎ **202 612 6800**); 5055 Wilshire Boulevard Suite 850, Los Angeles, CA 90036 (www.tourismturkey.org). **In the U.K.:** 4/F 29–30 St. James's St, London SW1A 1HB (☎ **020 7839 7778**, www.gototurkey.co.uk).

The Best Times to Go

May to June and **September to October** have a comfortable temperature (daytime 16°–25°C/61°–77°F) and many events. During hot, humid August, some top hotels offer discounts due to fewer business visitors, and many Istanbullus head to the south coast for holidays.

Business and opening hours alter during **Ramazan** (the month-long fasting from dawn to dusk). The Islamic lunar calendar is used, so its date moves approximately 11 days annually. Ramazan for 2012 begins July 20, and July 9 in 2013 (estimated). During this month, avoid eating, drinking, or smoking in the street out of respect for those fasting. Smaller restaurants, especially in conservative neighborhoods, may close all day; all places are generally busy for *iftar* (meal to break the fast) especially in Sultanahmet Park, a favorite for picnicking locals. Outside nightlife areas of Beyoğlu, Ortaköy, etc., some bars close for the whole month. During the two biggest religious festivals, **Şeker Bayram** (3-day festival marking the end of Ramazan) and **Kurban Bayram** (Feast of Sacrifice, 10 weeks later), many attractions and shops close for 2 days. Hotels and flights fill up in advance and are more expensive, and generally many people travel to, and from, Istanbul to visit family.

Festivals & Special Events

Most art and cultural festivals are organized by **Istanbul Kültür Sanat Vakfı** (Istanbul Foundation for Culture and Arts, ☎ **0212 334 0700**, www.iksv.org). **Pozitif** (☎ **0212 334 0100,** www.pozitif. info) organizes funky music events in the city. Most, including music, festivals and sports, can be booked at **Biletix** (various outlets inc Istiklal Kitabevi, 55 Istiklal Cad, www.biletix. com.tr.).

SPRING. The cultural year kicks off with **Istanbul International Film Festival** for 2 weeks in April with old, new, Turkish, and international films (with English subtitles) plus awards to honor top Turkish films and directors. Screened in six cinemas, mainly in Beyoğlu, tickets sell out fast. May's 3-week **International Istanbul Theater Festival** is a mix of overseas theater and dance companies, plus new productions from around Turkey. Performances take place at venues ranging from Hagia Eirene to tiny stages at museums. In May, music-lovers flock to the **Chill Out Festival** (www.chilloutfest.com) organized by Lounge 102 FM at Kemer Golf & Country Club, a 12-hour fest from jazz and funk to soul and hip-hop.

SUMMER. Since 2005, usually in May, the **Formula 1 Istanbul Grand Prix** at Istanbul Park attracts worldwide petrol-heads to the city's Asian outskirts. (Istanbul Park, Göçbeyli Köyü Yolu, ☎ **0216 677 1039**; www.istanbulparkcircuit.com.) June's 2-day music festival **One Love** (www.pozitif-ist.com) (formerly

Previous page: Istanbul sign posts.

AVERAGE TEMPERATURE AND RAINFALL IN ISTANBUL

	°C (LOW)	°C (HIGH)	°F (LOW)	°F (HIGH)	RAINFALL (CM)
Jan	3	8	37	46	10.9
Feb	3	9	36	48	9.2
Mar	3	11	37	52	7.2
Apr	7	16	45	61	4.6
May	9	22	48	54	3.8
June	16	25	61	77	3.4
July	18	28	64	82	3.4
Aug	19	29	66	84	3.0
Sept	16	24	61	75	5.8
Oct	13	20	55	68	8.1
Nov	9	15	48	59	10.3
Dec	5	11	41	52	11.9

known as Efes Pilsen One Love) has put on artists as varied as Gogol Bordello, Black Eyed Peas, and the Beastie Boys at an outdoor venue. The **International Istanbul Music Festival** (3 weeks in June, www.iksv. org/muzik) showcases over 500 artists, with over 20 performances from symphony orchestras and baroque music ensembles. Best are those performed at historic venues like the Archaeology Museum's gardens. **Istanbul Pride Week** (www. prideistanbul.org) in late June incorporates LGBT cultural events and meetings in various venues culminating in the march, growing in numbers since the first in 2003. The prestigious **International Istanbul Jazz Festival** (2 weeks in June, www.iksv.org/caz) has seen the likes of Herbie Hancock and Al Jarreau gracing the stages of jazz clubs and parks. **Rock 'n' Coke** (www. rockncoke.com) is Turkey's largest open-air music festival, attracting 50,000 with major acts (2011 saw Limp Bizkit and Skunk Anansie), in Hezarfen Airfield, outside the city.

FALL. Istanbul goes arty with Turkey's largest contemporary art show, the **International Istanbul Biennal** (www.iksv.org/bienal) lasting 3 months from September (next one 2013). Run by international guest curators, the city exhibits works by about 100 international artists in various venues. October sees runners compete in the **Istanbul Eurasia Marathon** (www. istanbulmarathon.org), the course passing through two continents. In October or November, **Contemporary Istanbul** (☎ 0212 244 7175, www.contemporaryistanbul.com), a selling fair at the Istanbul Convention and Exhibition Center, incorporates all arts from local and international galleries. Going since 1993, **Akbank Jazz Festival** (www. akbanksanat.com) favors fusion events at hip venues, with Brazilian or Middle Eastern beats, and plenty of Turkish musicians. Everything stops—including pedestrians and traffic—when the siren sounds on November 10 at precisely 9:05am to mark the **Anniversary of Atatürk's death.**

WINTER. **Efes Pilsen Blues Festival** (www.pozitif.info) warms up chilly evenings, with international blues artists performing with local artists, part of a tour through cities in Turkey and Russia. It's time to look to sunnier climes during February's **Eurasia Boat Show** (www.cnravrasya boatshow.com), a major selling fair of all things nautical at CNR Expo.

The Weather

Spring and fall are usually dry and sunny; summers (July–Aug) can be blisteringly hot and humid, not much fun on crowded transport but good to enjoy Bosphorus-front evenings in cafes, restaurants, and nightclubs. Some up-market terrace clubs and restaurants close in winter (mid-Oct–mid-May) or switch to indoor venues. December to February can be cold and wet with occasional snow, usually bringing chaos to the city.

Useful Websites

- **www.whatsonwhen.com**: Excellent events listings for Istanbul, including festivals and exhibitions.

- **www.mymerhaba.com**: Covers all Turkey with practical information, although the What's On section isn't very up to date.

- **www.todayszaman.com**: Online version of *Today's Zaman*, the English-language daily paper started in 2007, with good listings for Istanbul and the way to keep track of the volatile political situation before visiting.

- **www.hurriyetdailynews.com**: Online version of the English-language daily newspaper (formerly *Turkish Daily News*).

- **www.istanbulcityguide.com**: Good profile of the city, and information on music events in the upcoming week.

- **www.biletix.com**: Online booking agent for tickets for concerts, sporting events, and shows, plus details of their outlets.

- **www.iksv.org**: Organizers of the majority of Istanbul's culture and music festivals.

- **www.kultur.gov.tr**: Official website of the Turkish Ministry of Culture and Tourism.

- **www.tourismturkey.org**: Official Turkish tourism site in the U.S.

- **www.gototurkey.co.uk**: Official Turkish tourist site in the U.K.

- **www.pozitif-ist.com**: Listings of funky music events.

- **www.istanbul-ulasim.com.tr**: Official site for Istanbul's public transport, with route maps and ferry times (Turkish only).

- **www.iett.gov.tr**: Another part of the public transport site, with information on modes of transport and route planner (under construction at time of writing).

- **www.turkeytravelplanner. com**: Guide to the country written by U.S. travel writer Tom Brosnahan.

Cellphones (Mobiles)

Most U.K. phones can send and receive calls/SMS, and most tri-band cell phones from the U.S. work here—although roaming charges are expensive. The Turkish government has restricted visitors buying local SIM cards on "unregistered" phones (i.e. those brought from overseas). If it's your first time in Turkey, you can buy a 7-day SIM and have instant access. If not, then you have to register your phone, which can take several days. For longer stays, you can buy a cheap handset in Istanbul and a pay-as-you-go SIM card. Major hotels can help with phone rental. The main Turkish networks are Turkcell (www.turkcell. com.tr), Türk Telekom (www.turk telekom.com.tr), Avea (www.avea. com.tr), and Vodafone (www.voda fone.com.tr); all companies have branches around the city. Stick to Turkcell and Vodafone for your SIM card, and ask for packages for cheap text messages.

Car Rental

Driving in Istanbul is *really* not advisable; traffic jams are a nightmare, fuel is expensive, and public transport and taxis are relatively cheap. Most of all, it takes guts (foolhardiness?) to compete with local drivers. Major car-hire companies have counters at the airport terminals, plus offices around Taksim, although it's cheaper to book online in advance. Prices are comparatively high to back home. Try **Avis** (www.avis.com), **Budget** (www.budget.com), **Hertz** (www.hertz.com), and **National** (www.nationalcar.com); prices can vary wildly. Drivers must be 21 or over. Check the website of **Turkish Touring and Automobile Club** (www.turing.org.tr) for information on driving licenses and permits.

Getting **There**

By Plane

Atatürk International Airport is the main international airport, in Yeşilköy (☎ **0212 463 3000,** www.ataturkairport.com). Major **airlines** flying into Istanbul from the U.S. and U.K. include Turkish Airlines, Delta Airlines, and British Airways. Other U.S. airlines require changing in London or other major European cities. The airport is located 28 km (17 miles) west of the city center.

The **Havaş** airport bus departs from outside the arrivals hall, approximately every 30 minutes between 4am and 1am, ending in Taksim (Cumhuriyet Caddesi), stopping in Aksaray (for Sultanahmet), and Tepebaşı (inform the driver before you board). Tickets cost 11 TL (single), and the journey takes around 40 minutes, depending on traffic. Traveling to the airport, the bus leaves Taksim on the hour (4–7am) and then every half-hour (7:30am–midnight). Regular private minibuses go from Sultanahmet and the Old City (ask at your hotel).

Yellow **taxis** queue outside arrivals; check the meter is switched on (p 165). Fares are approximately 45 TL to Taksim (40 min) and 35 TL to Sultanahmet (30 min).

The cheapest option (great if no luggage!) is by **metro**, changing at Aksaray onto the tram (total 2.90 TL), taking around 50 minutes. The metro runs daily, approx 6am–midnight.

Istanbul's second airport, **Sabiha Gökçen International Airport** (☎ **0216 585 5000,** www.sgairport.com), is in Pendik on the Asian side. You'll land here from London with budget airlines **easyJet** (www.easyjet.com) and Turkish airline **Pegasus** (www.flypgs.com), which also has a great network of domestic flights throughout the country. Located 50km (31 miles) east of the city center, a half-hourly **Havaş** bus service (14 TL) takes approx 1 hour (much longer in traffic) to reach Taksim. The bus leaves the Taksim office every half-hour from 6am.

By Train

Most trains in Turkey (www.tcdd.gov.tr) are much slower, less regular, and cheaper (and in my opinion more pleasant, especially in a first-class sleeper) than the bus (see below). There are daily overnight services to Sofia (15 hours) and other European cities including Bucharest and Budapest departing from **Sirkeci** station. Trains to cities on the Asian side, including Ankara (express taking 5.5 hours), Kayseri, Gaziantep, and Van, plus daily to Iran, leave from **Haydarpaşa** station, near Kadıköy on the Asian side.

By Bus

Comfortable coaches are the preferred way to travel long distance, to other Turkish and European cities. The main bus station (otogar) is in Esenler, but you can book tickets in offices located on İnönü Caddesi in Gümüşsuyu, Sultanahmet, and Beşiktaş, from where private shuttle buses (servis) take you to the otogar. If you arrive in Istanbul by bus, ask the driver for the servis, or take the metro to Aksaray and change to the tram for Sultanahmet or Kabataş/Taksim. As well as national routes, international services include Sofia (8 hr), Thessaloniki (12 hr), and many other European cities. Welcoming extras on board include complimentary refreshments and personal TV/radio screens, and there are regular rest/food stops.

Reputable companies include **Varan** (19B İnönü Cad; ☎ **0212 251 7474**; www.varan.com.tr), **Ulusoy** (59 İnönü Cad; ☎ **444 1 888**; www.ulusoy.com.tr), and **Kamil Koç** (29 İnönü Cad; ☎ **444 0562**; www.kamilkoc.com.tr).

By Car

All roads lead to Istanbul! The highways are fast, new, and usually—unless you're driving into Istanbul on a Sunday evening—reasonably traffic-free. Most highways operate a toll fee of a few liras, not payable in cash; buy a pre-paid card in advance. The downside is that gas (petrol) in Turkey is almost the most expensive in the world, and the roads here are considered some of Europe's most dangerous. The speed limit is (120km/h) on highways. If you bring your own car into Turkey, ensure you have an international driving license, car registration documents, and international green card. (Check www.turing.org.tr for details.)

By Boat

Fast ferries run by IDO (www.ido.com.tr) across the Sea of Marmara to Yalova, connecting by road to cities including Bursa and Iznik. Sea transport to Odessa (Ukraine) and Bodrum (Turkey's south coast) was suspended in 2010.

Getting **Around**

By Public Transport

Istanbul's public transport system, run by IETT (www.iett.gov.tr), is always improving—although the city desperately needs an underground/subway system. An akbil (pay-as-you-go electronic "ticket") is recommended; buy a new one for a 6 TL deposit, then top up with cash (try 10 TL at a time) and "bleep" in as you board the bus, tram, local ferry, or metro. Look out for the white booths labeled "akbil satiş noktasi" at transport hubs including Taksim Square and Eminönü. At 1.65 TL for

each single journey, it is slightly cheaper and far more convenient, and there is a further discount (approx 50%) for connecting services taken within 90 minutes. It's possible to pay the driver in cash on board; some buses have a ticket seller at the front of the bus.

By Tram

The sleek tram (www.istanbul-ulasim.com.tr) from Kabataş to Zeytinburnu is one of the best ways to get around the Old City, with stops including Eminönü (Spice Market),

Sirkeci (train station), Sultanahmet (Blue Mosque), and Beyazit (Grand Bazaar). It crosses Galata Bridge and ends at Kabataş, from where the underground **funicular** goes up to Taksim, connecting with the **metro** (below).

In contrast, the **Nostaljic Tramvey** is a revival of Istanbul's historic tram system, now running from Taksim Square to Tünel. The 1.6-km (1-mile) journey down Istiklal Caddesi (8am–10pm) takes up to 15 minutes. Pay by *akbil* or 1 TL to the driver (they give change). This connects with the historic **Tünel,** one of the world's oldest underground routes, traveling 573m (1,879 ft.) between Karaköy and Tünel's main square (saving the steep uphill hike) between 7am–9pm.

By Taxi

You'll find yellow metered taxis all over Istanbul. Since 2010, there has been no difference between day- and night-time fares. If a driver attempts to fix a price in advance, or says the meter isn't working, don't take the ride (watch out for those around Sultanahmet), and ensure the meter is switched on as your journey starts. Most taxi drivers are decent, although some will try to take the longer, "scenic" route. Tipping is not required, although rounding up a couple of liras is appreciated. Avoid handing over large bills (20 TL or 50 TL) as drivers don't always keep much change—and ensure canny ones don't cheat you by substituting your 50 TL for a 5 TL. Take your hotel card for address details; few drivers speak English.

By Metro

The underground metro travels from Şişhane via Taksim to Hacıosman, passing through Şişli and 4. Levent. On a different line, the light metro

(also underground) runs from Aksaray to Otogar (main bus station) and Atatürk Havalimanı (airport).

By Bus

Most buses are green single-deckers, run by IETT, with hubs including Taksim Square, Eminönü, Beyazit, and Kabataş. There's a journey planner on their site (http://harita.iett.gov.tr). If you don't have an *akbil*, it's possible to pay the driver on boarding. Most services run between 6:30am and 11:30pm. Private blue buses (Özel Halk Otobüsleri) run roughly the same routes; pay cash on boarding. Single journeys are fixed fares of 1.65 TL.

By Boat

The network of fast catamarans, slow passenger ferries, and full-day excursions form an integral part of Istanbul, with routes crisscrossing the Bosphorus, the Golden Horn, and Marmara. From quick trips between Üsküdar and Beşiktaş to an evening sail up the Bosphorus, ferryboats are the most pleasant way to get around. The main departure points are Eminönü, Karaköy, Beş iktaş, and Kabataş on the European side, and Üsküdar and Kadıköy on the Asian. Pay for your journey by *akbil* (p 164) or jeton, except for private day trips on the Bosphorus. (Check www.ido.com.tr, and www. denturavrasya.com for various routes.)

By *Dolmuş* & Minibus

Yellow *dolmuş* (meaning "stuffed") minibuses operate like shared taxis on fixed routes, departing when full. Start and end points are fixed, but you can get off at any point, shouting *"inecek var"* to the driver to stop. You can flag the bus down anywhere on the route. Useful routes include İnönü Caddesi (off Taksim Square) to Teşvikiye, Taksim

The Savvy Traveler

to Aksaray, and Eminönü to Nişantaşı, which run until approx 2am. Fares are payable to the driver. Blue-and-white minibuses operate on longer distances from fixed points; look out for the big "D" sign by bus stops. A useful service runs between Beşiktaş and Sarıyer.

On Foot

Istanbul is best seen on foot, especially around the Old City and Beyoğlu. Watch out for the traffic, as Istanbul drivers have scant regard for cross-walks (zebra crossings), often make turns without looking out for pedestrians, and never use their indicators.

Fast **Facts**

ACCOMMODATION   Istanbul is geared to both tourists and business travelers, so the city has plenty of beds, from Ottoman-style traditional guesthouses to high-end international hotel chains. The number of suite hotels (almost self-contained apartments) and contemporary boutique hotels has shot up. Prices have increased substantially in recent years, now on a par with many European cities—Istanbul isn't the bargain it once was! For longer stays, look for good deals on apartments and suites (p 166). For short-term rental try ☎ **0212 251 8530,** www.istanbulholidayapartments. com; from U.S. and Canada ☎ **1-800-753-2877** (toll-free). Longer-term rental is available at www. istanbulrentals.com (☎ **0212 638 1215**). Don't arrange hotels on arrival at the airport, or from touts in the arrivals hall, as you're likely to get ripped off.

ATMS/EXCHANGE   Maestro, Cirrus, MasterCard, and Visa are accepted at **ATMs,** although some machines only deal with Turkish banks. Major banks may deal with American Express. *Döviz* (exchange bureaus) accept all major international currencies. Dotted around Istiklal Caddesi, Divanyolu in Sultanahmet up to Beyazit, and the Grand Bazaar, they don't charge commission. Count the notes out in front of the cashier to

prevent "errors." Banks usually charge a small commission to change money, often a bureaucratic process. Traveler's checks, although rare these days, are exchanged at banks, with commission.

BANKS   Banks open Monday to Friday 9am to 5pm; some close 12:30 to 1:30pm.

BUSINESS HOURS   Most stores open daily 10am–7pm, with many around Istiklal Caddesi open until 9pm; some small, independent stores close on Sundays. Most galleries and museums close on Mondays. Offices generally operate Monday–Friday, 9am–5pm.

CLOTHING   Men and women should avoid wearing shorts above the knee, and singlets (vest tops). For mosque visits, women will be given gowns to cover up if their clothing is revealing; carry a light wrap suitable to cover the hair and upper arms when necessary. Women wearing skimpy clothes are more likely to get unwanted attention, especially in the Old City. On a night out in Beyoğlu or Ortaköy, anything goes!

CONSULATES & EMBASSIES   **U.S. Consulate,** 2 Uçşehitler Sokaği, Istiniye, ☎ **0212 335 9000,** http:// istanbul.usconsulate.gov. **Canadian Consulate,** 16/F Tekfen Tower, 209 Büyükdere Cad, Levent 4, ☎ **0212 385 9700,** http://turkey.gc.ca. **U.K. Consulate,** 34 Meşrutiyet Cad,

Tepebaşı, ☎ **0212 334 6400,** http://ukinturkey.fco.gov.uk. **Irish Consulate,** 417 Meridyen İş Merkezi, Ali Riza Gurcan Cad, Merter, ☎ **0212 482 2434,** www. dfa.ie. **Australian Consulate,** 16/F Suzer Plaza, 15 Elmadağ Askerocaği Cad, Şişli, ☎ **0212 243 1333,** www. dfat.gov.au. **New Zealand Consulate,** 48 İnönü Cad, Taksim, ☎ **0212 244 0272,** www.nzembassy.com.

CREDIT CARDS Withdraw cash in Turkish liras from all ATMs with credit or Visa debit cards, usually with a commission of 2–4% (depending on your bank's rates). All hotels and restaurants (except the most basic) accept credit cards, especially Visa and MasterCard; fewer take American Express or Diners Club.

A PIN is required when using credit cards at all outlets. To report **lost or stolen** cards from Turkey **for U.S. card-holders:** American Express ☎ **001-715 343 7977;** Visa ☎ **00-800-13-535-0900;** MasterCard ☎ **00-800-13-887-0903.** For **U.K. card-holders:** Visa ☎ **00-800-13-535-0900.**

CUSTOMS It is forbidden to export genuine antiquities from Turkey. Bear this in mind if buying older goods (e.g. a carpet) and ask the dealer a certificate of authenticity (and get a receipt for all expensive items over $100). Check www. gumruk.gov.tr for details. It is officially forbidden to import any electronic items not for personal use.

DENTIST American Hospital and German Hospital (see "Hospitals") both have dental clinics.

DRUGS Don't even think of buying, taking, possessing, importing, or exporting any illegal drugs into Turkey. Possession of any illegal drugs (including cannabis) is considered a serious offence, with high penalties and harsh police treatment.

ELECTRICITY The current is 220 AC, 50Hz, with standard European-style two-pin plugs. Adaptors can be bought locally, or bring a multi-purpose traveling adaptor from home. U.S. visitors may need a voltage converter for laptops.

EMERGENCIES For ambulance ☎ **112;** Police ☎ **155;** Fire ☎ **110;** Traffic Police ☎ **154.**

GAY & LESBIAN TRAVELERS Istanbul is home to gay (and gay-friendly) bars and clubs (p 120), with increasingly liberal attitudes. Homosexuality is actually legal in Turkey, although generally not tolerated in this conservative country. In mid-2008, local courts shut down the human-rights organization **Lambdaistanbul** (LGBT Solidarity Association), organizers of Gay Pride, but it was reinstated after an appeal (Tel Sok 28/5; off Istiklal Cad; ☎ **0212 245 7068;** www.lambdaistanbul. org). **Mor Kedi** and **Sugarclub Café** (p 120) are both good meeting and information points for gay and lesbian visitors. The Gay Pride march culminates in a week of activities, usually held in June (www. prideistanbul.org).

HEALTH Even the locals don't drink tap water, so stick to bottled or filtered water. No inoculations are necessary for Istanbul. Avoid the mussels sold on street-carts— unless you have a cast-iron gut. If you have an upset stomach, stick to yogurt and plain rice, and black tea with sugar. If things get worse, visit the *eczane* (pharmacy) (p 168).

HOLIDAYS Public holidays: January 1 (New Year's Day), April 23 (National Sovereignty and Children's Day), May 19 (Atatürk Commemoration and Youth Sports Day), August 30 (Victory Day), October 29 (Republic Day). In addition, first 2 days of Şeker Bayram (from Aug 19 in 2012; Aug 8 in 2013) and Kurban Bayram (from Oct 28, 2012; Oct 15, 2013).

HOSPITALS For advice, call the Hospital Information Hotline on ☎ **0212 444 0911.** Some of the best private hospitals, with English-speaking staff, include **American Hospital**, Güzelbahçe Sok, Nişantaşı (☎ **444 3 777,** www.american hospitalistanbul.com); **German Hospital,** 119 Sıraselviler Cad, Taksim (☎ **0212 293 2150,** www.almanhastanesi.com.tr). Bring your credit card; payment is required at the time of treatment, with reimbursement through your insurance company.

INSURANCE Check your existing policies before you buy travel insurance to cover trip cancellation, lost luggage, theft, and medical expenses. Recommended U.S. insurers include **Access America** (☎ **1-800-284-8300,** www.access america.com); **Travel Assistance International** (☎ **800-821-2828,** www.travelassistance.com); and for medical insurance **MEDEX Assistance** (☎ **1-800-732 5309,** www.medexassist.com). Other travelers should shop around for the best deal from back home, and remember that **EHIC** cards for subsidized or free hospital treatment are not valid in Turkey, which is outside the E.U. Bring ID and credit cards in case you need emergency medical treatment.

INTERNET Most hotel rooms have Wi-Fi or cable Internet. Basic Internet cafes dot Beyoğlu and Sultanahmet; look for the "Internet" sign often in a window on the 3rd or 4th floor (approx 2 TL per hour), many with Skype facilities. Watch out for the different keyboard with Turkish characters (ç, ş, ı, etc.) when typing in Web addresses and passwords.

LOST PROPERTY If your credit cards are stolen, call your card company immediately and file a report with the police (p 167). If anything is lost or stolen, including your passport, go to the Tourist Police (below), who will help you fill out the necessary forms.

MAIL & POSTAGE Post offices—PTT—have prominent yellow-and-black signs, usually open Monday to Friday 9am to 5pm; the main office at Sirkeci (**Büyük Posthane Cad**) is open daily. Other useful branches are Yeniçarşı Cad, Galatasaray and 2 Cumhuriyet Cad, Taksim. PTT branches are the only places to buy postage stamps.

MONEY The currency of Turkey is the **Türk Lirası** (Turkish Lira) or TL. This replaced the old lira (TL) in 2005, knocking six zeros off the old notes (at that stage $1 = TL1,400,000!). Banknotes come in denominations of 5, 10, 20, 50, and 100 TL. The lira is divided into 100 kuruş; coins come in 1, 5, 10, 25, 50 kuruş and 1 TL. At the time of writing, $1 = 1.6 TL; £1 = 2.6 TL; €1 = 2.3 TL.

NEWSPAPERS & MAGAZINES English-language newspapers include *Hürriyet Daily News* (www.hurriyet dailynews.com) formerly the *Turkish Daily News;* and *Today's Zaman* (www.todayszaman.com). The monthly magazine *Time Out Istanbul* has arts and entertainment listings, available in larger bookstores and newsstands. *The Guide* (www.theguideistanbul.com) is a bi-monthly, mini-directory of restaurants, nightlife, and shops.

PASSPORTS It is compulsory to carry ID in Turkey at all times, so for tourists this means passports. Police carry out occasional spot checks, especially in bars, and if you don't have ID, you may even be taken to the police station. Leave a photocopy of your passport photo page and Turkish visa (p 170) in your hotel. Contact your consulate (p 166) if you lose your passport.

PHARMACIES There are pharmacies (*Eczane*) around the city, especially near the hospitals in Taksim (p 168). Local pharmacies take turns to provide a 24-hour service (*nobetci*), the address of which is posted on the windows. Some close on Sundays. Pharmacists provide basic medical services and sell some medication without prescription. Those in Beyoğlu and Sultanahmet probably speak some English.

POLICE   For emergencies ☎ **155;** Traffic police ☎ **154;** Tourist police: Yerebatan Caddesi, opposite Yerebatan Sarnıçı ☎ **0212 527 4503.**

SAFETY   Violent crime is rare in Istanbul, but minor, opportunistic crime exists. Watch your bags at all times, and be wary of pickpockets in crowded major sights and on public transport. You often see young solvent-sniffers asking for money on quiet Beyoğlu streets at night—walk briskly past. Avoid walking along unlit streets at night alone.

SMOKING   The smoking ban hit Turkey in July 2009, when all bars, restaurants, shops, and taxis were made smoke-free. Although this law is adhered to in most major hotels and restaurants, with a fine imposed for those breaking it, it's noticeable that things are definitely more relaxed in many bars and clubs (p 115).

TAXES   Turkish value-added tax (KDV) is 18% on most goods—8% on food—and included in the price. Foreign visitors can reclaim tax on all goods costing over 100 TL at shops with the "Tax Free Shopping" sign; ask for a full VAT receipt. This can be processed at the airport and a refund made in cash (Turkish liras) or to your credit card, with a small deduction. For more information, contact Global Refund Turkey, 29 Ferah Sokak, Teşvikiye. ☎ **0212 232 1121.** www.globalrefund.com.

TELEPHONES   For national telephone enquiries ☎ **118;** international operator ☎ **115.** The local code for Istanbul is ☎ 0212 for the European side and ☎ 0216 for the Asian side. Include the local code for all calls made within Istanbul. To dial Istanbul from overseas: ☎ 001 (or 00 from UK) + 90 (Turkey code) + 212 (or 216) + 7-digit local number. Public telephones only take cards; for local calls use a regular **telefon kartı,** which is inserted into the phone; for cheaper mobile and international calls buy a pre-paid discount calling card, scratch off the PIN and dial the access phone number. Use these in your hotel room to minimize extortionate phone charges, especially for overseas calls. Kiosks by public phones sell all types of cards, or buy from *bakkal* (grocery stores).

TIME ZONE   Turkey is 2 hours ahead of GMT, and 3 hours ahead between last weekend of March to last weekend of October.

TIPPING   Top restaurants usually include service charge (*servis dahil*) on your check, especially at hotels, but if service is good add an extra 5%, especially as many waiting staff survive on tips. If not included, leave a tip of around 10% at bars that give table service. Leave small change in teahouses. It's not necessary to tip cab drivers, just round up to the nearest lira. Pay tour guides about 10% if they are good, caretakers at mosques a few liras.

TOILETS (RESTROOMS)   Most toilets (*tuvalet*) in restaurants and bars are clean, and public lavatories usually have an attendant. Expect to pay between 50 Ks to 1 TL, and take the toilet paper if offered! The most basic ones (in parks and mosques) are squat toilets, with a flush or a tap. A pack of tissues and wet wipes is always handy to carry around. All mosques have a basic toilet.

TOURIST INFORMATION   **Atatürk International Airport** arrivals hall; **Sirkeci station** (to the left of the main entrance) ☎ **0212 511 5888; Sultanahmet Meydani** (square) ☎ 0212 518 1802; **opp Hilton Hotel** (Elmadağ) ☎ **0212 233 0592.** Merkez Caddesi, 1/F, no 6 (opp Atatürk Kültür Merkezi, Taksim Square) ☎ **0212 2465 313).** Unfortunately, the service and knowledge is poor at most offices, but at least you can pick up a free city map.

TRAVELERS WITH DISABILITIES With so many steep, cobbled, and narrow streets, Istanbul is difficult to get around in a wheelchair. Fortunately, access is improving, with lifts at all metro stations and easy access onto trams and some buses. Most hotels have elevators and disabled access rooms, although some "boutique" Ottoman and traditional hotels do not; check before booking.

VISAS U.S. and E.U. passport holders get a visa on arrival at the airport—head to the Visa counter just before immigration. Pay in cash only (dollars, euros, or pounds, depending on your nationality). Most visas are 3-month multiple entry (work forbidden). Check the Turkish Embassy in your country for costs to ensure you have adequate cash. At the time of writing, a visa for a British passport was £15, U.S. passport $20.

WOMEN Turkish men are renowned Romeos, so tread carefully. Traveling alone or in women-only groups can attract more attention, some of it unwanted. If you wish to discourage it, say you're married, and be firm but polite if hassling gets too much. Aksaray has pockets of red-light districts and "girlie bars" and can warrant hisses and too-close proximity; avoid eye contact and give these guys a wide berth. Long blonde hair attracts attention—if it all gets too much, tie it back or cover it up with a scarf or hat. Making a scene and getting the attention of locals will usually do the trick of chasing them away.

Istanbul: **A Brief History**

7TH CENTURY B.C. First settlement of Istanbul when Megarians flee the Dorian occupation of Greece.

680 B.C. Megarians cross the Marmara and settle in Chalcedon, today's Kadıköy.

660 B.C. Megarian commander, Byzas, leads settlement in Chalcedon, today's Sarayburnu, and names it Byzantium.

318 B.C. Byzantium taken over by Antigonus, commander of Alexander the Great.

A.D. 324 Constantine becomes head of the Roman Empire, making Byzantium the capital, and is the first Roman ruler to adopt Christianity.

330 Constantine I moves capital of the Roman Empire to Byzantium, renaming it Constantinople.

381 Constantinople becomes the seat of the Patriarch, nominal head of the Orthodox Church.

412 Theodosius II builds the city walls, enlarging the city.

532 Thousands killed and much of the city burnt in Nika insurrection, between the Greens and Blues at a Hippodrome chariot race. Emperor Justinian I rebuilds the city; rebuilding of Hagia Sophia starts.

1071 Byzantine army defeated by Seljuk Turks in the Battle of Manzikert and most of Anatolia is lost.

1082 Venetians allotted quarters in the city with special trading privileges, later joined by the Genoese.

1204 Fourth Crusade bursts into the city, forcing emperor into exile and imposing a new emperor. Venetians take control of the church. Crusaders rule until 1261, Constantinople's most disastrous period.

1299 The reign of Osman I (Osman Gazi), founder of the Ottoman Empire begins.

1422 Ottoman Sultan Murad II fails in his attempted siege of Constantinople.

1452 Mehmet II builds Rumeli Hisarı (fortress) to blockade the Bosphorus.

1453 Mehmet II begins conquest of Constantinople; after 53-day siege troops enter, on May 29 the city becomes third capital of the Ottoman Empire. The last Byzantine Emperor, Constantine XI, is killed in battle; the city is renamed Istanbul.

1455 Kapalı Çarşısı (Grand Bazaar) is built.

1457 Capital of the Ottoman Empire is transferred from Adrianople (Edirne) to Istanbul.

1459 Mısır Çarşısı (Spice Market) is built.

1520–66 Reign of Süleyman I (Süleyman the Magnificent)—conqueror, lawmaker, and commissioner of many magnificent mosques.

1839 Tanzimat reforms begin to modernize and revive Ottoman Empire, influenced by Europe, including secular schooling system and attempted equality.

1854 Crimean War sees Ottoman Turks side with British and French against the Russians. Florence Nightingale in charge of military hospitals in Selimiye Army barracks, near Üsküdar.

1915 Ottoman Empire sides with the Central Powers during World War I. Mustafa Kemal thwarts the Allies' attempt to take the Dardanelles, is hailed as a savior and promoted to colonel, one year later to General.

1918 Ottoman Empire is on the losing side of World War I; it is divided up between European powers.

1919 British and French occupy Istanbul; the empire is dissolved. Anatolia is under Greek occupation.

1920 Mustafa Kemal leads the Turkish War of Independence, leading to the abolition of the Ottoman Empire.

1923 Founding of the Republic of Turkey with Mustafa Kemal, now known as Atatürk, its leader; capital moves from Istanbul to Ankara.

1925 Gregorian calendar officially replaces the Islamic (lunar) calendar; the fez is prohibited.

1928 Turkey officially becomes secular when the clause retaining Islam as the state religion is removed from the constitution. Atatürk starts reforms to modernize Turkey.

1934 Women are given the vote. Atatürk proclaims Ayasofya, previously Hagia Sophia, a national museum.

1938 Atatürk dies on November 10 at 9:05am; the anniversary and exact time is marked every year. Ismet Inönü is the new president.

1945 Turkey declares war on Germany and Japan, but remains neutral during most of World War II, so no combat. Turkey joins the UN.

1955 Istanbul riots, forcing many Greeks to leave the city.

1960 Military coup against the ruling Democratic Party.

1965 Süleyman Demirel becomes prime minister, the first of seven terms of office.

1970s Large increase in Istanbul's population with migrants from rural Anatolia.

1971 Army forces Demirel's resignation following political violence.

1973 First bridge crossing the Bosphorus is completed, linking Istanbul's European and Asian sides.

1974 Turkish troops invade Northern Cyprus.

1980 Military coup follows political deadlock and imposes martial law. Curfew in Istanbul between 2 and 5am.

1982 Military coup and curfew ends; new constitution creates 7-year presidency.

1987 Turkey applies for full E.E.C. membership.

1993 Tansu Çiller becomes Turkey's first (and so far only) woman prime minister.

1999 PKK leader Abdullah Ocalan captured in Kenya; receives death sentence, later commuted to life imprisonment. August 17, huge earthquake reaching 6.7 on the Richter scale hits Izmit and damages many buildings in Greater Istanbul, killing more than 23,000 people.

2002 Turkish men no longer seen in law as head of the family, giving women full legal equality with men. Turkey reaches the semi-finals of the soccer World Cup, beaten by Brazil.

2003 Truck bombs kill a total of 53 people and wound 700 in attacks on Neve Shalom synagogue (Nov 15) and British Consulate (Nov 17). Al Qaeda claims responsibility.

2004 State TV broadcasts its first Kurdish-language program, previously banned in Turkey. Istanbul hosts the NATO summit.

2005 New Turkish Lira (TL) introduced, knocking off six zeros from the old lira. Negotiations for Turkey to join the EU officially launched after intense bargaining.

2006 Istanbul author Orhan Pamuk wins Nobel Prize in Literature. Marmaray, the transport tunnel being built under the Bosphorus to link the European and Asian sides of Istanbul, is delayed when a 4th-century port is uncovered and archeologists begin to excavate.

2007 Armenian community leader and newspaper editor of *Agos*, Hrant Dink, is assassinated outside his office in Istanbul by an ultra-nationalist, provoking outrage. AK Party wins parliamentary election led by PM Recep Tayyip Erdoğan.

2008 Turkish Parliament votes to lift the ban on women students wearing Islamic headscarf at university, provoking huge protests.

2009 Smoking ban comes into force in Turkey on July 1. State broadcaster TRT introduces its first Kurdish-language TV channel.

2010 Istanbul is European Capital of Culture. Plans are announced for Istanbul's first archeological park, the Küçükyalı ArcheoPark, the site of excavated 9th-century Byzantine treasures.

2011 Turkey enjoys a buoyant economic 2010: GDP grows to 7.3%, one of Europe's highest. Recep Tayyip Erdoğan's AK party wins a third term of office in the general election.

Art & Architecture **Highlights**

Byzantine Empire (330–1453)
This was the city's most significant period for art, beginning with Emperor Constantine building his new capital from A.D. 330, when many architects came from Rome and the style was Christian. Justinian (483–565) was the most influential Byzantine Emperor, rebuilding the battered city after the Nika Revolt in A.D. 532, creating present-day Istanbul's best-known landmarks with Hagia Sophia (p 7) a superb example. For the Byzantines, exteriors were unimportant, as attention went to the all-important interior, which glittered with religious art, mosaics, and frescoes—also seen in Kariye Museum (p 20).

Here, the central dome was adorned with a mosaic of *Christ Pantocrator*, below that angels and archangels, with figures of saints on the walls and often the Virgin Mary on a high dome. Figures were static with flat areas of color, frontal pose, and characteristic use of gold background. Below that would be the congregations, forming a microcosm of the universe. Justinian also constructed viaducts and underground cisterns, enlarging Emperor Constan-

tine's Yerebatan Sarnıçı (Basilica Cistern) in A.D. 532 (p 16).

Ottoman Empire (1453–1920s)
Soon after conquering the city in 1453, Mehmet II added minarets to churches and consecrated them as mosques. Figurative art was forbidden in Islam, seen as detracting from pious thoughts, so mosaics and frescoes were covered over—many to be revealed centuries later. The Ottoman Empire, considered the height of Turkish architecture, was renowned for its mosques, influenced by Seljuk, Byzantine, and Arabic design. The concept of the *külliye* (mosque complex, also a charitable foundation) flourished under Süleyman I (1494–1566), typically with the mosque in a walled courtyard, and outside a *medrese* (religious school), soup kitchens, orphanage, travelers' lodgings, hospital, and *hamam* (bath). Under Süleyman I, **calligraphic art** flourished especially the elaborate writing of Qur'ans, where Arabic script was written in highly decorative form. Later sultans developed their *tuğra*, a personal monogram with ornamental loops.
Mimar Sinan's mosques (p 11) typically

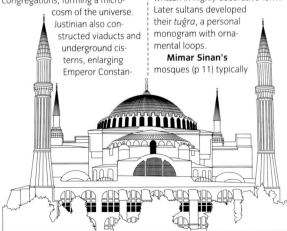

Hagia Sophia.

had cascading domes, appearing almost weightless. His Süleymaniye mosque (built 1550–57; p 75) is a masterpiece; a *külliye* built on one of the city's seven hills, using the vast central dome as its key feature, plus distinctive slender minarets, typically Ottoman. Typically, they had a vast inner space, huge central dome, plus semi-domes, vaults, and columns, creating space and serenity.

Sinan's *hamams*—best seen at Çemberlitaş Hamam (p 22) or Roxelana's baths (p 68)—also made full use of glorious domes.

Best seen in Rüstem Paşa mosque (p 9) and Sultanahmet (Blue) Mosque (p 15) are the use of **tiles,** especially from the city of Iznik. This made the most of abstract patterns, often designs of flowers and trees.

Turkish Baroque

The early 18th century marked the end of the classical period and a gradual Westernization of Ottoman art, using curves, floral patterns, and motifs best seen at the fountain of Ahmet III (1728) near Topkapı Palace's entrance. Such fountains usually had a large square block with wall fountains at the center of each facade, with the marble surfaces of the kiosk carved with floral patterns and decorated with calligraphic panels. The roof projected outward, forming large eves to shade the walls.

Late Ottomans & the Tanzimat Declaration

Under Abdülmecit I (1823–61), the Tanzimat Declaration (1839) was a series of modernizing reforms for the Ottoman Empire to compete with Europe. This created an ethnically diverse workforce, introducing talented artisans from Europe. Most significant were the Armenian-born **Balyan** family—a five-generation dynasty of Ottoman imperial architects (around 1700–1894)—who built in a Western European style, changing the architectural face of the country. Their mosques moved from spiritual ambience to the ornamental, as seen at Ortaköy mosque of 1854 (p 21), combining baroque, Romantic, and Oriental architecture. Other significant Balyan creations include Dolmabahçe (1856) and Beylerbeyi palaces (1865).

This period also saw Orientalist painters, and the first "proper" professional artists. Previously, Ottoman painting was restricted to portraiture of the sultans by Renaissance painters. From the 19th century, Istanbul was visited by European diplomats and merchants, and painters who depicted everyday Ottoman life. The late 19th century saw the first Ottoman painters travel

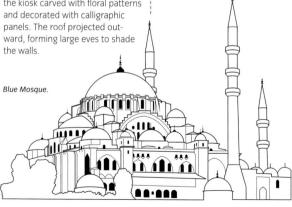

Blue Mosque.

Fountain of Ahmet III.

to Paris to study, like Osman Hamdi Bey (p 30) and Şeker Ahmet Paşa (1847–1907), ironically under the French Orientalist painters. They returned to Istanbul to establish the first art academies. Of those, Osman Hamdi is best known for his "Orientalist" style (as labeled in the West) depicting everyday scenes yet enhancing an "Eastern" ambience.

Turkish Republic

Art nouveau influenced the early 20th century; Italian architect Raimondo d'Aronco created modern structures using elements of Islamic architecture. Motifs from stonework, wood, wrought iron, and glass were a statement of social standing and modernization, especially in Beyoğlu (known as Pera pre-1923),

then the epitome of modern living. Today's Istiklal Caddesi (p 47) has superb exterior features from this era. Once Atatürk formed the Turkish republic in 1923 and shifted the capital to Ankara, modern architectural development stalled. The late 20th and early 21st centuries, however, have seen stunning contemporary additions, especially Kanyon (p 90) and the Kartal-Pendik Masterplan. This exciting new project, begun in 2008, is the urban transformation by Zaha Hadid (Iraqi-born architect, b 1950); her cutting-edge plans for a 555 sq.-hectare site stretching from the Marmara on the Asian side at Kartal Park to comprise business and residential towers (completion date tbc).

Useful **Phrases**

Most people working in hotels and restaurants speak a smattering of English, but don't bank on it elsewhere. A few letters are pronounced differently in Turkish but once you learn these you will find that the language is totally phonetic and so easy to read. If in doubt, put equal emphasis on each syllable, and pronounce every letter—for example don't fall into the trap of pronouncing "ph" like an "f." The main letters to look out for are **ç** (pronounced "ch", **ş** ("sh"), **c** ("j"), **ö** ("or," as in "work"), **ğ** (silent, just elongate the vowel following it), and **ı** ("e" as in "the"). Menu terms are in the Dining chapter (p 97).

Everyday Phrases

ENGLISH	TURKISH	PRONUNCIATION
Hello	merhaba	merhaba
How are you?	nasılsınız?	nasulsunuz?
Goodbye	güle güle	gul-eh gul-eh
Thank you (very much)	teşekkür (erderim)	teshekur erderim
Please	lütfen	lutfen
I don't know	bilmiyorum	bilmiyorum
Yes/No	evet/hayır	evet/hayur
How much?	Ne kadar/kaç lira?	ne kadar/kach lira?
I don't understand	anlamıyorum	anlamuh-yorum
I can't speak Turkish	Türkçe bilmiyorum	Turk-cheh bilmiyorum
Do you speak English?	Ingilizce biliyor musunuz?	Ingiliz-jeh biliyor musunuz?
Where is the... (toilet)?	(Tuvalet) ... nerede?	Tuvalet neh-reh-deh?
Can you write it down?	Yazar mısınız?	Yazar musunuz?
left/right	sol/sağ	sol/saah
Ladies	bayan	bay-an
Gents	bey	bey
mosque	camii	jar-mi
museum	müzesi	muh-zesi
church	kilise	kili-seh
OK, fine	tamam	tamam
Do you have any rooms?	Boş odanız var mı?	bosh odanuz var muh?
For one night	bir gece için	beer geh-jeh ichin
With shower	duşlu	dush-lu
Can I see the room?	Odayı görebilir miyim?	odayu gure-bilir miyim?
Do you have any...?	... var mı?	... var muh?
The room is ...	Oda...	oda...
too hot/ cold/small	cok sicak/ soguk/küçük	chok suhjak/ so-uk/kuchuk

ENGLISH	TURKISH	PRONUNCIATION
The check please	Hesap lütfen	hesap lut-fen
My name is...	Ismim...	ismim...
I don't feel well	Iyi hissetmiyorum	Iyi hisset-miyorum
I need a doctor	(Ingilizce bilen)	(Ingiliz-jeh bilen)
(who speaks English)	doktor lazım	doktor laz-um
When does it	Ne zaman	Neh zaman
open/close?	açilir/kapanır?	aji-lir/kapan-ur?
What time is it?	Saat kaç?	Saat kach?
It's 10 o'clock	Saat on	Saat on
It's 2:30	Saat iki buçuk	Saat iki buchuk
At what time?	Saat kaçta?	Saat kach-ta?

Numbers

NUMBER	TURKISH	PRONUNCIATION
1	bir	beer
2	iki	iki
3	üç	uch
4	dört	durt
5	beş	besh
6	altı	alt-uh
7	yedi	yedi
8	sekiz	sekiz
9	dokuz	dokuz
10	on	on
11	on bir	on beer
12	on iki	on iki
20	yirmi	yirmi
21	yirmi bir	yirmi beer
30	otuz	otuz
40	kırk	kurk
50	elli	el-li
60	altmış	alt-mush
70	yetmiş	yetmish
80	seksen	seksen
90	doksan	doksan
100	yüz	yewz
200	iki yüz	iki yewz
210	iki yüz on	iki yewz on

Days of the Week

ENGLISH	TURKISH	PRONUNCIATION
Monday	pazartesi	pazartesi
Tuesday	salı	sar-luh
Wednesday	çarşamba	char-shamba
Thursday	perşembe	per-shembeh
Friday	cuma	jumah
Saturday	cumartesi	jumar-tesi
Sunday	pazar	Pazar

Index

See also Accommodations and Restaurant indexes, below.

A

Abdülaziz I, 49, 63
Abdülhamid II, 21, 63
Abdulla (shop), 87
Accommodations. See also Accommodations Index
    best bets, 132
    maps, 133–135
    rates, 138
    resources, 166
Ada (cafe-bar), 116
Adalar Müzesi (Museum of Princes Islands), 146
Adnan & Hasan, 85
Aa, Mehmet, 15
Ahmet Çeşme, 67
Ahmet III, 61
Ahrida Synagogue, 71
Air travel, 163
Akaretler galleries, 32
Akbank Sanat, 122, 125
Al-Ansari, Abu Ayyub (Eyüp Sultan), 53
A La Turca, 84
Alay Köşkü, 94
Alcohol, 118
Ali Textile, 85
Alkazar Sinemasi, 47
Al-Ma'mun, Caliph, 93
Anadolu Kavağı, 17
Angelique (club), 112, 118
Antikacilar Çarşısı, 61–62
Antiques, 61–62, 84
Aqueduct of Valens (Bozdoğ Kemeri), 42
Araf Café Bar, 127
Arap Camii (Arab Mosque), 58, 59
Archeological Park, 67
Architecture, 173–175
Arkeoloji Müzesi (Archaeology Museum), 14–15
Armaggan (shop), 87
Armenian Church of Three Altars (Üç Horan Ermeni Kilisesi), 49
Arnoux, J.A., 50
Art galleries and museums, 28–33
    Art on the Gallery, 32
    Galerist, 31, 32
    highlights, 173–175
    Istanbul Modern, 17, 30
    Kariye Müzesi, 20, 41–42
    Misir Apartmanı, 31–32
    Pera Müzesu, 30–31
    Rampa, 32
    Sakıp Sabanı Müzesi, 33
    santralistanbul, 3, 32–33, 36
    Taksim Art Gallery, 47
    Taksim Cumhuriyet Sanat Galerisi, 31
    Türk ve Islam Eserleri Müzesi, 151
    TÜRVAK, 32
Art On the Gallery, 32
Askeri Müzesi (Military Museum), 38
Aslanım, 112, 114
Atatürk, Mustafa Kemal, 38, 47, 96
Atatürk Kültür Merkezi, 125
Atik Valide Külliye, 62
At Meydanı (Hippodrome), 44, 68
ATMs, 166
Avrupa Pasajı, 49
Ayasofya. See Hagia Sophia
Aya Triada Church, 47–48
Aya Yorgi Manastır (St. George Monastery), 147
Ayder Leather, 86
Ayios Fokas Rum, 22
Ayvansary neighborhood, 55
Aznavur, Hovzep, 50

B

Bab Bowling Café, 122, 129
Bab-us Selam (Gate of Salutations), 25
Babylon (music venue), 122, 127
Backgammon, 3
Badehane (bar), 112, 114
Bahar Korçan (shop), 86
Balart, 72
Balat neighborhood, 70–73
Balyan, Sarkis, 63
Balyan, Senekerim, 75
Banks, 166
Banu, Valide Nur, 62
Bars, 114–120
    cafe-, 116–118
    DJ, 118–120
    gay and lesbian, 117, 120
    restaurant, 116–118
Basilica Cistern (Yerebatan Sarnıçı), 16–17, 43–44
Bath, Turkish. See hamam (Turkish bath)
Baths of Roxelana (Haseki Hürrem Hamamı), 68

Bazaars. See also Kapalı Carşısı
    Beyazıt, 74–78
    Booksellers Bazaar, 77
    Camii Kebir Sokak, 54
    Dolapdere Bazaar, 4, 90
Bektas, Cengiz, 73
Benedict XVI, Pope, 50
Berg, Mike, 31
Beşiktaş FC, 122, 129
Beta (shoe shop), 86
Bey, Osman Hamdi, 14, 30, 31
Beyazit, 4, 74–78
Beyazit II, 49, 59, 77
Beyazit II Complex (Ikinci Beyazit Külliyesi), 157
Beyazit Camii, 76–77
Beyazit Kulesi (Beyazit Tower), 75
Beyazit Meydanı, 76
Beylerbeyi Sarayı (Beylerbeyi Palace), 22, 63
Beyoğlu district, 136
Beyoğlu Iş Merkezi, 89
Bigudi (bar), 120
Bike rentals, 145, 157
Biletix, 127
Blachernae Church, 55
Blue Mosque (Sultanahmet Camii), 7, 15–16
Boat travel, 164, 165. See also Ferries
Books, 77, 84–85
Booksellers Bazaar (Sahaflar Çarşısı), 77
Bora, Banu, 87
Borusan Muzik Evi, 125
Borusan Philharmonic Orchestra, 125
Bosphorus Bridge, 22
Bosphorus Cruise, 17
Bozdoğ Kemeri (Aqueduct of Valens), 42
Bozok, Murat, 106
Bukoleon Sarayı, 44
Bursa, 148–153
Buses, 157, 164, 165
Business hours, 89, 166
Büyükada Iskele, 146
Büyüksaray Mozaik Müzesi (Mosaic Museum), 44
Büyük Valide Han, 78
Büyük Yeni Han, 78
By Retro, 86
Byzantine Empire, 40–44

C

Cable-car. See Teleferik
Çadır Köşkü, 21
Café Meşale, 112, 116
Caferağa Medresesi, 67, 90
Çakmak, Fevzi, 47

Çakmakçılar Yokuşu, 78
Calligraphy Museum, 76
Camii Kebir Sokak, 54
Çam Limanı, 145–146
Camondo, Avram, 57–58
Camondo Staircase
   (Kamondo Merdivenleri),
   57–58
Çankaya Caddesi, 146
Canonica, Pietro, 47
Carpets, 85, 86, 90
Cars, 163, 164
Casa Dell'Art (Mısır
   Apartmanı), 31–32, 50
Çavuş Hamam, 71
Çekirge neighborhood, 152
Celebi, Evlia, 158
Çelebi, Hazerfan Ahmet, 57
Çelikkol, Şinasi, 153
Cellat Çeşmesi (Fountain of
   the Executioner), 25
Cell phones, 162
Cemal Reşit Rey Konser
   Salonu, 125
Çemberlitaş Hamam, 22
Cemil Topuzlu Açıkhava,
   122, 125
Chalayan, Hussein, 31
Chamber of Holy Relics
   (Topkapı Palace), 27
Children, activities for
   Aqueduct of Valens, 42
   in Beyazit, 75, 77–78
   bowling, 129
   on Constantinople tour,
      41–44
   in Eminönü and
      Sultanahmet, 65–69
   in Eyüp, 53, 54
   in Fener and Balat,
      72, 73
   full-day tours, 7–9, 11,
      14–17, 20–22
   horseracing, 129
   at Istiklal Caddesi,
      48, 50, 51
   at Karagöz Müzesi,
      152–153
   in Karaköy
      neighborhood, 57–59
   at Maarif Caddessi, 155
   at Makedonya Kulesi,
      156
   at Ottoman Folk
      Costumes and
      Jewelry Museum, 153
   in restaurants, 102–108
   shopping, 84
   special-interest tour,
      34–39
   at Topkapı Palace,
      25–27
   at Uludağ, 151, 152
   in Üsküdar, 61–63
Chris Kami, 88
Churches. See also
   Mosques; Synagogues
   Aya Triada Church,
      47–48
   Blachernae Church, 55
   Church of St. Savior in
      Chora, 41–42
   Church of the Panaghia
      Kamariotissa, 145
   Dominican Church of SS
      Peter and Paul, 57
   Hagia Eirene, 25, 122,
      126
   Hagia Sophia, 7, 11, 44,
      67, 76
   Hagios Nikolaos Church,
      145
   Panaghi ton Mongolon,
      72
   St. Antoin di Padua, 50
   St. George Monastery,
      147
   St. George's Church,
      72–73
   Santa Maria Draperis,
      50
   Surp Hirestagabet
      Ermenikilisesi, 71
   Sveti Stefan, 73
   Üç Horan Ermeni
      Kilisesi, 49
Church of St. Savior in
   Chora, 41–42
Church of the
   Pammakaristos (Fethiye
   Camii), 42, 72
Church of the Panaghia
   Kamariotissa, 145
Cigarette smoking, 115, 169
Cinema, 32
Çinili Camii (Tiled Mosque), 62
Çinili Köşk (Tiled Pavilion), 15
Cite de Pera, 48–49
Clock Tower (Saat Kulesi), 156
Clothes, 86–87, 166
Clubs, 118–120
Coastline, 3
Cocoon (carpet shop), 85
Coffee, 4
Column of Porphyrogenitus
   (Hippodrome), 68
Concerts
   opera, 126
   rock and jazz, 127, 128
Constantine I, 44
Constantinople, 40–44, 58
Consulates, 166–167

Corridor of Concubines
   (Topkapı Palace), 26
Corvus Wine & Bite, 112, 114
Credit cards, 167
Cuisine, 106. See also Dining
Çukurcuma, 4
Cumhuriyet Anıtı (Republic
   Memorial), 47
Currency, 168
Customs, 167

D
Dance performances,
   125–127
Day trips
   Bursa, 148–153
   Edirne, 154–158
   Princes' Islands,
      144–147
Denizler Kitabevi, 84
Deniz Lisesi, 145
Dentists, 167
Dersaadet (cafe-bar),
   3, 112, 116
Design Zone, 88
Devrim, Nejad Melih, 30
Dining. See also Restaurant
   Index
   best bets, 98
   maps, 99–101
Diramalilar Motorsiklet &
   Bisiklat, 157
Disabilities, travelers with,
   170
Divan Yolu, 43–44
DJ bars, 118–120
Dogzstar (club), 112, 118
Dolapdere Bazaar, 4, 90
Dolmabahçe Sarayı
   (Dolmabahçe Palace),
   20–21, 38
Dolmuş minibuses, 165–166
Dolmuş, 151
Dominican Church of SS
   Peter and Paul, 57
Dondurma stalls, 38
Dösim G.E.S., 85, 90
Drugs, 167

E
Edel Jewels, 88
Edirne, 154–158
Edirnekapı, 41
Edirne Tourist Office, 157
Efendi, Hristaki Zografos, 48
Efes beer, 118
Egyptian Obelisk, 44, 68
Ela Cindoruk-Nazan Pak, 88
Elaidi (shop), 86
Elaidi, Mehtap, 86
Electricity, 167
Embassies, 166–167

Emergency services,
167, 169
Eminönü neighborhood, 39,
64–69
Emirgan Park, 33, 96
Eski Camii (Old Mosque),
148, 157
Eski Kaplica, 152
Event listings, 127
Exchange rate, 166, 168
Eyüp, 52–56
Eyüp Meydanı, 53
Eyüp Sultan Heights, 55
Eyyub-el-Ensari Türbesi, 53

F

Fabrics, 85, 86
Fenerbahçe FC, 129, 130
Fener neighborhood, 70–73
Feray, Ayfer, 47
Ferries, 3, 17, 147, 151
Festivals, 160–161
Fethiye Camii (Church of the
Pammakaristos), 42
5.Kat (bar), 112, 114–115
Food shopping, 87
Football clubs, 4, 129–130
Fortress of Europe (Rumeli
Hisarı Müzesi), 4, 39
Forum of Theodosius, 76
Fossati, Gaspare, 57
Fototrek Fotograf Merkezi
(Mısır Apartmanı), 31–32
Fountain of the Executioner
(Cellat Çeşmesi), 25
Freedom Square (Hürriyet
Meydanı), 76
French Cultural Center, 125
Full-day tours
one day, 6–11
two days, 12–17
three days, 18–22

G

Galata. See Karaköy
neighborhood
Galata Evi (Galata House), 57
Galata Köprüsü (Galata
Bridge), 10, 39
Galata Kulesi (Galata Tower),
4, 10, 11, 57
Galata Mevlevihanesi
Müzesi, 51
Galatasaray FC, 130
Galatasaray Lisesi, 49
Galeri Hediye, 85, 86
Galeri Nev (Mısır Apartmanı),
31
Galerist (Mısır Apartmanı),
31, 32
Galip Dede Caddesi, 3
garajistanbul, 122, 126

GarajistanbulPro, 126
Gate of Salutations (Bab-us
Selam), 25
Gavand, Eugene Henri, 57
Gay and lesbian travelers,
117, 120, 167
Gazi, Orhan, 149–150, 151
Gazi, Osman, 53, 149–150
Ghetto (club), 122, 128
Gizli Bahçe, 115
Göktuğ, Mete, 57
Göktuğ, Nadire, 57
Golden Rose (shop), 89
Gonül Paksoy (shop), 87
Gotlar Sütunu (Goth's
Column), 94
Government tourist
offices, 160
Grand Bazaar. See Kapalı
Çarşısı
Grand Synagogue, 155
Great Mosque (Ulu Camii), 149
Great Palace, 44
Greek Orthodox
Patriarchate, 72–73
Green Mosque (Yeşil
Camii), 150
Green Tomb (Yeşil Türbe), 150
Gülbaba's Tomb, 49
Gülhane Park, 39, 92–96
Güneş Carpet & Kilim
House, 86

H

Hafız Mustafa, 87
Hagia Eirene, 25, 122, 126
Hagia Sophia, 7, 11, 44,
67, 76
Hagios Nikolaos Church, 145
Hamam (Turkish bath), 22,
151, 152
Handicrafts, 87–88
Harem (Dolmabahçe
Palace), 20
Harem (Topkapı Palace),
14, 25–26
Haremlique (shop), 87–88
Haseki Hürrem Hamamı
(Baths of Roxelana), 68
Hasırcılar Caddesi, 65
Hatice Turhan Valide Sultan
Türbesi, 65–66
Hayal Kahvesi, 128
Health, 167
Hippodrome (At Meydanı),
44, 68
Holidays, 167
Holy Angels Armenian
Church (Surp Hirestagabet
Ermenikilisesi), 71
Homer Kitabevi, 84

Homewear, 87–88
Hor Hor Bit Pazari, 84
Horseracing, 129
Hospitals, 168
Hotels. See Accommodations
Index
Hürriyet Daily News, 127
Hürriyet Meydanı (Freedom
Square), 76

I

Ibraham I, 8, 94
İç Bedesten, 9
Ikinci Beyazit Külliyesi
(Beyazit II Complex), 157
Imperial Gate (Dolmabahçe
Palace), 21
Imperial Hall (Topkapı
Palace), 26
Indigo (club), 118
İnönü, Ismet, 47
İnönü stadium, 4
Insurance, 168
Internet access, 168
Ipekci, Cemil, 88
Iskele, 22
Iskele Camii (Mihrimah
Sultan Camii), 61
Ismail, Khedevi, 96
İş Merkezi, 3
Ismet İnönü Evi, 145
Istanbul
favorite moments in,
3–4
history of, 170–172
maps, 2
Istanbul Culinary Institute, 31
Istanbul Islam Bilim ve
Teknoloji Tarihi Müzesi
(Istanbul Museum of the
History of Science and
Technology in Islam), 93
Istanbul Jazz Center, 128
Istanbul Kitapçısı, 84
Istanbul Kültür Sanat
Vakfi, 127
Istanbul Modern, 17, 30
Istanbul Music Festival, 126
Istanbul University, 75
Istiklal Caddesi, 11, 46–51
Istiklal Kitabevi, 84
Istiklal Nostaljic Tram, 37–38

J

James Joyce Irish Pub, 115
Jazz, 127, 128
Jewelry, 88, 89
Jewish community, 58, 59,
71, 155
Jewish Museum of Turkey
(Türk Musevileri Müzesi),
59

John XXIII, Pope, 50
Jolly Joker Balans, 119
Justinian I, 7, 43, 44, 69

K

Kadıköy fish market, 3
Kadin Eserleri Kütüphanesi
  (Women's Library and
  Information Center), 73
Kafe Ara, 4
Kalenderhane Camii, 43
Kami, Chris, 88
Kamondo Merdivenleri
  (Camondo Staircase),
  57–58
Kampanaki, 47
Kanyon, 90
Kapalı Çarşısı (Grand Bazaar),
  8–9, 77–78, 89, 90, 149
Karaburçak, Ihsan Cemal, 30
Karagöz and Haciabat
  Monumental Grave, 153
Karagöz Müzesi, 152–153
Karakedi Plak Evi, 85
Karaköy neighborhood, 56–59
Kare Deri (shop), 89
Karinca (shop), 88
Kariye Müzesi, 20, 41–42
Kaymakam headquarters,
  146
Kennedy Caddesi, 3, 69
Kiğılı, 87
Kilims, 85, 86
Kiraç, Inan, 30
Kiraç, Suna, 30
Kırkpınar Evi, 155
Kız Kulesi (Maiden's/
  Leander's Tower), 63
Koç, Rahmi, 37
Kösem, Mahpeyker, 62
Kösem, Valide Sultan, 78
Koza Han, 149
Küçük Ayasofya Camii, 68–69
Kukurtlu Kaplica, 152
Kumpir stalls, 22
Kurakahveci Mehmet Efendi
  (shop), 87
Kuum Saati, 104
K.V. (bar), 112, 115

L

Leander's Tower (Kız Kulesi),
  63
Levant Koleksiyon, 84
Liquor, 118
Lodging. *See*
  Accommodations
Lost property, 168
Loti, Pierre, 54, 55
Lucca (bistro bar), 112, 118

M

Maarif Caddessi, 155
Magazines, 168
Mahmud II, 75
Maiden's Tower (Kız
  Kulesi), 63
Mail, 168
Makedonya Kulesi, 156
Malls, 89–90
Malta Köşkü, 21
Mapplethorpe, Robert, 31
Markets
  antique, 61–62
  Pigeon, 41
  Selimiye Arasta, 158
  shopping in, 89–90
  spice. *See* Mısır Çarşısı
Mehmet II, 8, 39, 43, 53, 59
Mehter band, 21
Meriç Bridge (Meriç
  Köprüsü), 155
Meriç Köprüsü (Meriç
  Bridge), 155
Metochites, Theodore,
  20, 41
Metro, 165
Midnight Express, 87
Mihrimah Sultan Camii, 61
Military Museum (Askeri
  Müzesi), 38
Million Stone, 43
Mimar Sinan Çarşısı, 61
Miniatürk, 36
Minibuses, 165–166
Mısır Apartmanı, 31–32, 50
Mısır Çarşısı (Spice Market),
  3, 9, 65, 89, 90
Mobile phones, 162
Monastery of the
  Pantocrator (Zeyrek
  Camii), 42
Mongeri, Giulio, 50
Mor (shop), 89
Mor Kedi, 120
Mosaic Museum (Büyüksaray
  Mozaik Müzesi), 44
Mosques. *See also*
  Churches; Synagogues
  Arap Camii, 58, 59
  Atik Valide Külliye, 62
  Beyazit Camii, 76–77
  Çinili Camii, 62
  Eski Camii, 148, 157
  Fethiye Camii, 42, 72
  at Ikinci Beyazit
    Külliyesi, 157
  Kalenderhane Camii, 43
  Küçük Ayasofya Camii,
    68–69
  Mihrimah Sultan
    Camii, 61
    at Muradiye
      Complex, 152
  Ortaköy Camii, 22
  Rüstem Paş Camii, 9
  Selimiye Camii, 158
  Süleymaniye Camii,
    4, 8, 75
  Sultanahmet Camii,
    7, 15–16
  Sultan Camii, 53
  Ulu Camii, 149
  Yeni Camii, 65
  Yeni Valide Camii, 61
  Yeşil Camii, 150
  Zal Mahmoud Paşa
    Camii, 54
  Zeyrek Camii, 42
Movie halls, 127
Muammer Karaca
  Tiyatrosu, 126
Mumcu, Tayfun, 87
Muradiye Complex, 152
Murat II, 152
Murat III, 42
Murat V, 21
Museum of Ancient
  Orient, 15
Museum of Energy, 36
Museum of Princes Islands
  (Adalar Müzesi), 146
Museum of Turkish and
  Islamic Arts (Türk ve Islam
  Eserleri Müzesi), 151
Music
  rock and jazz, 127, 128
  shopping for, 84–85
  venues for, 125–127
Muslu, Esra, 106
Mustafa II, 61
Mustafa III, 78
Muteferrika, 77

N

Nadir Shah throne (Topkapı
  Palace), 27
Nardis Jazz Club, 128
Naval High School, 145
Neighborhood walks
  Beyazit's bazaars and
    mosques, 74–78
  Eminönü to
    Sultanahmet, 64–69
  Eyüp's sacred sites,
    52–56
  Fener & Balat, 70–73
  Istiklal Caddesi, 46–51
  Tünel to Karaköy, 56–59
  Üsküdar, 60–63
New Mosque (Yeni
  Camii), 65
Newspapers, 168

Nightlife
  bars, 114–116
  best bets, 112
  cafe-bars and
    restaurant bars,
    116–118
  clubs and DJ bars,
    118–120
  for gay and lesbian
    travelers, 120
  maps, 113–114
Nublu (cafe-bar), 122, 128

O
Oil wrestling, 156
Old Mosque (Eski Camii),
  157, 158
Opera, 126
Ortaköy, 21–22
Ortaköy Camii, 22
Ortaköy Craft Market, 90
Osmanlı Bankası Müzesi
  (Ottoman Banking
  Museum), 58
Osmanoğlu, 3
Otherside The Club, 120
Ottoman Banking Museum
  (Osmanlı Bankası
  Müzesi), 58
Ottoman Folk Costumes and
  Jewelry Museum (Uluumay
  Osmanlı Kıyafetleri ve
  Takıları Müzesi), 153
Outdoor activities, 92–96
Özel Femer Rum Lisesi, 72
Öztaraçı, Güneş, 86

P
Palace Museum Collection
  (Saray Müzesi
  Koleksiyonları), 21
Palace of Constantine
  Porphyrogenitus (Tekfur
  Sarayı), 41
Panaghi ton Mongolon (St.
  Mary of the Mongols), 72
Parks
  Archeological Park, 67
  Emirgan Park, 33, 96
  Gülhane Park, 39, 92–96
  Sultanahmet Park, 7
  Tophane Park, 149
  Yıldız Park, 21, 96
Paşa, Hacı Ivaz, 150
Paşa, Koca Reşit, 77
Paşa, Semsi, 62
Paşa, Zal Mahmoud, 54
Paşabahçe (shop), 88
Pasha, Abbas Halim, 50
Passports, 168
Pera Müzesi, 30–31

Performing arts
  best bets, 122
  classical music, 125–127
  dance, 125–127
  maps, 123–124
  rock and jazz music,
    127, 128
  theater, 125–127
Perşembe Pazarı Caddesi, 58
Phaeton, traveling by, 145
Pharmacies, 168–169
Pia (cafe-bar), 118
Pierre Loti Heights, 55
Pierre Loti Kahvesi, 4
Pigeon Market, 41
Pistachios, 3
Police, 169
Post office, 66, 168
Princes' Islands, 3, 144–147
Public transport, 164
Puppetry, 152–153

R
Rahmi Koç Museum, 37
Reina (club), 119
Republic Memorial
  (Cumhuriyet Anıtı), 47
Restaurants. See Restaurant
  Index
Restrooms, 169
Rock music, 127, 128
Rose garden (Gülhane Park),
  93–94
Roxelana, 8, 68
Roxy (club), 119
Royal Carriages, 25
Rumeli Han, 47
Rumeli Hisarı Müzesi
  (Fortress of Europe), 4, 39
Rüstem Paş Camii, 9

S
Saat Kulesi (Clock Tower), 156
Safety, 117, 169
Şah (bar), 116
Sahaflar Çarşısı (Booksellers
  Bazaar), 77
St. Antoin di Padua, 50
St. George Monastery (Aya
  Yorgi Manastır), 147
St. George's Church, 72–73
St. Mary of the Mongols
  (Panaghi ton Mongolon), 72
St. Nikolaos, 145
St. Stephen of the Bulgars
  (Sveti Stefan), 73
Sakıp Sabanı Müzesi, 33
Santa Maria Draperis, 50
santralistanbul, 3, 32–33, 36
Saray Müzesi Koleksiyonları
  (Palace Museum
  Collection), 21

Schools
  Deniz Lisesi, 145
  Istanbul University, 75
  Özel Femer Rum
    Lisesi, 72
Science museum, 93
Sea buses, 147
Sefahathane, 116
Selamlik (Dolmabahçe
  Palace), 20
Selimiye Arasta, 158
Selimiye Camii, 158
Selimiye Vakif Müzesi
  (Selimiye Foundation
  Museum), 158
Şemsi Ahmet Paşa
  Külliye, 62
Serpentine Column
  (Hippodrome), 68
Servis (shuttle minibus), 157
Sesler, Selim, 127
Sevan Bıçakcı, 89
Shopping
  antiques and vintage,
    61–62, 84
  best bets, 80
  books and music, 84–85
  carpets, kilims and
    fabrics, 85, 86, 90
  clothes and
    accessories, 86–87
  food, 87
  homewear and
    handicrafts, 87–88
  jewelry, 88, 89
  maps, 81–83
  markets and malls,
    89–90
Sightseeing, 10
Sinan, Mimar, 8, 11, 61, 62,
  68, 75–76, 158
Sirkeci Garı & Müzesi, 66–67
Sirkeci PTT & Müzesi
  (Sirkeci Post Office and
  Museum), 66
Smoking, 115, 169
Soccer clubs, 4, 129–130
Soğukçeşme Sokak, 67
Sound and Light shows, 16
Spanish Inquisition, 58
Spas, 152. See also Hamam
  (Turkish bath)
Special-interest tours
  arty Istanbul, 28–33
  Byzantine
    Constantinople,
    40–44
  for children, 34–39
  Topkapı Palace, 24–27
Spice Market. See Mısır
  Çarşısı

Spoonmaker's Diamond
(Topkapı Palace), 27
Sports
soccer clubs, 4,
129–130
wrestling, 156
Sublime Porte, 94, 95
Sugarclub Cafe, 120
Süleyman I, 8, 11
Süleymaniye Camii, 4, 8, 75
Sultan, Gülnuş Emetullah
Valide, 61
Sultan, Kösem, 66
Sultan, Valide Safiye, 61
Sultanahmet Camii (Blue
Mosque), 7, 15–16
Sultanahmet district, 7,
64–69, 136
Sultanahmet Park, 7
Sultan Camii, 53
Supper Club, 119
Süreyya Opera House,
122, 126
Surp Hirestagabet
Ermenikilisesi (Holy Angels
Armenian Church), 71
Sveti Stefan (St. Stephen of
the Bulgars), 73
Swedish Consulate, 51
Synagogues. See also
Churches; Mosques
Ahrida Synagogue, 71
Grand Synagogue, 155

T

Taksim Art Gallery, 47
Taksim Cumhuriyet Sanat
Galerisi, 31
Taksim Maksemi (Water
Distribution Center), 47
Taksim Square, 47
Tamirane (cafe), 122, 128
Taxes, 169
Taxis, 151, 165
Tekfur Sarayı (Palace of
Constantine
Porphyrogenitus), 41
Tek Yon (club), 112, 120
Teleferik (cable-car), 4, 54,
151, 152
Telephones, 162, 169
Theater, 125–127
Theodosian walls, 55
Theodosius, 76
Theophilos, 44
360Istanbul (restaurant-bar),
31, 50, 112, 119, 120
Tickets, 127, 128
Tiled Mosque (Çinili Camii), 62
Tiled Pavilion (Çinili Köşk), 15
Time Out Istanbul, 127
Time zone, in Istanbul, 169

Tipping, 169
Toilets, 169
Tomb(s), 49, 149–150
of Beyazit II, 77
in Eyüp, 54, 55
Eyyub-el-Ensari
Türbesi, 53
Hatice Turhan Valide
Sultan Türbesi, 65–66
of Mimar Sinan, 75–76
Soğukçeşme Sokak, 67
Tophane Park, 149
Topkapı Dagger, 27
Topkapı Sarayı (Topkapı
Palace), 14, 24–27
Tourist information, 169–170
Train travel, 69, 163
Tram, 164–165
Transportation, 69, 163–166
Treasury (Topkapı Palace),
14, 27
Tünel, 56–59
Turhan, Hatice, 65–66
Türker İnanoğlu Foundation
Cinema Theatre Museum
(TÜRVAK), 32
Turkish bath. See Hamam
Turkish Jockey Club, 129
Turkish language, 10, 110,
176–177
Türk Musevileri Müzesi
(Jewish Museum of
Turkey), 59
Türk ve İslam Eserleri Müzesi
(Museum of Turkish and
Islamic Arts), 151
TÜRVAK (Türker İnanoğlu
Foundation Cinema
Theatre Museum), 32

U

Üç Horan Ermeni Kilisesi
(Armenian Church of
Three Altars), 49
Ulu Camii (Great Mosque), 149
Uludağ (mountain), 151, 152
Uluumay, Esat, 153
Uluumay Osmanlı Kıyafetleri
ve Takıları Müzesi
(Ottoman Folk Costumes
and Jewelry Museum), 153
Urart (shop), 88
Üsküdar, 60–63

V

Valens viaduct, 16
Valide Han, 9
Veliefendi, 122, 129
Veysel, Aşik, 95, 96
Vintage items, 84
Visas, 170
Vodina Caddesi, 72

W

Walking around, 166
Water Distribution Center
(Taksim Maksemi), 47
Weather, 162
Whirling Dervish Ceremony,
51, 122, 126, 127
Wilhelm II, 68
Wine, 118
Women, 170
Women's Library and
Information Center (Kadın
Eserleri Kütüphanesi), 73
Wrestling, 156

Y

Yeni Camii (New Mosque),
4, 65
Yeni Kaplica, 152
Yeni Valide Camii, 61
Yerebatan Sarnıcı (Basilica
Cistern), 16–17, 43–44
Yeşil Camii (Green Mosque),
150
Yeşil Ev, 116
Yeşil Türbe (Green Tomb),
150
Yıldız Palace, 96
Yıldız Park, 21, 96
Yıldız Porcelain Factory &
Museum, 21
Yıldız Sarayı Palace, 21
Yoros Castle, 17

Z

Zal Mahmoud Paşa Camii, 54
Zeyrek Camii (Monastery of
the Pantocrator), 42
Zincirli Han, 9

Accommodations

A'jia, 132, 135
Anemon Galata, 135
Ansen 130, 135, 136
Ayasofya Konakları, 136
Büyük Londra Otel, 136
Çırağan Palace Kempinski,
21, 136
Dersaadet, 136–137
Eklektik Guest House,
132, 137
Erboy Hotel, 137
Four Seasons Hotel, 67, 132,
137, 140
Four Seasons Hotel—
Istanbul at the Bosphorus,
137–138
Galata Residence, 58, 132,
138
Hanedan, 138
Hotel Empress Zoe, 132, 138

Hotel Niles, 132, 138
Hotel Sapphire, 139
The House Hotel, 139
Lush Hip Hotel, 139
Marigold Thermal & Spa Hotel, 151
Marions Suites, 139–140
Marmara Pera Hotel, 106
Mavi Ev (Blue House), 132, 140
Mövenpick, 132, 140
Peninsula, 132, 140
Pera Palace Hotel, 101, 132, 140
Pera Tulip Hotel, 140, 141
Radisson Blu Bosphorus Hotel, 132, 141
Safran Otel, 151
Şebnem, 141
Shangri-La, 140
Side Hotel & Pension, 141
Sirkeci Konak Hotel, 132, 141
Sumahan on the Water, 132, 141
Tan Hotel, 132, 142
Villa Zurich, 142
W Hotel, 32, 132, 142
Witt Istanbul Suites, 132, 142
Yeşil Ev, 116, 142

Restaurants

Agatha, 98, 101
Asitane, 101–102
Bab-i Hayat, 9, 102
Balıkçı Sabahattin, 98, 102
Balkan Piliç Lokantası, 158
Banyan, 102
Boncuk, 102
Börekci, 72
Borsa, 102

Büyükada Kultur Evi, 147
Caferağa Medresesi, 67, 90
Cakirağa Cay Evi, 41
Canim Ciğerim, 98, 102
Çapari Arif, 103
Cezayir, 103, 112, 116
Çiya, 98, 103
Dai Pera, 98, 103
Derviş, 15
Doğa Balık, 103, 142
Doğatepe Cafe & Restaurant, 117
D'Or, 151
Dubb, 98, 103
Erenler, 77
Eyüp Sultan Meydanı, 53
Feriye Lokantası, 98, 104
Haci Baba, 104
Hala, 98, 104
Hamdi et Lokantası, 104
The House Café, 104, 117
Hünkar, 104
Istanbul Culinary Institute, 31, 104
Istanbul Modern Cafe & Restaurant, 104
Kafe Ara, 98, 104–105
Kanaat Lokantası, 61
Karaköy Balıkcıar Çarşısı, 59
Kariye Pembe Köşk, 20
Kebapcı Iskender, 153
Konyalı, 26, 67
Kule Cay Bahcesi cafe, 39
Kurucu Ali Baba, 8
Lale Bahçesi, 75
Leb-i Derya, 105, 118
Lokanta, 105
Lokanta Helvetia, 98, 105
Lucca, 112, 118
Malta Köşkü, 21

Markiz Patisserie, 50
Mekan, 105
Melekler, 106
Mikla, 106
Mimolett, 98, 106
Mistanbul, 63
Moreish, 106
Müzedechanga, 107
Nu Teras, 107, 119
Otantik, 107
ottosantral, 33, 36
Özsüt, 18
Pano Şeraphanesi, 115, 116
Pierre Loti Kahvesi, 54
Pitti, 135
Poseidon, 107
Protokol Evi, 156
Rumeli, 107
Rumeli Iskele, 107
Şar, 108
Seasons, 108
Set Üstü Çay Bahçe, 95
Sirkeci Balıkcısı, 108
Sofyalı, 98, 108
Sunset Grill & Bar, 108–109
Sütiş, 47
Tarihi Haliç Işkembecisi, 73
360Istanbul, 31, 50, 112, 119, 120
Topaz, 98, 109
Vefa Bozacısı, 42–43
Vogue, 98, 109
Yeni Camii Parkı, 65
Yücetepe Kir Gazinosu, 147
Zeyrekhane, 42
Zuma Istanbul, 109

Photo Credits

Front cover (L-R): © Shutterstock; © Steve Hodder / Fotolibra; © James Sparshatt / Axiom. Back cover: © Peter Chambers / Alamy Images. All images: © Emma Levine with the following exceptions: Courtesy of Four Seasons Hotel: p 137 bottom. Courtesy of IKSV Archives: p 121. Courtesy of Lush Hotel: p 139. Courtesy of Moevenpick Hotel: p 132. © Istanbul Modern: p 30. © Neil Setchfield / Alamy: p 16 bottom. © Rebecca Erol / Alamy: p 31. © sean sprague / Alamy: p 126. © Sunset Grill & Bar, Istanbul: p 109. © Yildirim Celik: p 33 bottom, p 87, p 98, p 108, p 149–p 153.